Lecture Notes in Artificial Intelligence   6572

Edited by R. Goebel, J. Siekmann, and W. Wahlster

Subseries of Lecture Notes in Computer Science

W0090963

Ron van der Meyden   Jan-Georg Smaus (Eds.)

Model Checking and Artificial Intelligence

6th International Workshop, MoChArt 2010
Atlanta, GA, USA, July 11, 2010
Revised Selected and Invited Papers

 Springer

Series Editors

Randy Goebel, University of Alberta, Edmonton, Canada
Jörg Siekmann, University of Saarland, Saarbrücken, Germany
Wolfgang Wahlster, DFKI and University of Saarland, Saarbrücken, Germany

Volume Editors

Ron van der Meyden
University of New South Wales
School of Computer Science and Engineering
Sydney 2052, Australia
E-mail: meyden@cse.unsw.edu.au

Jan-Georg Smaus
Albert-Ludwigs-Universität Freiburg
Institut für Informatik
79110 Freiburg, Germany
E-mail: smaus@informatik.uni-freiburg.de

ISSN 0302-9743   e-ISSN 1611-3349
ISBN 978-3-642-20673-3   ISBN 978-3-642-20674-0 (eBook)
DOI 10.1007/978-3-642-20674-0
Springer Heidelberg Dordrecht London New York

Library of Congress Control Number: 2011926039

CR Subject Classification (1998): I.2.3, I.2, F.4.1, F.3, D.2.4, D.1.6

LNCS Sublibrary: SL 7 – Artificial Intelligence

Typesetting: Camera-ready by author, data conversion by Scientific Publishing Services, Chennai, India

Printed on acid-free paper

Springer is part of Springer Science+Business Media (www.springer.com)

Preface

This volume provides a snapshot of current work on the interaction of model checking and artificial intelligence. It is based on revised versions of a selection of the papers presented at the 6th Workshop on Model Checking and Artificial Intelligence (MoChArt), held as a satellite workshop of the Conference of the Association for the Advancement of Artificial Intelligence in Atlanta, Georgia, USA, in July 2010, as well as papers contributed subsequent to the workshop.

Model checking is an approach to verification based on the idea of representing the system of interest as a *model*, a semantic structure of which one can say that it supports the truth or falsity of a formula of a logic. Typically, the model describes the states of the system and its evolution over time, and the logic is a modal logic that describes the possible temporal behaviors of the system. A model checker is a software system that takes as inputs representations of the system and its specification in modal logic, and computes whether the specification holds in the system.

The interactions between model checking and artificial intelligence are rich and diverse. Originating in the 1980s as an approach to the verification of concurrent hardware processes and computer network communications protocols, model checking has found application in an increasingly broad range of areas. These days, model checking is applied by researchers working on computer software such as hardware device drivers and operating systems kernels, cryptographic protocols, and Web services protocols. Artificial intelligence applications include planning, stochastic process models, normative systems, autonomous robots, economic game theory models, and other forms of multi-agent systems. This broadening of the application area has also led to a broadening of the range of modal logics studied in the field, and there are now model checkers whose specification language is able to express modalities such as knowledge, belief, probability, strategy and obligation as well as time. Such modalities are of particular interest in areas of artificial intelligence dealing with autonomous and multi-agent systems.

In principle, a model checker conducts an exhaustive examination of the state space of the system in order to determine whether the specification holds. Underpinning the success of the area is a range of sophisticated optimization techniques and heuristic algorithms that enable this computation to be performed efficiently rather than by a brute force search. In this regard, model checking has benefited from a range of ideas from artificial intelligence, where efficient search over large and complex state spaces has long been a topic of interest. Ideas transferred from artificial intelligence to model checking include satisfiability solving, search heuristics such as A^*, and planning approaches to counter-example construction.

The MoChArt series of workshops aims to provide a forum for researchers interested in these interactions between artificial intelligence and model checking. Previous editions of MoChArt were held with ECAI 2002, IJCAI 2003, CONCUR 2005, ECAI 2006 and ECAI 2008. For the 2010 edition at AAAI, the Program Committee carefully evaluated submissions for quality and relevance to the MoChArt theme, leading to a selection of papers that were presented at the workshop and distributed among the participants as AAAI working notes. The papers presented in this volume include revised versions of a selection of the papers presented at the workshop.

Several themes are touched upon by these papers. Concerning general search algorithms, the paper by Edelkamp and Sulewski describes the use of the graphical processing unit (GPU) for external memory breadth-first search.

The potential for the application of AI techniques to automated program verification is explored in the paper by Edelkamp, Kellershoff and Sulewski, which deals with the transformation of the problem of verification of C code to problems of action planning.

A strongly represented theme at the workshop was multi-agent systems and epistemic logic, building a bridge between AI concepts and model checking. The paper by Alechina, Logan, Nguyen and Rakib deals with abstraction for specifications concerned with resource requirements in multi-agent systems. Abstraction is also a key concern in the paper by Lomusciou, Qu and Russo, which considers automatic data abstraction in model-checking multi-agent systems. This paper is one of three dealing with epistemic logic. Huang, Luo and van der Meyden present results on improvements to bounded model checking for an extension of CTL with epistemic operators. Finally, Luo, Su, Gu, Wu and Yang study epistemic model checking of the Herbivore protocol, which involves knowledge and anonymity.

Several papers presented at the workshop have not been included in this volume, for a variety of reasons, including conflicts with publication in other venues. Stefan Leue presented an algorithm for finding the k shortest paths in graph, a problem which is relevant, among others, for stochastic model checking. Siddharth Srivastava spoke on computing applicability conditions for plans with loops, with various results conerning termination and other behaviors of transition systems applying not just to a particular planning formalism, and hence of interest to the model-checking community. There was also lively discussion on the general direction of the field, and on how best to foster interaction between the model-checking and artificial intelligence communities.

In addition to these improved versions of papers from the workshop working notes, this volume also contains an extended abstract of the invited talk presented at the workshop by Hector Geffner, who spoke on planning with incomplete information, stressing that while logic and theory are needed in planning, the bottom line is heavily empirical.

To round out the topics treated with a contribution to the theory of model checking, there is also a paper contributed after the event by Kupferman and Rosenberg, dealing with lower bounds for transformations from LTL to Deterministic Büchi automata.

Taken together, the papers in this volume provide a good sample of current research, and are representative of the diversity of interactions mentioned above and the quality of the field.

All papers in this volume were carefully reviewed by our Program Committee members or external reviewers. Our thanks go to the Program Committee and these reviewers for their diligent work in reviewing the submissions, to AAAI for hosting the meeting and handling logistics, to Springer for publication of these proceedings, to the creators of the wonderful EasyChair conference management system, and, of course, to the contributing authors.

December 2010   Ron van der Meyden
                                                                  Jan-Georg Smaus

Conference Organization

Program Chairs

Ron van der Meyden   University of New South Wales, Sydney, Australia
Jan-Georg Smaus   Albert-Ludwigs-Universität Freiburg, Germany

Program Committee

Rajeev Alur   University of Pennsylvania, USA
Massimo Benerecetti   Università di Napoli "Federico II", Italy
Alessandro Cimatti   IRST, Trento, Italy
Stefan Edelkamp   Universität Bremen, Germany
Enrico Giunchiglia   Università di Genova, Italy
Patrice Godefroid   Microsoft Research, Redmond, USA
Aarti Gupta   NEC Laboratories America, Princeton, USA
Klaus Havelund   NASA Jet Propulsion Laboratory & Caltech, USA
Orna Kupferman   Hebrew University, Israel
Marta Kwiatkowska   University of Oxford, UK
Alessio Lomuscio   Imperial College London, UK
Charles Pecheur   Université catholique de Louvain, Belgium
Doron Peled   Bar Ilan University, Israel
Jussi Rintanen   NICTA & Australian National University, Australia
Michael Wooldridge   University of Liverpool, UK

External Reviewers

Xiaowei Huang
Gavin Lowe

Table of Contents

Planning with Incomplete Information
(Invited Paper)

Hector Geffner

ICREA & Universitat Pompeu Fabra
Roc Boronat 138, 08018 Barcelona, Spain
hector.geffner@upf.edu
http://www.dtic.upf.edu/~hgeffner

Abstract. Planning is concerned with the development of solvers for a wide range of models where actions must be selected for achieving goals. In these models, actions may be deterministic or not, and full or partial sensing may be available. In the last few years, significant progress has been made, resulting in algorithms that can produce plans effectively in a variety of settings. These developments have to do with new formulations, inference techniques, and transformations. In this paper, I review some of these developments, focusing on those pertaining to planning with incomplete information.

1 Introduction

The problem of creating agents that can decide what to do on their own has been at the center of AI research since its beginnings. One of the first AI programs to tackle this problem, back in the 50's, was the General Problem Solver (GPS) that selects actions for reducing a difference between the current state and a desired target state [1]. Ever since then, this problem has been tackled in a number of ways in many areas of AI, and in particular in the area of Planning.

The problem of selecting actions for achieving goals, however, even in its most basic version – deterministic actions and complete information – is computationally intractable [2]. Under these assumptions, the problem of finding a plan becomes the well-known problem of finding a path in a directed graph whose nodes, that represent the possible states of the system, are exponential in the number of problem variables.

Until the middle 90's in fact, no planner or program of any sort could synthesize plans for large problems in an effective manner from a description of the actions and goals. In recent years, however, the situation has changed: in the presence of deterministic actions and full knowledge about the initial situation, classical planning algorithms can find plans quickly even in large problems with hundred of variables and actions [3, 4]. This is the result of new ideas, like the automatic derivation of heuristic functions [5, 6], and a established empirical methodology featuring benchmarks, comparisons, and competitions. Moreover, many of these planners are *action selection mechanisms* that can commit to the next action to do in real-time without having to construct a full plan first [7].

R. van der Meyden and J.-G. Smaus (Eds.): MoChArt 2010, LNAI 6572, pp. 1–11, 2011.

These developments, however, while crucial, do not suffice for producing autonomous agents that can decide by themselves what to do in environments where the two assumptions above (deterministic actions, complete information) do not apply. The more general problem of selecting actions in uncertain, dynamic and/or partially known environments arises in a number of contexts (a rover in Mars, a character in a video-game, a robot in a health-care facility, a softbot in the web, etc.), and has been tackled through a number of different methodologies:

1. *programming-based:* where the *desired behavior is encoded explicitly* by a human programmer in a suitable high-level language,
2. *learning-based:* where the *desired behavior is learned automatically* from trial-and-error experience or information provided by a teacher, or
3. *model-based:* where *the desidered behavior is inferred automatically* from a suitable description of the actions, sensors, and goals.

None of these approaches, however, or a combination of them, has resulted yet in a solid methodology for building agents that can display a robust and flexible behavior in real time in partially known environments. Programming agents by hand puts all the burden in the programmer that cannot anticipate all possible contingencies, leading to systems that are brittle. Learning methods such as reinforcement learning [8], are restricted in scope and do not deal with the problem of incomplete state information. Finally, traditional model-based methods, when applied to models that are more realistic than the ones underlying classical planning, have difficulties scaling up.

Planning in Artificial Intelligence represents the model-based approach to autonomous behavior: a planner is a solver that accepts a model of the actions, sensors, and goals, and produces a controller that determines the actions to do given the observations gathered (Fig. 1). Planners come in a great variety, depending on the types of models they target. Classical planners address deterministic state models with full information about the initial situation [9]; conformant planners address state models with non-deterministic actions and incomplete information about the initial state [10, 11], POMDP planners address stochastic state model with partial observability [12], and so on.

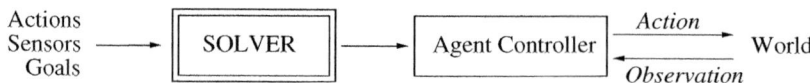

Fig. 1. Model-based approach to intelligent behavior: the next action to do is determined by a controller derived from a model of the actions, sensors, and goals

In all cases, the models of the environment considered in planning are intractable in the worst case, meaning that brute force methods do not scale up. Domain-independent planning approaches aimed at solving these planning models effectively must thus *recognize* and *exploit* the structure of the individual problems that are given. The key to exploiting this structure is *inference*, as in other AI models such as Constraint Satisfaction Problems and Bayesian Networks [13, 14]. In the paper, we will go over the inference techniques that have been found computationally useful in planning with incomplete information.

The paper is organized as follows. We consider the model, language, and inference techniques developed for classical planning, conformant planning, and planning with sensing, in that order. We focus on inference techniques of two types: heuristic functions and transformations.

2   Classical Planning

Classical planning is concerned with the selection of actions in environments that are *deterministic* and whose initial state is *fully known*. The model underlying classical planning can be described as a state space containing

- a finite and discrete set of states S,
- a *known initial state* $s_0 \in S$,
- a set $S_G \subseteq S$ of goal states,
- actions $A(s) \subseteq A$ applicable in each $s \in S$,
- a *deterministic transition function* $s' = f(a, s)$ for $a \in A(s)$, and
- *uniform action costs* $c(a, s)$ equal to 1.

A solution or *plan* in this model is a sequence of actions $a_0, \ldots, a_n$ that generates a state sequence $s_0, s_1, \ldots, s_{n+1}$ such that a_i is applicable in the state s_i and results in the state $s_{i+1} = f(a_i, s_i)$, the last of which is a goal state.

The cost of a plan is the sum of the action costs, which in this setting, corresponds to plan length. A plan is optimal it is has minimum cost, and the cost of a problem is the cost of an optimal plan.

Domain-independent classical planners accept a compact description of the above models, and automatically produce a plan (an optimal plan if the planner is optimal). This problem is intractable in the worst case, yet currently large classical problems can be solved using heuristic functions derived from the problem encodings.

A simple but still common language for encoding classical planning problems is Strips [9]. A problem in Strips is a tuple $P = \langle F, O, I, G \rangle$ where

- F stands for set of all *atoms* (boolean vars),
- O stands for set of all *operators* (actions),
- $I \subseteq F$ stands for the *initial situation*, and
- $G \subseteq F$ stands for the *goal situation*.

The actions $o \in O$ are represented by three sets of atoms from F called the Add, Delete, and Precondition lists, denoted as $Add(o)$, $Del(o)$, $Pre(o)$. The first, describes the atoms that the action o makes true, the second, the atoms that o makes false, and the third, the atoms that must be true for the action o to be applicable.

A Strips problem $P = \langle F, O, I, G \rangle$ encodes the state model $\mathcal{S}(P)$ where

- the states $s \in S$ are *collections of atoms* from F,
- the initial state s_0 is I,
- the goal states s are those for which $G \subseteq s$,
- the actions a in $A(s)$ are the ones in O such that $Prec(a) \subseteq s$, and
- the next state is $s' = f(a, s) = (s \setminus Del(a)) \cup Add(a)$.

All areas in Planning, and in particular Classical Planning, have become quite empirical in recent years, with competitions held every two years, and hundreds of benchmark problems available in PDDL, a standard syntax for planning that extends Strips [15].

The classical planners that scale up best can solve large problems with hundreds of fluents and actions [16, 17]. These planners do not compute optimal solutions and cast the planning problem P as an *heuristic search problem* over the state space $\mathcal{S}(P)$ that defines a directed graph whose nodes are the states, whose initial node is the initial state, and whose target nodes are the states where the goals are true [18]. This graph is never made explicit as it contains a number of states that is exponential in the number of fluents of P, but can be searched quite efficiently with current heuristics.

Heuristic functions $h(s)$ provide an estimate of the cost to reach the goal from any state s, and are derived automatically from a relaxation (simplification) of the problem P [19]. The relaxation most commonly used in planning, called the delete-relaxation and denoted as P^+, is obtained by removing the delete lists from the actions in P. While finding the *optimal* solution to the relaxation P^+ is still NP-hard, finding just one *solution* is easy and can be done in low polynomial time.

The *additive heuristic*, for example, estimates the cost $h(p; s)$ of achieving the atoms p from s through the equations [18]:

$$h(p; s) = \begin{cases} 0 & \text{if } p \in s \\ h(a_p; s) & \text{otherwise} \end{cases}$$

where a_p is a *best support* for p in s defined as

$$a_p = \operatorname{argmin}_{a \in O(p)} h(a; s)$$

$O(p)$ is the set of actions that add p in P, and $h(a; s)$ is

$$h(a; s) = cost(a) + \sum_{q \in Pre(a)} h(q; s) \ .$$

The cost of achieving the goal G from s is then defined as

$$h_{add}(s) = \sum_{p \in G} h(p; s) \ .$$

The heuristic h_{add} is not admissible (it's not a lower bound) but is informative and its computation involves the solution of a shortest-path problem in *atom space* as opposed to *state space*. A plan $\pi^+(s)$ for the relaxation P^+ can be obtained from the heuristic $h_{add}(s)$ by simply collecting the *best supports* recursively backwards from the goal [20]. This is actually the technique used in the state-of-the-art planner LAMA [17], winner of the 2008 International Planning Competition, that defines the heuristic $h(s)$ as the cost of this 'relaxed plan', and uses it in problems where action costs are not uniform. The search algorithm in LAMA is (greedy) best first search with the evaluation function $f(s) = h(s)$ and two open lists rather one, for giving precedence to the actions applicable in the state s that are most relevant to the goal according to $\pi^+(s)$; the so-called helpful actions [7].

3   Incomplete Information

The good news about classical planning is that it works: large problems can be solved quite fast, and the sheer size of a problem is not an obstacle to its solution. The bad news is that the assumptions underlying classical planning are too restrictive. We address now the problems that arise from the presence of *uncertainty* in the initial situation. The resulting problems are called *conformant* as they have the same form as classical plans, namely plain action sequences, but they must work for each of the initial states that are possible.

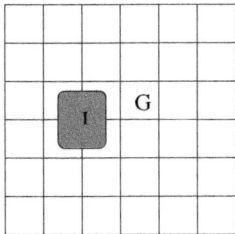

Fig. 2. A problem involving incomplete information: a robot must move from an uncertain initial location I shown in gray, to the target cell G with certainty. For this, it must locate itself into a corner and then head to G.

An example that illustrates the difficulties that arise from the presence of incomplete information in the initial situation is shown in Fig. 2. It displays a robot that must move from an uncertain initial location I, shown in gray, to the target cell G that must be reached with certainty. The robot can move one cell at a time, without leaving the grid: moves that would leave the agent out of the grid have no effects. The problem is very much like a classical planning problem except for the uncertain initial situation I. The solutions to the problem, however, are quite different. Indeed, the best *conformant plan* for the problem must move the robot to a corner first, and then head with certainty to the target

G. For example, for being certain that the robot is at the left lower corner of the grid, the robot can move *left* three times, and *down* three times. Notice that this is the opposite of reasoning by cases; indeed, the best action to do from each of the possible initial locations is not to move left or right, but up or right. Yet such moves would not help the robot reach the goal with certainty.

The model for the conformant planning problem is the model for classical planning but with the initial state s_0 replaced by a non-empty *set* S_0 of possible initial states. The Strips syntax for the problem $P = \langle F, O, I, G \rangle$ is also extended to let I stand for a *set of clauses* and not just a set of atoms, and O to include actions with effects L, positive or negative, that are *conditional* on a set of literals $L_1, \ldots, L_n$, written as $L_1, \ldots, L_n \to L$, where each L_i and L are positive or negative literals.

Conformant planning problems are no longer path-finding problems over a directed graph whose nodes are the *states* of the problem, but rather path-finding problems over a directed graph whose nodes are *sets of states*, also called *belief states* [21]. Belief states express the states of the world that are deemed possible to the agent. Thus, while in classical planning, the size of the (state) space to search is exponential in the number of variables in the problem; in conformant planning, the size of the (belief) space to search is exponential in the number of states. Indeed, conformant planning is harder than classical planning, as even the verification of conformant plans is NP-hard [22].

Conformant planners such as Contingent-FF, MBP, and POND [23–25], address the search in belief space using suitable belief representations such as OBDDs, that do not necessarily blow up with the number of states deemed possible, and heuristics that can guide the search for the target beliefs. Another approach that has been pursued recently, that turned out to be the most competitive in the 2006 Int. Planning Competition, is to automatically transform the conformant problems P into classical problems $K(P)$ that are solved by off-the-shelf classical planners.

The translation $K(P) = K_{T,M}(P)$ of a conformant problem P involves two parameters: a set of *tags* T and a set of *merges* M [26]. A tag t is a set (conjunction) of literals in P whose status in the initial situation I is not known, and a merge $m \in M$ is a collection of tags $t_1, \ldots, t_n$ that stands for the DNF formula $t_1 \vee \cdots \vee t_n$. Tags are assumed to represent consistent assumptions about I, i.e. $I \not\models \neg t$, and merges represent disjunctions of assumptions that follow from I; i.e. $I \models t_1 \vee \cdots \vee t_n$.

The fluents in $K_{T,M}(P)$, for the conformant problem $P = \langle F, O, I, G \rangle$ are of the form KL/t for each $L \in F$ and $t \in T$, meaning that "it is known that if t is true in the initial situation, L is true". In addition, $K_{T,M}(P)$ includes extra actions, called *merge actions*, that allow the derivation of a literal KL (i.e. KL/t with the "empty tag", expressing that L is known unconditionally) when KL/t' has been obtained for each tag t' in a merge $m \in M$ for L.

Formally, for a conformant problem $P = \langle F, O, I, G \rangle$, the translation defines the *classical problem* $K_{T,M}(P) = \langle F', O', I', G' \rangle$ where

$$F' = \{KL/t, K\neg L/t \mid L \in F\}$$
$$I' = \{KL/t \mid \text{if } I \models t \supset L\}$$
$$G' = \{KL \mid L \in G\}$$
$$O' = \{a : KC/t \to KL/t, \ a : \neg K\neg C/t \to \neg K\neg L/t$$
$$\mid a : C \to L \text{ in } P\} \cup \{\bigwedge_{t \in m} KL/t \to KL \mid m \in M_L\}$$

with t ranging over T and with the preconditions of the actions a in $K_{T,M}(P)$ including the literal KL if the preconditions of a in P include the literal L.

When $C = L_1, \ldots, L_n$, the expressions KC/t and $\neg K\neg C/t$ are abbreviations for $KL_1/t, \ldots, KL_n/t$ and $\neg K\neg L_1/t, \ldots, \neg K\neg L_n/t$ respectively. A rule $a : C \to L$ in P gets mapped into "support rules" $a : KC/t \to KL/t$ and "cancellation rules" $a : \neg K\neg C/t \to \neg K\neg L/t$; the former "adds" KL/t when the condition C is known in t, the latter undercut the persistence of $K\neg L/t$ except when (a literal in) C is known to be false in t.

The translation $K_{T,M}(P)$ is *sound*, meaning that the classical plans that solve $K_{T,M}(P)$ yield valid conformant plans for P that can be obtained by just dropping the merge actions. On the other hand, the *complexity* and *completeness* of the translation depend on the choice of tags T and merges M. The $K_i(P)$ translation, where i is a non-negative integer, is a special case of the $K_{T,M}(P)$ translation where the tags t are restricted to contain at most i literals. $K_i(P)$ is exponential in i and complete for problems with *conformant width* less than or equal to i. The planner T_0 feeds the $K_1(P)$ translation into the classical FF planner [7] and was the winning entry in the Conformant Track of the 2006 IPC [27].

4   Sensing and Finite-State Controllers

Most often problems that involve *uncertainty* in the initial state of the environment or in the action effects, also involve some type of *feedback* or *sensors* that provide partial state information. As an illustration of a problem of this type, consider the simple grid shown on the left of Fig. 3, where an agent starting in some cell between A and B, mut move to B, and then to A. In this problem, while the exact initial location of the agent is not known, it is assumed that the marks A and B are *observable*.

The solutions to problems involving observations can be expressed in many forms: as contingent plans [23], as policies mapping beliefs into actions [12], and as *finite-state controllers*. A finite-state controller that solves the problem above is shown on the right of Fig. 3. An arrow $q_i \to q_j$ between one controller state q_i and another (or the same) controller state q_i labeled with a pair O/a means to do action a and switch to state q_j, when o is observed in the state q_i. Starting in the controller state q_0, the controller shown tells the agent to move right until observing B, and then to move left until observing A or B (the observation '-' means no observation).

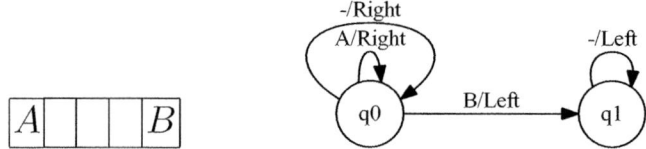

Fig. 3. *Left:* A problem where an agent, initially between A and B, must move to B and then back to A. *Right:* A finite-state controller that solves the problem.

Finite-state controllers such as the one displayed above have two features that make them more appealing than contingent plans and POMDP policies: they are often very *compact*, and they often quite *general* too. Indeed, the problem above can be changed in a number of ways and the controller shown would still work. For example, the *size of the grid* can be changed from 1×5 to $1 \times n$, the agent can be placed *initially* anywhere in the grid (except at B), and the actions can be made *non-deterministic* by the addition of 'noise'. This generality is well beyond the power of contingent plans or exact POMDP policies that are tied to a particular state space. For these reasons, finite-state controllers are widely used in practice, from controlling non-playing characters in video-games [28] to mobile robots [29, 30]. Memoryless controllers or policies [31] are widely used as well, and they are nothing but finite-state controllers with a single state. The additional states provide finite-state controllers with memory that allows different actions to be taken given the same observation.

The benefits of finite-state controllers, however, come at a price: unlike contingent trees and POMDP policies, they are usually not derived automatically from a model but are written by hand; a task that is not trivial even in the simplest cases. There have been attempts for deriving finite-state controllers for POMDPs with a given number of states [32–34], but the problem can be solved approximately only, with no correctness guarantees.

Recently, we have extended the translation-based approach to conformant planning presented above [26], to derive finite-state controllers [35]. For this, the *control problem* P is defined in terms of a *conformant problem* with no preconditions, extended with a set O of *observable fluents*. The solution to the problem P is defined in terms of *finite state controllers* $\mathcal{C}_N$ with a given number N of *controller states*. This rules out sequential plans as possible solutions, as they would involve a number of controller states equal to the number of time steps in the plan.

The controller $\mathcal{C}_N$ is a set of tuples $t = \langle i, o, a, k \rangle$ that tell the agent to do a and switch to state q_k when the observation is o and the controller state is q_i. The key result is that a finite-state controller $\mathcal{C}_N$ that solves P can be obtained from the *classical plans* of a *classical problem* P_N obtained by a suitable translation from P, O, and N. The key idea in the translation is to replace each action a in P by an action $a(t)$, for each $t = \langle i, o, a, k \rangle$, so that the effects $C \to C'$ of a in P become effects $q_i, o, C \to \neg q_i, q_k, C'$ of $a(t)$ in P_N. That is, the effects of the action a are made conditional on the observation o and state q_i in the actions $a(t)$ where $t = \langle i, o, a, k \rangle$.

Fig. 4 shows a more challenging problem solved in this way, resulting in a very compact and general controller. In the problem, shown on the left, a visual-marker (a circle on the lower left) must be moved on top of a green block . The observations are whether the cell currently marked contains a green block (G), a non-green block (B), or neither (C); and whether this cell is at the level of the table (T) or not ('-'). The visual marker can be moved one cell at a time in the four directions. This is a problem à la Chapman or Ballard, that have advocated the use of deictic representations of this sort [36, 37]. The finite-state controller that results for this problem is shown on the right. Interestingly, it is a very compact and general controller: it involves two states only and can be used to solve the same problem for any number and arrangement of blocks. See [35] for details.

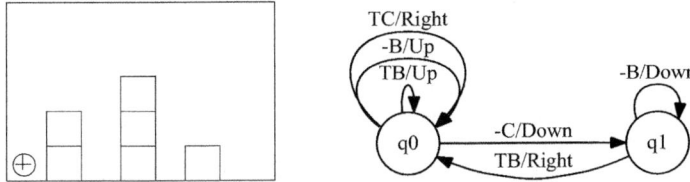

Fig. 4. *Left:* Problem where visual-marker (circle on the lower left) must be moved on top of a green block. The observations are whether the cell currently marked contains a green block (G), a non-green block (B), or neither (C); and whether this cell is at the level of the table (T) or not (−). *Right:* Finite-state controller that solves the problem for any number and arrangement of blocks.

5   Summary

I have reviewed some of the formulations, transformations, and inference techniques that have been found useful for planning for incomplete information. While planning with incomplete information can be cast as a search problem in belief space, the techniques that we have presented aim to exploit the finer propositional structure of planning problems, and in particular, the performance of classical planners. The area of planning with incomplete information has matured much in the last few years, both theoretically and experimentally, although further work is required to scale up to problems of real size. This is the challenge for the next few years; many of the basic ideas are already in place.

Acknowledgments. This paper is a revision of [38]. It's joint work with a number of students and colleagues, in particular Blai Bonet and Hector Palacios. I thank Jan-Georg Smaus and Ron van der Meyden for the invitation to MoChaArt. The author is partially supported by grant TIN2009-10232,MICINN, Spain.

References

1. Newell, A., Simon, H.: GPS: a program that simulates human thought. In: Feigenbaum, E., Feldman, J. (eds.) Computers and Thought, pp. 279–293. McGraw Hill, New York (1963)
2. Bylander, T.: The computational complexity of STRIPS planning. Artificial Intelligence 69, 165–204 (1994)
3. Blum, A., Furst, M.: Fast planning through planning graph analysis. In: Proceedings of IJCAI 1995, pp. 1636–1642. Morgan Kaufmann, San Francisco (1995)
4. Kautz, H., Selman, B.: Pushing the envelope: Planning, propositional logic, and stochastic search. In: Proc. AAAI, pp. 1194–1201 (1996)
5. McDermott, D.: Using regression-match graphs to control search in planning. Artificial Intelligence 109(1-2), 111–159 (1999)
6. Bonet, B., Loerincs, G., Geffner, H.: A robust and fast action selection mechanism for planning. In: Proceedings of AAAI 1997, pp. 714–719. MIT Press, Cambridge (1997)
7. Hoffmann, J., Nebel, B.: The FF planning system: Fast plan generation through heuristic search. Journal of Artificial Intelligence Research 14, 253–302 (2001)
8. Sutton, R., Barto, A.: Introduction to Reinforcement Learning. MIT Press, Cambridge (1998)
9. Fikes, R., Nilsson, N.: STRIPS: A new approach to the application of theorem proving to problem solving. Artificial Intelligence 1, 27–120 (1971)
10. Goldman, R.P., Boddy, M.S.: Expressive planning and explicit knowledge. In: Proc. AIPS 1996 (1996)
11. Smith, D., Weld, D.: Conformant graphplan. In: Proceedings AAAI 1998, pp. 889–896. AAAI Press, Menlo Park (1998)
12. Cassandra, A., Kaelbling, L., Littman, M.L.: Acting optimally in partially observable stochastic domains. In: Proc. AAAI, pp. 1023–1028 (1994)
13. Dechter, R.: Constraint Processing. Morgan Kaufmann, San Francisco (2003)
14. Pearl, J.: Probabilistic Reasoning in Intelligent Systems. Morgan Kaufmann, San Francisco (1988)
15. McDermott, D.: The 1998 AI Planning Systems Competition. Artificial Intelligence Magazine 21(2), 35–56 (2000)
16. Helmert, M.: The Fast Downward planning system. Journal of Artificial Intelligence Research 26, 191–246 (2006)
17. Richter, S., Helmert, M., Westphal, M.: Landmarks revisited. In: Proc. AAAI, pp. 975–982 (2008)
18. Bonet, B., Geffner, H.: Planning as heuristic search. Artificial Intelligence 129(1-2), 5–33 (2001)
19. Pearl, J.: Heuristics. Addison-Wesley, Reading (1983)
20. Keyder, E., Geffner, H.: Heuristics for planning with action costs revisited. In: Proc. ECAI 2008 (2008)
21. Bonet, B., Geffner, H.: Planning with incomplete information as heuristic search in belief space. In: Proc. of AIPS 2000, pp. 52–61. AAAI Press, Menlo Park (2000)
22. Haslum, P., Jonsson, P.: Some results on the complexity of planning with incomplete information. In: Biundo, S., Fox, M. (eds.) ECP 1999. LNCS, vol. 1809, pp. 308–318. Springer, Heidelberg (2000)
23. Hoffmann, J., Brafman, R.: Contingent planning via heuristic forward search with implicit belief states. In: Proc. ICAPS, pp. 71–80 (2005)

24. Bertoli, P., Cimatti, A., Roveri, M., Traverso, P.: Planning in nondeterministic domains under partial observability via symbolic model checking. In: Proc. IJCAI 2001 (2001)
25. Bryce, D., Kambhampati, S., Smith, D.E.: Planning graph heuristics for belief space search. Journal of AI Research 26, 35–99 (2006)
26. Palacios, H., Geffner, H.: From conformant into classical planning: Efficient translations that may be complete too. In: Proc. 17th Int. Conf. on Planning and Scheduling, ICAPS 2007 (2007)
27. Bonet, B., Givan, B.: Results of the conformant track of the 5th int. planning competition (2006), http://www.ldc.usb.ve/~bonet/ipc5/docs/results-conformant.pdf
28. Buckland, M.: Programming Game AI by Example. Wordware Publishing Inc., Plano (2004)
29. Murphy, R.R.: An Introduction to AI Robotics. MIT Press, Cambridge (2000)
30. Mataric, M.J.: The Robotics Primer. MIT Press, Cambridge (2007)
31. Littman, M.L.: Memoryless policies: Theoretical limitations and practical results. In: Cliff, D. (ed.) From Animals to Animats 3. MIT Press, Cambridge (1994)
32. Meuleau, N., Peshkin, L., Kim, K., Kaelbling, L.P.: Learning finite-state controllers for partially observable environments. In: Proc. UAI, pp. 427–436 (1999)
33. Poupart, P., Boutilier, C.: Bounded finite state controllers. In: Proc. NIPS, pp. 823–830 (2003)
34. Amato, C., Bernstein, D., Zilberstein, S.: Optimizing memory-bounded controllers for decentralized pomdps. In: Proc. UAI (2007)
35. Bonet, B., Palacios, H., Geffner, H.: Automatic derivation of memoryless policies and finite-state controllers using classical planners. In: Proc. Int. Conf. on Automated Planning and Scheduling, ICAPS 2009 (2009)
36. Chapman, D.: Penguins can make cake. AI magazine 10(4), 45–50 (1989)
37. Ballard, D., Hayhoe, M., Pook, P., Rao, R.: Deictic codes for the embodiment of cognition. Behavioral and Brain Sciences 20(4), 723–742 (1997)
38. Geffner, H.: Inference and learning in planning (extended abstract). In: Gama, J., Costa, V.S., Jorge, A.M., Brazdil, P.B. (eds.) DS 2009. LNCS, vol. 5808, pp. 1–12. Springer, Heidelberg (2009)

External Memory Breadth-First Search with Delayed Duplicate Detection on the GPU

Stefan Edelkamp and Damian Sulewski

TZI, Universität Bremen, Germany
{edelkamp,sulewski}@tzi.de

Abstract. We accelerate breadth-first search by delegating complex operations to the graphics processing unit (GPU). The algorithm exploits external memory: if the state space becomes too large to be kept in main memory, it is maintained I/O-efficiently on disk.

As in many other approaches for external memory graph search, we apply delayed duplicate detection. The search proceeds in breadth-first layers with increasing minimum distance from the start state. For each layer stored on disk, we load chunks into the systems memory, which are forwarded to the memory on the graphics card. Here we test if outgoing transitions are enabled and generate all successors. Finally, we eliminate duplicates delayed by sorting on the GPU. Even facing the overhead of I/O access, noticeable overall speed-ups are obtained.

1 Introduction

Thanks to a continuous improvement of algorithms, but also because of the increasing power of the graphics processing units (GPUs), search engines have been able to successfully cope with complexity and tackle a wide range of problems.

Modern GPUs are not only powerful, but also parallel programmable processors featuring high arithmetic capabilities and memory bandwidths. Its rapid increase in both programmability and capability has inspired researchers to map computationally challenging, complex problems to it. These efforts in general purpose programming on the GPU (GPGPU) have positioned it as a compelling alternative to traditional microprocessors in high-performance computing. Since the memory transfer between the graphics card and the main board (using the express bus) is extremely fast, GPUs have become candidates to speed-up large-scale computations like sorting [35].

The GPU's architecture being based on the requirements for visualizing data is very different to multi-core processors build to manipulate data. It accumulates a huge number of cores in one chip, but the programming and computational models are different from each other. GPU programming requires a special compiler, which translates the code to native instructions. The number of cores on the GPU exceeds the one on the CPU, but they are limited to streamed processing. The architecture is that of a vector computer following the *single instruction multiple data* (SIMD) paradigm with the same function running on all processors. While cores on a multi-core processor work autonomously, the operations

R. van der Meyden and J.-G. Smaus (Eds.): MoChArt 2010, LNAI 6572, pp. 12–31, 2011.

of cores on the GPU are strongly correlated. The GPU supports different layers for accessing memory, forbids common writes to a memory cell and a limited form of concurrent read.

In the research field of Artificial Intelligence (AI), external memory breadth-first search [31] branch-and-bound [44] , and A* [16] have been studied and solved challenging problems. Optimal solutions to AI problems with state spaces of more than a quintillion (10^{18} or a billion times a billion) have been obtained. In extreme cases, weeks of computation time, gigabytes of main memory and terabytes of hard disk space have been invested to solve search challenges.

For example, the state space of the Fifteen Puzzle has been completely generated with external memory breadth first search in several weeks of computation time using 1.4 terabytes of disk space [33]. Memory saving strategies like bitvector compression in external memory breadth-first search apply in case of inversible hash functions [32]. The approach has been successfully ported on the GPU [20] but is less general than the delayed detection of duplicates.

In model checking, external memory BFS is sufficient for the verification of safety properties. Moreover, variants of it are in use to generate counter-examples of minimal length [21]. As identified e.g. in [6], complete state space construction via external memory BFS is the performance bottleneck for large-scale model checking. Last, but not least, it is essential for constructing the state space on hard disk for a perfect hash function, the basis for semi-external [17] and flash-memory efficient model checking [18]. After having generated the state space its compression in form of a memory based hash function is considerably fast. In order to avoid the problem of accessing swap space on external memory (thrashing), several other large-scale model checking attempts [34,15] also refer to variants of external memory model checking.

An internal memory (RAM) approach to explicit-state GPU-based model checking [4,3] transforms model checking to a matrix multiplication problem to apply fast operations on the graphics card. The speed-ups are considerable, but the approach applies to small state spaces only. We propose a conceptually different algorithm, suited to parallel model checking large models. In such large-scale verificationWhile our GPU-based algorithm also applies to internal memory model checking, our interest is in efficiency advances in exploring state spaces which exceed the available RAM. For showing significant results the verified model or, in other words, the number of reachable states in the state space, has to be big enough to occupy all fragment processors and overcome the slow-down imposed by copying the data.

This paper applies GPGPU technology to external memory state space generation using external memory breadth-first search (BFS) in implicit graphs that are generated via repeatedly applying transitions. Our work extends a technical report [19] that restricts to advances in the sorting process for the delayed detection of duplicates, a commonly used technique to avoid random look-up in external memory search. This revision covers the entire search process, including the test for the enabledness of transitions and generating the successors.

Our focus is external memory breadth-first search (BFS) to generate the entire state space in implicit graphs that are generated via repeatedly applying transitions. While external memory BFS for explicit graphs is studied by algorithm engineers [37,36], external memory BFS is relevant for both model checking and artificial intelligence.

We are interested in sorting based external-memory BFS [27] that leads to three computationally intensive tasks applied to each BFS layer which are all portable to the GPU:

- for each state in the layer test the applicability of outgoing transitions.
- generate the set of successors for all states and enabled transitions.
- apply delayed duplicate detection by sorting and scanning all successors.

For all three stages we obtain significant individual speed-ups of more than one order of magnitude in analyzing benchmark protocols on the GPU[1]. The overhead in combining the results of the different stages in the CPU and the I/O bandwidth limitation limits the, still noticeable, overall speed-ups.

The paper is structured as follows. We next review large-scale explicit state space generation and the issue of delayed duplicate detection. Then an overview on the GPU architecture used is provided. Next, we turn to GPU-based BFS and provide details on delayed duplicate elimination, transition checking and successor generation and supply a note on their complexities. Finally, we present empirical results in various benchmark protocols and discuss future research avenues.

2   External-Memory Breadth-First Search

External memory searching in a graph has to prevent revisiting of already explored states, so that states that have been processed have to be recognized and a generated state can be checked against the set of visited ones. Due to the huge number of states and in some cases their large sizes, time and memory demands rise rapidly.

To release RAM, states have to be written to disk. A check, whether a state has been visited, now involves accessing the disk (I/O). Here, an important aspect is to access the data in blocks to reduce the I/O waiting time per state and to be able to increase bandwidth by connecting multiple external devices. Different disk-based solutions to this problem have been published [15,6,5]. In [15], the authors avoid nested DFS for accepting cycle detection by reducing the liveness to a safety problem [40]. The I/O-efficient solution was further improved by guided and parallel search. Another disk-based algorithm for LTL model checking [5] avoids the increase in space, but does not operate on-the-fly. The algorithm given in [6] is both on-the-fly and linear in the space requirements, but its worst-case time complexity is large.

---

[1] Hashing contributes only a small fraction to the overall performance so that we compute the hash values in by the CPU. There is a recent study for advanced incremental hashing in SPIN [38] with moderate but visible performance gains.

In delayed duplicate detection [28] individual checks against the set of visited states are postponed and performed in a bulk operation to amortize the cost of I/O. Duplicates have to be eliminated both within one layer and with respect to previous layers. The additional efforts for detecting duplicates late slows down the verification, so that various improvements for BFS space generation have been studied: resisting revisiting states in large search depths [6], or layered duplicate detection, sacrificing completeness [34].

Hash-based delayed duplicate detection for external memory breadth-first search has successfully been applied to puzzles like the Towers-of-Hanoi problem [29]. For the example of the 30-disc 4-peg Towers-of-Hanoi problem the approach divides the state uniquely by the location of the discs. Using two bits per disc this gives a total of 60 bits. The discs are divided into the 16 largest and 14 smallest discs. States are written to the file based on the position of the 16 largest discs. Thus, all states in any given file have the 16 largest discs in identical positions, and any set of duplicate nodes must be confined to the same file. This allows to read one file at a time into a hash table in memory, detect and merge any duplicate nodes in that file, and write out just one copy to an output file. A similar approach has been applied to the 15-Puzzle [30], where representation of a state corresponds to 64 bit, but hash functions that take the first few tiles and the remaining tiles, the space required for the entire puzzle could be reduced to about 1.4 terabytes. For hash-based delayed duplicate detection, however, implicit assumptions on the regularity of the domain apply that illustrate the differences to be applied in model checking domains.

Semi-external model checking [17] is one of the fastest methods for large-scale verification of LTL properties. It exploits the power of perfect hash functions and maintains the state space in compressed form by externally constructing a RAM-based mapping from states to indices. After generating the state space via BFS on disk, a space-efficient minimum perfect hash function [10,8] is computed and used to address collision-free bit-state hash tables. In other words, it reinvents immediate duplicate detection e.g. for depth-first model checking algorithms.

Assumed a perfect hash function is known prior to the search external two-bit breadth-first search by [32] integrates a tight compression method into an I/O efficient algorithm. It applies a space-efficient representation in breadth-first search with two frontier bits per state, an idea that goes back to [14].

To tackle the intrinsic hardness of large search problems in AI, sparse-memory and disk-based algorithms are in joint use. Examples are frontier search with duplicate detection schemes (being either delayed [31] or structured [44]). Especially on multiple disks, instead of I/O waiting time due to disk latencies, the computational bottleneck for these external-memory algorithms is internal time, so that a rising number of parallel search variants have been studied [33,45,15].

In [20] a smooth interplay of a bitvector state space representation and parallel computation on the GPU is proposed. It is shown how to efficiently rank and unrank states on the GPU. To map the search space to a bit-vector GPU-based two-bit BFS, and, for limited space, one-bit variants are studied.

3   GPU Programming

The design of our model checking algorithm is closely related to the architecture of GPUs. Thus, insights into this architecture are essential.

The application of the modern GPUs goes far beyond the realm of graphics applications. They can be seen as general purpose multi-threaded data parallel co-processors. However, there are substantial architectural differences between GPUs and CPUs, including the new generations of multi-core processors. This imposes restrictions on the programs that can run on GPUs. Consequently, one has to cope with several new challenges when developing model checking algorithms for GPUs. The latter can significantly differ not only compared to their sequential counterparts, but also to the multi-core and distributed (cluster-based) analogues.

Harnessing the power of GPUs is facilitated by the new APIs for general computation on GPUs. CUDA is an interface from NVIDIA where programs are basically extended C programs. To this end CUDA features extensions like: special declarations to explicitly place variables in some of the memories (e.g., shared, global, local), predefined keywords (variables) containing the block and thread IDs, synchronization statements for cooperation between threads, run-time API for memory management (allocation, deallocation), and statements to launch functions on GPU.

CUDA enforces a program architecture which provides flexibility and minimizes the dependence of the software from the concrete GPU. A CUDA program consists of a *host* program which runs on the CPU and a set of CUDA *kernels*. The kernels, which are the parallel parts of the program, are launched on the GPU device from the host program, which comprises the sequential parts. The CUDA kernel is a parallel program that is executed as a set of *threads*. Each thread of the kernel executes the same code. Threads of a kernel are grouped in *blocks* that form a *grid*. Each thread block of the grid is uniquely identified by its block ID and analogously each thread is uniquely identified by its thread ID within its block. The dimensions of the thread and the thread block are specified at the time of launching the kernel. Blocks of a grid are ordered as an one- or two-dimensional array dividing the block ID in x and y axis component, while the threads of a block are ordered in up to three dimensions. A thread is then identified uniquely by the x, y ans z axis component of the thread ID.

The GPU offers three different kind of memories that differ substantially in access speed (latencies). This has important implications for the efficiency of the CUDA programs.

The memory hierarchy loosely maps to the program thread-block-kernel hierarchy. Each thread has its own *on-chip registers* which are fast and *off-chip local memory*, which is quite slow. Per block there is also an on-chip *shared memory*(SRAM). Threads within a block cooperate via this memory. If more than one block is executed in parallel then the shared memory is equally split between them. The whole grid – all blocks and threads within them – have access to the off-chip *global memory* (Video RAM, or VRAM) at the speed of RAM. The host has read and write access to the VRAM, but cannot access the other memories

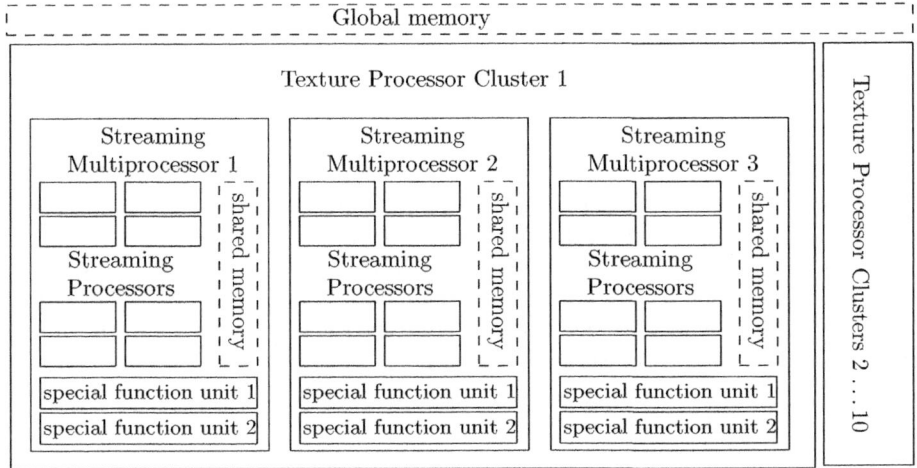

Fig. 1. Sample GPU Architecture

(registers, local, shared). Thus, as such, global memory is used for communication between the host and the kernel. Threads within a block can communicate also via light-weight synchronization barriers.

The GPU architecture, as shown exemplary in 1, consists of a set of multiprocessor units called streaming multiprocessors (SMs). Each SM contains a set of processor cores called streaming processors (SPs). The NVIDIA GeForce GTX280, which we are using for the experiments in this paper, has 30 SMs each consisting of 8 SPs, which gives in total 240 SPs.

Analogously with the memory model, there is a similar correspondence between the CUDA logical (programming) hierarchy and the physical (hardware) hierarchy of the GPU. Each thread is assigned to one processor (SP), whereas several threads can be executed alternately. Similarly, each block is mapped to one multiprocessor (SM), whereas each multiprocessor can execute several blocks. The logical kernel architecture allows flexibility: the GPU can schedule the blocks of the kernel depending of the concrete hardware architecture in an optimal way which is completely transparent for the user. Each multiprocessor performs computations in SIMT (Single Instruction Multiple Threads) manner, which means that the same instruction is executed for each thread independently with its own instruction address and local state (registers and local memory).

Due to the above described specific logical and physical architectures, GPU programs often require optimization techniques which are quite different compared to the multi-core and distributed parallel programming contexts. These idiosyncrasies of the GPU programming are mainly visible in the optimization of memory latencies, synchronization, thread mapping, the data layout in the memory, and data reuse.

Communication with the off-chip device memory is relatively slow compared to the enormous peak computational power. This is usually the main performance bottleneck. To fully exploit the capacity of the GPU parallelism this memory latency must be minimized. Another issue that can lead to a performance degradation is unnecessary synchronization between thread blocks. The inter-thread communication within a block is cheap via the fast shared memory, but the accesses to the global and local memories are more than hundred times slower.

Unlike the CPU threads, the GPU threads are very light-weight with negligible overhead of creation and switching. This allows GPUs to use thousands of threads whereas multi-core CPUs use only a few. Usually more threads and blocks are created than the number of SPs and SMs, respectively, which allows GPU to maximally use the capacity via smart scheduling - while some threads/blocks are waiting for data, the others which have their data ready are assigned for execution. Thus, another way to maximize the parallelism is by optimizing the thread mapping. This is often tightly coupled with the optimization of the memory access. One should strive towards an alignment of the data in the memory such that threads of the same block access memory locations which are as close as possible. In this case we have so-called coalesced accesses. Thus, threads that access physically close memory locations should be grouped together such that they can be provided data with the same memory access. Finally, in order to minimize the access to the slow global memory, one should exploit data reuse. The parts of the computation are localized to thread blocks which are synchronized as loosely as possible. These threads use local data as much as possible and the global results are written only at the end of the computation.

4   External Memory Breadth-First Search on the GPU

In the following, we provide the essentials for large-scale breadth-first explicit-state model checking on the GPU. We show how to test enabledness for a set of states in parallel, and – given all sets of applicable transitions – how to generate the successor state sets accordingly. Duplicate detection is delayed. We restrict to BFS, generating the entire search space. This is sufficient for verifying safety properties. As said, exploring large state spaces with breadth-first search on disk is an essential step for semi-external LTL model checkingL [17]. Our setting, illustrated in Fig. 2, indicates the interplay of the different kinds of memory and the partition of it into cells and of processing units into cores. The intuition behind our approach to external memory BFS is to dispatch set operations to the GPU.

The pseudo-codes display a fine-grained algorithm, separating the selection of the transitions from their application. For the sake of clarity, the transfer from

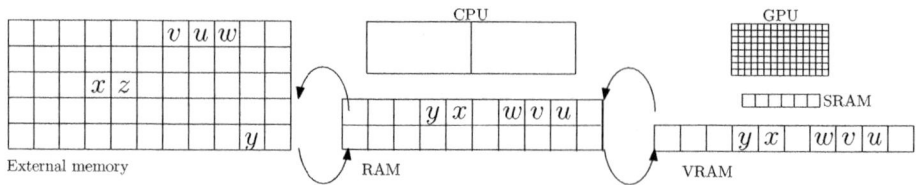

Fig. 2. External-Memory Search on the GPU

Procedure GPU-BFS
Input: Initial state s, transition conditions *guards* and updates *effects*
Output: State space
  $g := 0$; $Layer[g] := \{s\}$
  while $(Layer[g] \neq \emptyset)$
    $Layer[g + 1] := SuccLayer := EnabledLayer := LayerPart := EnabledLayerPart := \emptyset$
    for each $s \in Layer[g]$
      $LayerPart := LayerPart \cup \{s\}$
      if $|LayerPart| = |\text{VRAM}|$
        $Enabledlayer := EnabledLayer \cup GPU\text{-}CheckEnabledness(LayerPart, guards)$
        $LayerPart := \emptyset$
    $EnabledLayer := EnabledLayer \cup GPU\text{-}CheckEnabledness(LayerPart, guards)$
    for each $(s, b) \in EnabledLayer$
      $EnabledLayerPart := EnabledLayerPart \cup \{(s, b)\}$
      if $|EnabledLayerPart| = |\text{VRAM}|$
        $SuccLayer := SuccLayer \cup GPU\text{-}ExpandLayer(EnabledLayerPart, effects)$
        $EnabledLayerPart := \emptyset$
    $SuccLayer := SuccLayer \cup GPU\text{-}ExpandLayer(EnabledLayerPart, effects)$
    for each $s \in SuccLayer$
      $H[hash(s)] := H[hash(s)] \cup \{s\}$
      if $|H[hash(s)]| = H[hash(s)].\max$ **then**
        $Sorted := GPU\text{-}DetectDuplicates(H)$
        $CompactedLayer := ScanAndRemoveDuplicates(Sorted)$
        $DuplicateFreeLayer := SubtractDuplicates(CompactedLayer, Layer[0..g])$
        $Layer[g + 1] := Merge(Layer[g + 1], DuplicateFreeLayer)$
        $H[0..m] := \emptyset$
    $Sorted := GPU\text{-}DetectDuplicates(H)$
    $CompactedLayer := ScanAndRemoveDuplicates(Sorted)$
    $DuplicateFreeLayer := SubtractDuplicates(CompactedLayer, Layer[0..g])$
    $Layer[g + 1] := Merge(Layer[g + 1], DuplicateFreeLayer)$
    $g := g + 1$
  return $Layer[0..g - 1]$

Fig. 3. Large-Scale Breadth-First Search on the GPU

hard disk to RAM (and back) for layers that do not fit in RAM is hidden in the set based representation, so is the transfer from RAM to VRAM.

For each BFS layer the state space enumeration is divided into three computational stages (see Alg. 3). The GPU functions needed for state exploration are displayed in Alg. 4 and 5. In the first stage, a set of enabled transitions is generated by copying the states to the global memory on the graphics card and replacing them by a bitvector of enabled transitions. In the second stage, sets of all possible successors are generated. For each enabled transition a pair, joining the transition ID and the explored state, is copied to the VRAM. Each state is replicated by the number of successors it generates in order to avoid memory to be allocated dynamically. The third stage removes all duplicates by hashing the successors to buckets, which are indexed by the hash value, and by sorting the buckets in the GPU. Adjacent duplicates are removed in a first scan, followed by scans to remove duplicates from previous layers.

For accelerating the exploration of states, we executed both the enabledness check and the generation of successors on the GPU, parallelizing (the essentials of) the entire model checking process. We exploit the fact that the order of explorations in one BFS-layer does not matter, so that no communication between the threads nor explicit load balancing is required. Each processor is simply assigned to its share and starts operating. Duplicate detection is delayed. Moreover, we separate the search frontier from the closed set of states, as only the first one needs to be accessible in uncompressed form.

In the state exploration routine, first we check all transitions and then we fire the enabled ones. Since the GPU can not access RAM and pointer manipulation on it is limited, it is necessary to rewrite the transition guard labels to be evaluated. This description has to be efficient in memory and evaluation time, since the size of the VRAM is small taking into account the high number of cores on the GPU. Furthermore, all transitions should be moved into one memory block to take advantage of fast block transfer on the express bus.

We rewrite the guards in reverse Polish notation [12], i.e., a postfix representation of Boolean and arithmetic expressions. This yields a pointer-free, compact and flat representation of the transition guards. Converting the protocol to such a notation and transferring it to the GPU is executed before the model checking process starts. Moreover, additional static information about the structure of the postfix representation, needed to evaluate a guard is copied to seperate memory blocks. This information includes, e.g. the offset of the guards for each process and the starting position of guards depending on the state a process is in[2]. For the application of a transition to a given state, similar to processing the guards, the effect expressions have been rewritten in reverse Polish notation. Since this static representation resides in the GPU's VRAM for the entire checking process and since it is addressed by all instances of the same kernel function, its access is fast. The cause is that broadcasting is an integral operation on most graphics cards.

4.1   Checking Enabledness on the GPU

Exploiting data reuse we make use of the fact that the state, copied to the GPU is obsolete once it has been evaluated for active transitions. On the other hand the indices of the transitions have to be transfered to the host for further proceeding and the global memory should contain a maximum number of states to utilize most of the fragment processors. This observation immediately leads to filling the complete VRAM with states and overwriting them with the indices. Considering the fact that a state and the number of all transitions in the model are both fixed and known prior to the search we arrive at a bitvector representation for communicating the active transitions from the GPU to the host. A check weather the number of transitions exceeds the size of the bitvector representation of a state is performed once and more space is reserved if needed.

According to that the VRAM is filled with states from the *Open* list in the first statge, see Algorithm 3. Then, Alg. 4, executed on the GPU, computes a

---

[2] We assume the transitions to be sorted by the outgoing state.

GPU-Kernel CheckEnabledness
Input: $Layer = \{s_1, \ldots, s_k\}$
    $guards$
Output: $ELayer = \{(s_1, \boldsymbol{b_1}), \ldots, (s_k, \boldsymbol{b_k})\}$
   for each group g do
     for each thread t do in parallel
      $i := SelectState(Layer, g, t)$
      $\boldsymbol{b_i} := CheckTransition(guards, s_i)$
      $ELayer := ELayer \cup \{(s_i, \boldsymbol{b_i})\}$
   return $ELayer$

GPU-Kernel ExpandLayer
Input: $ELayer = \{(s_1, \boldsymbol{b_1}), \ldots, (s_k, \boldsymbol{b_k})\}$
    $effects$
Output: $SLayer = \{s_1, \ldots, s_l\}$
   for each group g do
     for each thread t do in parallel
      $i := SelectTransition(ELayer, g, t)$
      $s_i := ExpandStates(effects, s_i, \boldsymbol{b_i})$
      $SLayer := SLayer \cup S_i$
   return $SLayer$

Fig. 4. Checking Transitions on the GPU (left). Expanding Layer on the GPU (right).

GPU-Kernel DetectDuplicates
Input: H (unsorted)
Output: H (partially sorted)
   for each group g do
    $i := SelectTable(H, g)$
    $H'[i] := ParallelSort(H[i])$
   return H'

Fig. 5. Detecting Duplicates via Sorting on the GPU

bitvector b of transitions, with bit b_i denoting, whether or not transition i applies. The entire array, whose size is equal to the number of available transitions, is initialized to false. Each thread reads one single state at a unique position defined by its ID and computes the set of its enabled transitions. For the implementation, after having checked all transitions for enabledness, the bitvectors are copied back to RAM.

To evaluate a postfix representation of a guard, one scan through its representation suffices. The maximal length of a guard times the number of groups thus determines the parallel running time, as for all threads in a group, the check for enabledness is executed concurrently.

4.2 Generating the Successors on the GPU

After having fixed the set of applicable transitions for each state, generating the successors on the GPU is relatively simple. Each thread needs two informations to generate a successor; the parent and an index of a transition it has to apply. We tested two strategies, copying the states as one set and the corresponding transition indices as the second set, and as a second strategy, creating a pair of state and transition index and copy a set of this pairs to the GPU. While the first strategy involves a second access to the global memory on the GPU, the second strategy involves copying the pairs into a buffer in RAM. An experimental evaluation identified the second strategy as superior.

Therefore, we replicate each state to be explored by the number of enabled transitions on the CPU. Moreover, we attach the ID of the transition that is enabled together with each state. Then, we move the array of states to the GPU and generate the successors in parallel overwriting the parent state.

Each state to be explored is overwritten with the result of applying the attached transition, which often results in small changes to the state vector. Finally, all states are copied back to RAM. The run-time is determined by the maximal length of an effect times the number of groups, as for all threads in a group we generate the successors in parallel.

4.3   Delayed Duplicate Detection on the GPU

For the delayed elimination of duplicates, we sort a BFS layer wrt. a comparison function that operates on states. The array is then scanned and adjacent duplicates are removed. As mentioned above, considering its strong set of assumptions of orthogonal[3], disjoint[4] and inversible[5] hash functions, hash-based delayed duplicate detection as proposed by [33] is not available for general explicit-state model checking. Therefore, we propose a hybrid of sorting- and hash-based delayed duplicate detection, sorting buckets that are filled by applying a first level hash function. The hidden objective of this approach is that hashing in RAM allows distant data moves, while sorting only induces local changes and can be accelerated on the GPU.

GPU-based sorting won the 2006 Indy PennySort category of the TeraSort competition [22], a sorting benchmark testing performance for database operations. Since then, various GPU sorting algorithms have been proposed, including MP5[6] GPU BITONIC SORT [7] and GPU QUICKSORT [13]. Probably the best general GPU sorting algorithm is one by Sanders et al. [35], whose source has not yet been released.

Depending on the external-memory model checker in use, sorting often consumes the largest amount of time. Consequently, we first parallelized the efforts for delayed duplicate detection by calling a state vector comparison function for both mentioned GPU sorting algorithms. The initial results, documented in [19], were disappointing. Even after further refinements, the best improvement we could achieve wrt. CPU QUICKSORT was about 20%.

In further evaluation of both routines we found out that the sorting speed highly depends on the size of the sorted elements, in our case the binary vectors of the states. This correlates with the observation that intensive access to the global memory should be avoided as much as possible. Moving large amounts of data in the VRAM generates large idle times for the threads which wait for the data, reducing the computation speed.

---

[3] Two hash functions h_1 and h_2 are orthogonal, if for all states s, and s' with $h_1(s) = h_1(s')$ and $h_2(s) = h_2(s')$ we have $s = s'$.

[4] Two hash functions h_1 and h_2 on $s = (s_1, .., s_n)$ are disjoint, if $h_1(s) = h_1(s_{i_1}, .., s_{i_k})$ and $h_2(s) = h_2(s_{i_{k-1}}, .., s_{i_n})$ and $k \in \{i_1, .., i_n\} = \{1, .., n\}$.

[5] A perfect hash function h is called inversible, if given $h(s)$, state s can be reconstructed.

[6] `courses.ece.uiuc.edu/ece498/al/mps/MP5-TopWinners/kaatz/`
`MP5-parallel_sort.zip`

As described in detail in [19] BITONIC SORT consists of two phases. In the first one a block of threads is used to sort a subset of all elements that fits into the SRAM, then the sorted subsets are joint invoking intensive access to the VRAM. The crucial observation is, the first phase accesses the global memory only once for reading and after sorting once for writing so it is fast compared to the second phase. Therefore, we employed hash-based partitioning on the CPU in order to distribute the elements into buckets of adequate size and use only the first phase of BITONIC SORT.

The state array to be sorted is scanned once. Using the hash function h and a distribution of the VRAM into p blocks, a state s is written to the bucket with index $h'(s) = h(s) \bmod p$. On the first overflow in one of the buckets, all remaining places in all buckets are set to a pre-defined illegal state vector that realizes the largest possible value in the total ordering of states. This hash-partitioned vector is copied to the graphics card and the buckets are sorted in parallel. A crucial observation is that the array is fully sorted wrt. to the extended comparison function operating on pairs $(h'(s), s)$. The sorted vector is copied back from VRAM to RAM, and the array is compacted by eliminating duplicates with another scan through the elements. Subtracting visited states is made possible by scanning all previous layers residing on disk. Finally, we flush the current, duplicate-free BFS layer to disk and iterate.

As long as the files do not exceed the GPUs memory, the above exploration strategy is sufficient. If a layer becomes too large to be sorted on the GPU, we split the search frontier into parts that fit in the VRAM. This yields additional state vector files to be subtracted to obtain a duplicate-free layer. For the case that subtraction becomes harder, we can exploit hash-partitioning – inserting previous states into files partitioned by the same hash value – a technique inspired by hash-based duplicate detection [33] and implemented in structured duplicate detection [44]. Provided that the sorting order is first on the hash value and then on the state, after the concatenation of files (even if sorted separately) we obtain a total order on the sets of states. This implies that we can restrict duplicate detection including subtraction to states with matching hash values.

The shorter the state vector, the more elements fit into one bucket, and the better the expected speed-up on the GPU. For improving the sorting performance we, therefore, compressed the state vectors to 64 bits [41]; Two independent 32-bit hash functions h_1 and h_2 were chosen randomly from a set of universal hash functions. The state vector for s is compressed to $(h_1(s), h_2(s), a(s))$, where $a(s)$ is the index of the state vector residing in RAM that is needed for state exploration. The values $(h_1(s), h_2(s), a(s))$ are then sorted lexicographically on the GPU.

For deriving an estimate on the probability of a false positive, we assume a space of $n = 2^{30}$ states universally hashed to the $m = 2^{64}$ possible bitvectors of length 64. According to the birthday problem [9], The probability of having no duplicates is $m!/(m^n(m-n)!)$. resolves to 0.9692, such that we have a chance of less than 96.92% to have no collision during the search. But how much less can this be? For a better confidence on our algorithm, we need a lower bound. We have $m!/(m^n(m-n)!) \geq (1-n/m)^n$. For our case this resolves to $(1-2^{-34})^{2^{30}} = (0.99999999994179233909)^{1073741824} = 0.9394$. Hence, we have a confidence of such that we arrive at a confidence of at least 93.94% that no duplicate arises.

An alternative way of computing the error probability is as follows. There are $2^{30}(2^{30}-1)/2$ pairs of states (x,y), where $x < y$. For a random hash function h, and for any such pair, the probability that $h(x) = h(y)$ is $1/2^{64}$. Therefore, the expected number of hash conflicts is $(2^{30}(2^{30}-1)/2)/2^{64} = (2^{60}-2^{30})/2^{65} = 1/2^5 - 1/2^{35} \leq 0.03126$, certifying that with a chance of more than a 99.68%, no false positive has been produced, while traversing the entire state space.

In contrast, single bit-state hashing with a 8 GB-sized hash table results in an expected number of about $(2^{30}(2^{30}-1)/2)/2^{36} \approx 2^{23}$ hash conflicts (see [24] for an analysis of single, double, and multi bit-state hashing). Moreover, missing a duplicate harms, only if the missed state is the exclusive way to reach the error in the system. In the search spaces we looked at the 64 bit compression did not miss any single state! If the above certified confidence is still too small, one can re-run the experiment with another set of hash functions, as in the Supertrace algorithm [23].

Exploiting parallel computation does not change the access times to the hard disk. According to the external-memory model of Vitter and Shriver [43], BFS on implicitly generated state space graphs $G = (V, E)$ that appear in model checking still has an I/O complexity of $O(sort(|E|) + locality \cdot scan(|V|))$, where $sort(N)$ is the effort to sort N states on disk, $scan(N)$ is the effort to read (or write) N states sequentially from disk, and locality is the length of the largest back-edge in the BFS enumeration of the state space graph [25].

Keeping the list of states in each bucked sorted as in ordered hashing [26] can accelerate the search on the CPU. However, this requires additional work for insertion and does not speed up the computation if compared to sorting the buckets on the GPU. Nonetheless, we implemented one refinement to detect some duplicates quickly. We check the state to be inserted into a bucket against its top element.

5 Experiments

We implemented our algorithms in DiVinE (DIstributed VerIficatioN Environment)[7] with CUDA kernel functions linked to it. Models are taken from the BEEM library [39]. We use an NVIDIA geForce 280 GTX (MSI) graphics card (with 1 GB VRAM and 240 streaming processors) to measure the impact of the GPU. RAM amounts to 12 GB, of which only 4 GB were usable due to the 32-bit implementation of the used DiVinE version, and the external storage encompasses 600 GB distributed on 3 hard disks connected via software RAID0 (achieving up to 240 MB/sec while sequential reading). The CPU of the PC is an Intel Core i7 CPU 920 @ 2.67GHz. Only one core was utilized due to the underlying implementation of DiVinE.

---

[7] Version: 0.7.1 found at: anna.fi.muni.cz/divine

For comparing delayed duplicate detection strategies, we tested different sorting strategies [19]: the built-in CPU QUICKSORT implementation, the GPU QUICKSORT implementation of [13] and a BITONIC SORT routine[8], all adapted to sort state vectors instead of numbers. At the end, we adapted BITONIC SORT and hash partitioning as well as state compression to 64 bit as motivated above.

Table 1 displays the total run-times of the model checker subject to CPU- and GPU-based state space exploration on disk for the selected benchmarks protocols. We observe that using the GPU induces the model checker to perform consistently better. The impact is even more obvious for the larger Peg Solitaire instance. To get CPU data in a feasible amount of time, we draw an experiment terminating Peg Solitaire after layer 17, when it had generated about 10% of all unique states and show the results in the last line. While the state space of the At.7 protocol is larger than that of the partially generated Peg Solitaire instance, surprisingly, the total time for generating it on the CPU is smaller[9]. This is due to the fact that the out degree of the Peg Solitaire protocol is much higher. We observed that 90% of the generated successors are duplicates which are discarded. For the sake of completeness we tried to compare the algorithm with the latest DiVinE-MC implementation and the latest Spin (5.2.4) binaries. Since DiVinE-MC and Spin are only able to check instances that fit into RAM (both were allowed to use 12 GB), we see that they are not terminating on most models. If they do they are much faster, since both checkers use hashing for state storage, which is very fast compared to our implementation that uses sorting-based delayed duplicate detection for an increased external-memory performance[10].

The individual speed-ups for enabling transitions, successor generation and sorting are depicted in Table 2. It shows the protocol and its checked property in the leftmost column. The remaining columns are divided into three parts showing the different stages. The timing information is the sum of the efforts for all BFS Layers in the state space generating process. The table strongly suggests that the GPU should be used to perform similar tasks on all threads. The table clearly shows that the impact of the GPU is larger for enabling the transitions than for generating the successors. This is due to the fact that the task of checking each transition for activeness is equal for all threads in one group and can be run simultaneously. To explore a state, each thread chooses a transition, according to its number, and applies it. In the worst case each thread applies a different transition, reducing the amount of parallelism in memory access. The last part of the table shows a sorting speed-up that differs widely between instances. This was a surprising result, since we expected that the work of sorting is the same on all

---

[8] Used sources available at courses.ece.illinois.edu/ece498/al/HallOfFame.html

[9] Even though AT.7 has more states, the size of a state is much smaller.

[10] We also looked into (though not directly comparable) data of a DiVinE based external-model checker [6] exploring the related Szymanski 5 (P4) protocol with 419,183,762 states on a different architecture (2 GHz Intel Xeon PC, 2 GB RAM, and 60 GB disk space). The results for full reachability in 51h 20m without and 17h 54 m with revisiting resistance still indicate that our running times are competitive with other external exploration engines.

Table 1. Comparing GPU- with CPU-based Performances (The CPU instance of Peg-Solitaire has been stopped in BFS-Layer 17, o.o.m denotes out of memory)

Protocol and Instance	State Space (in GB)			Runtimes in HH:MM			
	Num. of States	uncomp.	compr.	DiVinE	Spin	CPU	GPU
Telephony.6	1,495,154,914	69.0	12	o.o.m	o.o.m	4:42	3:03
Telephony.7	21,960,309	1.1	0.168	0:01	0:00.5	0:04	0:02
Telephony.8	854,245,188	43.0	6.4	o.o.m	o.o.m	2:22	1:09
Szymanski.5	79,518,741	3.8	0.6	0:03	0:01	0:12	0:08
Anderson.8	538,699,094	26.0	4.1	o.o.m	o.o.m	1:32	0:47
At.7	819,243,858	34.0	6.2	o.o.m	o.o.m	1:56	0:45
Peg Solitaire.6	2,383,981,575	134.0	18	o.o.m	o.o.m	o.o.t.	14:57
(first 17 layers)	246,328,560	13.8	1.8			11:52	1:20

Table 2. Comparing GPU- with CPU-based Performances in each enhanced stage

Protocol and Instance	Enabling Transitions			Generating Successors			Sorting		
	CPU	GPU	Spdup	CPU	GPU	Spdup	CPU	GPU	Spdup
Telephony.6	3,654s	115s	31.7	1,964s	301s	6.5	4,372s	180s	24.3
Telephony.7	59s	1s	59.0	28s	4s	7.0	62s	41s	1.51
Telephony.8	2,362s	78s	30.2	1193s	196s	6.1	2,447s	134s	18.3
Szymanski.5	188s	5s	37.6	74s	12s	6.2	193s	82s	2.4
Anderson.8	720s	24s	30.0	734s	121s	6.0	1,585s	153s	10.4
At.7	1,727s	46s	37.5	801s	140s	5.7	2,002s	86s	23.2
Peg Solitaire.6		1,308s			1,815s			557s	
(first 17 layers)	32,226s	429s	75.6	4.088s	448s	9.1	3,220s	129s	25.0

instances, where a constant number of buckets (VRAM/SRAM) with an in average constant number of elements (SRAM/64/8/2) is sorted. Looking carefully at the state space can clarify why the speed-up differs. Since the maximal BFS depth varies, and the size of the BFS layers is different between the instances, sorting is not a unified task. The small speed-up of the Szymanski instance can be explained by a large number of small layers, where, for each layer, all buckets have to be copied to the GPU.

Finally, we ran a profiler to uncover remaining performance bottlenecks. A detailed profile for the Solitaire.6 Protocol (explored up to BFS-Level 17) is provided in Table 3. We see that a lot of the time is lost in pre- and post-processing the data. The term that harms most is due to the subtraction of previous layers, for which strategies like revisiting resistance [6] and layered duplicate detection [34] should apply. Using multiple external drives would also reduce the impact of reading and writing and yielding a better factor.

Computing (and storing) the hash values on the CPU is the second largest problem, which might also be exported to the GPU. As illustrated in [19] after generating the successors, and sorting eliminating duplicates can be accelerated elegantly by computing prefix sums (which is native on many graphics cards).

Some of the deficiencies contribute to the fact that we have split the model checking process on the GPU into three disjoint stages. A tighter integration of

Table 3. Comparison of CPU and GPU times for the distinct stages on the first 17 BFS layers of the Solitaire protocol. (The CPU experiment was stopped due to obvious suboptimal performance).

Operation	CPU Time	GPU Time	Ratio
Reading Search Frontier States from HDD	397s	402s	
Find active Transitions (on the GPU incl. Transfer)	32,226s	429s	75.11
Applying Transitions (on the GPU incl. Transfer)	4,088s	448s	9.13
Compressing States (Hash Function and Bucketing)	877s	1,488s	
Sorting Compressed States	3,220s	129s	24.96
Subtracting Previous Layers Read from HDD	1,538s	1,577s	
Writing Duplicate-Free Layer File to HDD	29s	45s	
Appending Full States to Search Frontier on HDD	146s	160s	
Other memory operations	178s	167s	
Total Time	42,699s	4,845s	9.61

the stages is expected to further speed-up the computation as it avoids moving the data between VRAM and RAM. A similar solution in external-memory algorithm designs is called pipelining [1], where one stage directly pipes its output in form of streamed buffers as an input to the next stage. Property checking is turned off: we restrict to efficient state space exploration.

Disk-based solutions often do not exploit parallelism, parallel solutions often do not look at I/O, the other ones we have tried to cover. We recognize that there is still remaining work in enlarging the set of experiments for a clearer picture on the state-of-the-art in external memory BFS. We would love to have cross-compare to CMurphi (e.g., in [11]), but it does not parse Promela or DVE, so we would have had to hand-code models to compare directly. Due to personal changes in the PARADISE group, experimenting with other I/O versions of DiVinE was little difficult. We have, however, compare to I/O-HSF-SPIN [25]. The full exploration of peg-solitaire-6 took 21GB and 12h:06m.

6   Conclusion and Discussion

Parallelism is the future of computing; microprocessor development efforts will concentrate on adding cores rather than increasing single-thread performance. The purpose of the paper is to show that large-scale external memory search on the GPU has the potential for growing towards an exciting research field. We exemplarily looked at external memory BFS, showing significant advances for analyzing large state spaces.

The contribution of this paper is that (to the best of our knowledge) it is the first attempt to perform external memory BFS with delayed duplicates detection on GPU. Comparing to other multi-core and GPU-based exploration engines typically runs out of memory, this algorithm is capable to handle much bigger state spaces. Comparing to the same algorithm running on CPU, especially in sorting we observe significant speed-ups. The individual gains are remarkable, and likely increase on multiple cards.

We successfully attacked three causes of bad performance of a CPU model checker: transition checking, successor generation and delayed duplicate detection. Our advances lead to significant individual speed-ups of up to factor 75. In the course of this research project we observed that subtraction of states of one layer even wrt. the entire set of previous layers is not as inefficient in practice as we have expected. This is due to the large number of successors that are already eliminated within one layer. Hence, transition enabledness, successor generation and sorting were identified as the main performance bottlenecks in large instances.

We encountered that the results on the software RAID are generally better than on a single HDD. We observe speed-ups of up to one order of magnitude exceed the number of cores on our PC. This will no longer be true for the dual 6-core CPUs available from Intel. Nonetheless, better speed-ups are certainly possible. Multiple Nvidia GPUs can be used in SLI mode and the Fermi architecture (e.g. located on the GeForce GTX 480 graphics card) will go far beyond the 240 GPU cores we had access to.

Given that disk-based algorithms often take days of computation, we are convinced that even moderate speed-ups for generating state spaces on disk are crucial. We observe that multi-core parallelizations usually does not extend to checking large systems beyond main memory [42] work on muti-core model checking [2].

Current graphics cards have a hierarchical memory structure, with local, shared, global, constant and texture memory together with different fragment processor units. Additionally facing the uncontrolled scheduling algorithm implemented on the graphics card a fine-grained theoretical time complexity analysis matching the observed performance is involved. The computational model for the GPU relates to the SIMD (Single Instruction Multiple Data) CREW (Common Read Exclusive Write) PRAM model, but this is a very rough characterization. More refined models are needed.

Of course, improving the overall speed-up is subject to further research. Besides the subtraction of previous layers, moving states and hashing takes most of the time, and shall be considered next.

The presented algorithm might be extended to run on clusters by storing the open list on a shared external space, dividing a BFS layer into partitions, and expanding them on different nodes. Duplicate checking has, of course, to be synchronised. The algorithm can in principle be applied to any external memory BFS. Given the GPU implementation, it is also easy to derive a multi-core version. The inverse, however, is not true. Considering the fundamental difference in the architectures, specialized solutions developed for multi-core model checking may not easily transfer to the GPU.

The actual code is written for CUDA supporting NVIDIA hardware. For other vendors the implementation of the pseudo-code algorithms have to be adapted. One also may combine the three stages into two avoiding some transfer between RAM and VRAM. Our core design objective, however, was to maximize memory usage to increase parallelism on the card. As other external-memory algorithms like External A* [25] are also streamed, they suggest to be executed on the GPU.

References

1. Ajwani, D., Dementiev, R., Meyer, U.: A computational study of external-memory BFS algorithms. In: ACM-SIAM Symposium On Discrete Algorithms (SODA), pp. 601–610 (2006)
2. Barnat, J., Brim, L., Ročkai, P.: Scalable multi-core LTL model-checking. In: Bošnački, D., Edelkamp, S. (eds.) SPIN 2007. LNCS, vol. 4595, pp. 187–203. Springer, Heidelberg (2007)
3. Barnat, J., Brim, L., Češka, M.: DiVinE-CUDA: A Tool for GPU Accelerated LTL Model Checking. Electronic Proceedings in Theoretical Computer Science (PDMC) 14, 107–111 (2009)
4. Barnat, J., Brim, L., Češka, M., Lamr, T.: CUDA accelerated LTL Model Checking. In: International Conference on Parallel and Distributed Systems (ICPADS 2009), pp. 34–41 (2009)
5. Barnat, J., Brim, L., Šimeček, P.: I/O efficient accepting cycle detection. In: Damm, W., Hermanns, H. (eds.) CAV 2007. LNCS, vol. 4590, pp. 281–293. Springer, Heidelberg (2007)
6. Barnat, J., Brim, L., Šimeček, P., Weber, M.: Revisiting resistance speeds up I/O-efficient LTL model checking. In: Ramakrishnan, C.R., Rehof, J. (eds.) TACAS 2008. LNCS, vol. 4963, pp. 48–62. Springer, Heidelberg (2008)
7. Batcher, K.E.: Sorting networks and their applications. AFIPS Spring Joint Computing Conference 32, 307–314 (1968)
8. Belazzougui, D., Botelho, F.C., Dietzfelbinger, M.: Hash, displace, and compress. In: Fiat, A., Sanders, P. (eds.) ESA 2009. LNCS, vol. 5757, pp. 682–693. Springer, Heidelberg (2009)
9. Bloom, D.: A birthday problem. American Mathematical Monthly 80, 1141–1142 (1973)
10. Botelho, F.C., Ziviani, N.: External perfect hashing for very large key sets. In: ACM Conference on Information and Knowledge Management (CIKM), pp. 653–662 (2007)
11. Brizzolari, F., Melatti, I., Tronci, E., Penna, G.D.: Disk based software verification via bounded model checking. In: Asia-Pacific Software Engineering Conference (APSEC), pp. 358–365 (2007)
12. Burks, A.W., Warren, D.W., Wright, J.B.: An analysis of a logical machine using parenthesis-free notation. Mathematical Tables and Other Aids to Computation 8(46), 53–57 (1954)
13. Cederman, D., Tsigas, P.: A practical quicksort algorithm for graphics processors. In: Halperin, D., Mehlhorn, K. (eds.) Esa 2008. LNCS, vol. 5193, pp. 246–258. Springer, Heidelberg (2008)
14. Cooperman, G., Finkelstein, L.: New methods for using Cayley graphs in interconnection networks. Discrete Applied Mathematics 37/38, 95–118 (1992)
15. Edelkamp, S., Jabbar, S.: Large-scale directed model checking LTL. In: Valmari, A. (ed.) SPIN 2006. LNCS, vol. 3925, pp. 1–18. Springer, Heidelberg (2006)
16. Edelkamp, S., Jabbar, S., Schrödl, S.: External A*. In: Biundo, S., Frühwirth, T., Palm, G. (eds.) KI 2004. LNCS (LNAI), vol. 3238, pp. 226–240. Springer, Heidelberg (2004)
17. Edelkamp, S., Sanders, P., Šimeček, P.: Semi-external LTL model checking. In: Gupta, A., Malik, S. (eds.) CAV 2008. LNCS, vol. 5123, pp. 530–542. Springer, Heidelberg (2008)

18. Edelkamp, S., Sulewski, D.: Flash-efficient LTL model checking with minimal counterexamples. In: International Conference on Software Engineering and Formal Methods (SEFM), pp. 73–82 (2008)
19. Edelkamp, S., Sulewski, D.: Model checking via delayed duplicate detection on the GPU. Technical Report 821, Technische Universität Dortmund. Presented on the 22nd Workshop on Planning, Scheduling, and Design PUK 2008 (2008)
20. Edelkamp, S., Sulewski, D., Yücel, C.: Perfect hashing for domain-dependent planning on the gpu. In: International Conference on Automated Planning and Scheduling, ICAPS (2010) (to appear)
21. Gastin, P., Moro, P.: Minimal counterexample generation for SPIN. In: Bošnački, D., Edelkamp, S. (eds.) SPIN 2007. LNCS, vol. 4595, pp. 24–38. Springer, Heidelberg (2007)
22. Govindaraju, N.K., Gray, J., Kumar, R., Manocha, D.: GPUTeraSort: High performance graphics coprocessor sorting for large database management. In: International Conference on Management of Data (SIGMOD), pp. 325–336 (2006)
23. Holzmann, G.: The Spin Model Checker: Primer and Reference Manual. Addison-Wesley, Reading (2004)
24. Holzmann, G.J.: An analysis of bitstate hashing. Formal Methods in System Design 13(3), 287–305 (1998)
25. Jabbar, S.: External Memory Algorithms for State Space Exploration in Model Checking and Action Planning. PhD thesis, Technical University of Dortmund (2008)
26. Knuth, D.E.: The Art of Computer Programming. Addison-Wesley, Reading (1973)
27. Korf, R.: Delayed duplicate detection: extended abstract. In: International Joint Conference on Artificial Intelligence (IJCAI), pp. 1539–1541 (2003)
28. Korf, R.: Best-first frontier search with delayed duplicate detection. In: National Conference on Artificial Intelligence (AAAI), pp. 650–657 (2004)
29. Korf, R., Felner, A.: Recent progress in heuristic search: A case study of the Four-Peg Towers of Hanoi problem. In: International Joint Conference on Artificial Intelligence (IJCAI), pp. 2334–2329 (2007)
30. Korf, R., Schultze, P.: Large-scale parallel breadth-first search. In: National Conference on Artificial Intelligence (AAAI), pp. 1380–1385 (2005)
31. Korf, R.E.: Breadth-first frontier search with delayed duplicate detection. In: MOCHART, pp. 87–92 (2003)
32. Korf, R.E.: Minimizing disk I/O in two-bit-breath-first search. In: National Conference on Artificial Intelligence (AAAI), pp. 317–324 (2008)
33. Korf, R.E., Schultze, T.: Large-scale parallel breadth-first search. In: National Conference on Artificial Intelligence (AAAI), pp. 1380–1385 (2005)
34. Lamborn, P., Hansen, E.: Layered duplicate detection in external-memory model checking. In: Havelund, K., Majumdar, R. (eds.) SPIN 2008. LNCS, vol. 5156, pp. 160–175. Springer, Heidelberg (2008)
35. Leischner, N., Osipov, V., Sanders, P.: GPU sample sort. CoRR, abs/0909.5649 (2009)
36. Mehlhorn, K., Meyer, U.: External-memory breadth-first search with sublinear I/O. In: Möhring, R.H., Raman, R. (eds.) ESA 2002. LNCS, vol. 2461, pp. 723–735. Springer, Heidelberg (2002)
37. Munagala, K., Ranade, A.: I/O-complexity of graph algorithms. In: SODA, pp. 687–694 (1999)
38. Nguyen, V.Y., Ruys, T.C.: Incremental hashing for SPIN. In: Havelund, K., Majumdar, R. (eds.) SPIN 2008. LNCS, vol. 5156, pp. 232–249. Springer, Heidelberg (2008)

39. Pelánek, R.: BEEM: Benchmarks for Explicit Model Checkers. In: Bošnački, D., Edelkamp, S. (eds.) SPIN 2007. LNCS, vol. 4595, pp. 263–267. Springer, Heidelberg (2007)
40. Schuppan, V., Biere, A.: Efficient reduction of finite state model checking to reachability analysis. International Journal on Software Tools for Technology Transfer (STTT) 5(2-3), 185–204 (2004)
41. Stern, U., Dill, D.L.: Combining state space caching and hash compaction. In: Methoden des Entwurfs und der Verifikation digitaler Systeme. GI/ITG/GME Workshop, vol. 4, pp. 81–90. Shaker Verlag, Aachen (1996)
42. Verstoep, K., Bal, H., Barnat, J., Brim, L.: Efficient Large-Scale Model Checking. In: International Symposium on Parallel and Distributed Processing, IPDPS (2009)
43. Vitter, J.S., Shriver, E.A.M.: Algorithms for parallel memory; I: two-level memories, II: hierarchical multilevel memories. Algorithmica 12(2/3), 110–169 (1994)
44. Zhou, R., Hansen, E.A.: Structured duplicate detection in external-memory graph search. In: National Conference on Artificial Intelligence (AAAI), pp. 683–689 (2004)
45. Zhou, R., Hansen, E.A.: Parallel structured duplicate detection. In: National Conference on Artificial Intelligence (AAAI), pp. 1217–1222 (2007)

Program Model Checking via Action Planning

Stefan Edelkamp[1], Mark Kellershoff[2], and Damian Sulewski[1]

[1] TZI, University of Bremen, Germany
[2] TU Dortmund, Germany

Abstract. In this paper we present steps towards a prototype implementation of a C++ software model checker based on AI planning technology. It parses source code annotated with assertions and translates it into the planning domain description language to invoke recent planners. Lifted back to the source code level, computed plans then serve as counterexamples. As the approach can participate from efficient planner in-built search heuristics, the verification procedure is directed. For the translation process, different aspects like parsing, generation of a dependency graph, slicing, property conversion, and data abstraction are described. The program model checker has been embedded as a plugin in the Eclipse software development environment, resulting in an interactive debugging aid. First empirical findings compare the approach with an existing directed program model checker parses the same input and executes object code.

1 Introduction

The implementation of correct software is an everyday challenge and crucial for the development safety-critical systems. Severe software failures such as the explosion of the Ariane 5 rocket due to an arithmetic overflow [29], the zapping of six Lockheed's F-22 Raptor by international date line[1], and the power shutdown for about 3 hours of the USS Yorktown due to a failure in the arithmetic exception handling[2], are only a few examples to illustrate the importance of the automated verification of systems.

The verification task becomes harder, when *concurrent threads* are involved, since the order of instruction execution is hard to predict and often not known in advance. Moreover, by the current rise in the number of processor cores, concurrent programming becomes a necessity, especially considering the continuous economic pressure for software development companies.

Model checking [14] is a formal method to increase the correctness of non-deterministic system designs by detecting errors (like violated assertions or deadlocks) that otherwise would require intensive code reviewing efforts. The main disadvantage of model checking for software verification is that it relies on a formal model of the software system to be checked, which might be unavailable, or inconsistent wrt. the ongoing development of the source code.

In contrast to classical model checking, *program model checking* aims at the automated verification of software in source code [34,52]. The advantage of these approaches is that there is no additional modeling error. As a push-button technology, program model checking requires tremendous computational power.

---

[1] http://www.dailytech.com/article.aspx?newsid=6225
[2] http://www.wired.com/science/discoveries/news/1998/07/13987

R. van der Meyden and J.-G. Smaus (Eds.): MoChArt 2010, LNAI 6572, pp. 32–51, 2011.
© Springer-Verlag Berlin Heidelberg 2011

For traditional model checkers, property specifications are often provided in some form of temporal logic, which (in automata-based model checking) can be compiled into (Büchi) automata to be able to explore a lifted state space graph. In program models checkers, however, mainly *safety errors* are validated. To facilitate program model checking by calling the verification engine during the course of programming, a few checker specific commands for source code annotation are needed, e.g., to cluster code into *atomic blocks*, to *lock* and *unlock* the access to shared variables, and to state *assertions* that should hold at a specific point in the program.

The choice of the language C++ to be checked is imposed by its wide-spread use and the lack of automated adequate bug-finding support. Besides ordinary debuggers there are advanced tools like *valgrind*[3] that are able to find memory leaks, and static analysis tools like *Orion* [17] that are very effective in reducing programming errors in practice. Debugging concurrent programs, however, imposes another challenge on top of these tools.

There is continuous research suggesting that search heuristics included into a *directed model checker* can outpace traditional model checkers a sizable number of problems (see survey in [26]). The rationale of applying heuristics is that – due to the large size of the global system state spaces – correctness is often infeasible to check, and for falsification states *closer* to the error can be priortized.

This paper proposes a program model checker that automatically converts C++ source into an action planning model in *PDDL* [47,27]. Guidance is then applied implicitly by exploiting planning heuristics. Besides opening an exciting research field to the planning community the core rationale to work on a PDDL model rather than to extend a program model checker is the growing body of results in designing accurate search heuristics via selecting any of a wide range of advanced heuristic search planners. Since current PDDL is inherently static, there are several restrictions to the expressiveness of the sources that can be processed. But the results of our prototype indicates visible advantages at least for simple benchmarks problems. As arithmetics are essential to follow the flow of control in most programs, we mainly concentrate on mapping numeric aspects. Besides *slicing* the program without loss of information, we have implemented a transformation into Level 2 PDDL and, for the case when a program cannot be searched completely, data abstraction converts infinite state variables to finite ones, into Level 1 PDDL. Various dependencies of variables are detected automatically by examining the parse of the source.

The paper is structured as follows. First, we recall action planning and the program domain description language. Next, options for program model checking of C++ source code is reviewed. To draw a connection between the two exploration objectives we review some related work on system verification via planning. Then, we address the translation process in a running example. We highlight various aspects of our program model checker prototype, including the extension of a C++ parser, the automated construction of the dependency graph, its integration as a Eclipse-plugin, as well as and the application of (semi-)automated abstractions. We provide some empirical data for a cross-comparison with a directed program model checker that executes programs on the assembly level and conclude.

---

[3] http://valgrind.org

2   Action Planning

In domain-independent action planning, a running system must be able to find plans and to exploit search knowledge fully automatically. In this paper we restrict to *deterministic planning* (each action application produces exactly one successor) with no uncertainty in the environment and no observation to infer otherwise inaccessible state variables. The input of a planning problem consists a set of state variables, an initial state in form of value assignments to the variables, a goal (condition), and a set of actions consisting of lists of preconditions and effects. A plan is a sequence of actions that eventually maps the initial state into one that satisfies the goal (condition).

The *problem domain description language* PDDL [47] allows flexible specifications of domain models and problem instances. Starting from problems described in STRIPS notation, PDDL has grown to an enormous expressive power, including large fragments of first-order logic to combine propositional expressions, numerical state variables to feature the handling of real-valued quantities, and constraints to impose additional conditions on the set of valid plans. The agreed standard for PDDL encompasses the following levels of expressiveness.

Level 1: Propositional Planning This level includes all sorts of propositional description languages. It unifies STRIPS-type planning with the *abstract description language* (ADL). ADL allows typed domain objects and any bounded quantification over these as well as negated and disjunctive preconditions, and conditional effects. While the former two language extensions can be easily compiled away by introducing negated predicates and by splitting the operators, the latter ones are *essential* in the sense that their compilation induces an exponential increase in the problem specification. Propositional planning is decidable, but PSPACE-hard [7].

Level 2: Metric Planning This level introduces numerical state variables, so-called *fluents*, and an objective function to be optimized (the *domain metric*) that judges plan quality. Instead of Boolean values to be associated with each grounded atom, the language extension enables the processing of continuous quantities, an important requirement for modeling many real-world domains. The growing expressiveness comes at a high price. Metric planning is not decidable even for very restricted problem classes [35]. This, however, does not mean that metric planners cannot succeed in finding plans for concrete problem instances.

More levels and features have been attached to this hierarchy. Level 3 introduces *duration*, which denotes action execution time. The duration can be a constant quantity or a numerical expression dependent on the assignment to variables [27]. Two different semantics been been proposed. In *PDDL semantics* each temporal action is divided into an initial, an invariant, and a final happening. Many temporal planners, however, assume the simpler *black-box semantics*. Domain axioms in form of *derived predicates* introduce recursion, while *timed initial facts* allow execution deadlines to be specified [40]. Newer developments of PDDL focus on temporal and preference constraints for plans [28]. Higher levels support continuous processes and triggered events [27].

The results of the biennial *international planning competitions* (started in 1998) show that planners keep aligned with the language extensions, while preserving good performances in finding and optimizing plans. Besides algorithmic contributions, the achievements also refer to the fact that computers have increased in their processing power and memory resources. As a consequence, modern action planning is apparently suited to provide prototypical solutions to specific problems. In fact, action planning becomes more and more application-oriented.

3   Program Model Checking

The ultimate goal of software model checking is to check programs as a push-button technology to be used directly within the process of programming. Most advances, however, are due to *bug-hunting*. If program model checker finds a counterexample of program instructions, which e.g., leads to a failed assertion, the corresponding system state violates a Boolean expression on the set of state variables.

Program Model Checking via Executables. For this case, at least in theory, there are no syntactic or semantic restrictions to the programs that can be checked as long as they can be compiled to an executable. A state vector is essentially composed of the stack contents and machine registers of the running threads, together with the lock- and the memory-pool. These pools store the set of locked resources and the set of dynamically allocated memory regions. The other parts of the state vector contain the program's global variables. Program model checkers are frequently composed on top of a virtual machine that has been extended to analyze programs along different execution branches. Checkers like the Java PathFinder (JPF) [33,53], the State Exploring Assembly Model Checker (StEAM) [46], or the .NET model checker (Moon Walker) [18], analyze a program as an object code or byte code executable.

Program Model Checking via Translation. Instead of producing a binary for execution, other approaches like the Bounded Model Checker for ANSI-C programs (CBMC) [11] perform symbolic simulation on the program. They translate a program to a theorem prover input via unrolling loops to some depth, and feed a SAT or SMT solver for verifying it. C++ input is converted into goto-programs via tools like goto-cc, while data abstractions have been used in [12]. Via introducing random variables, in TCBMC (p)threads have been translated to CMBC [50] and in a preliminary experiment successfully compared to Microsoft's ZING [2]. Similar experiments have been conducted in [15].

As for our research we need both C++-input and threads, we have had difficulties in comparing with tools like (T)CBMC directly. Hence, we cross-compare our prototype with our assembly-level program model checker StEAM [46,48]. For better scalability, it has been externalized [22], such that it efficiently exploits hard disk space much larger than the RAM. Furthermore, StEAM has been parallelized [23], such that it can work more efficiently in multi-processor or cluster environments. StEAM parses C++, has the same in- and output behavior, and shares the same frontend. Program model checking in StEAM performs a search on the level of machine code instructions, compiled, e.g., from a C++ source. The compiled code is stored in ELF, a common object file format for binaries. Moreover, the virtual machine was extended with multi-threading, which makes it also possible to model-check concurrent programs.

The tool automatically detects deadlocks during the program exploration. A thread can require and release exclusive access to a resource). When a thread attempts to lock an already locked resource, it must wait until the lock is released by the thread which holds it. A deadlock arises, where all running threads wait for a lock to be released.

The state representation is large and one may like to conclude, that program model checking machine code is infeasible due to the memory required to store the visited states. In practice, however, most states of a program differ only slightly from their immediate predecessors. If memory is only allocated for changed components, by using pointers to unchanged components in the predecessor state, it is possible to explore large parts of the programs state space, before running out of memory.

Heuristic guidance has been successfully included to improve error detection, see e.g., [31]. States are evaluated by a estimator function, measuring the distance to an error state, so that states closer to the faulty behavior have a higher priority and are considered earlier in the exploration process. An appropriate example for the detection of deadlocks is the *most-block heuristic*. It favors states, for which more threads are blocked. Another established estimate used for error detection in concurrent programs is the *interleaving heuristic*. It relies on a quantity for maximizing the interleaving of thread executions. The heuristic do not assign values to states but to paths. The objective is that by prioritizing interleavings concurrency bugs are found earlier in the exploration process. The *lock heuristic* additionally prefers states with many variable locks and threads alive. Locks are the obvious precondition for threads to become blocked and only threads that are still alive, can get in a blocked mode in the future.

4   Model Checking via Planning

At least conceptually, both action planners and model checkers apply a domain-inde-pendent exploration of so-called *Kripke structures*, i.e., state space graphs labeled with atomic propositions. *Planning via model checking* [8] considers the integration of ver-ification technology (mainly in form of BDDs [6]) into action planners [9,10]. The in-verse is less frequently reported, even though SATPLAN [43] inspired bounded model checking [4] and documents a successful knowledge transfer in the opposite direction.

Considering the rising effectiveness of heuristics in planning (see e.g., [36,32,37]), a natural question was to apply heuristics to enhance error detection in model checking. Directed model checkers [24,45,54] have been successfully equipped with heuristics to provide short traces to programming errors time- and space-efficiently.

The effectiveness of translating model checking input directly into PDDL avoids the source code extension of an existing model checker and allows to interact with different kinds of planners. The success of such prototype compilations has been documented by a series of preceding papers.

LTL Model Checking Input. A prototype compiler from a restricted subset of SPIN's[4] input language Promela [42] into PDDL exploits the representation of pro-tocols as communicating finite state machines [19][5].

---

[4] http://spinroot.com

[5] One implication was to validate state properties in communication protocols, in particular, deadlocks, as planning benchmarks in international planning competitions [41].

CTL Model Checking Input. The translation of (nu)SMV[6] input to PDDL to run a heuristic search planner with promising results in a simple but scaling (Dining Philosopher) example has been discussed in [1].

μ-calculus Model Checking Input. To solve μ-calculus model checking problems[7], practical models and properties from data-flow analysis were transformed to parity game graphs, which, in turn, were compiled to planner input [3].

Petri Net Model Checking Input. Finding a particular marking in *Petri nets* corresponding to a property violation can be reduced to traversing a state space of sets of reachable markings[8]. Typical exploration approaches are undirected and do not take into account any knowledge about the structure of the Petri net. In [20] a PDDL model to apply heuristic search for enhanced exploration has been proposed. This translation has been included to counterexample-guided abstraction-refinement [44], while [5] consider the directed unfolding of Petri nets.

Graph Transformation Model Checking Input. Graphs are suitable modeling formalisms for software systems involving aspects such as communication, object orientation, concurrency, mobility, and distribution. State spaces of such systems can be modeled by graph transition systems, which are basically systems whose states and transitions reflect graphs and graph morphisms. Inspired by Groove[9], and directed graph transformation [21], modeling of graph transition systems in PDDL and the application of heuristic search planning for their analysis has been proposed [25][10].

5   Parsing

In model checking software, state spaces are analyzed that have non-deterministic effects. Such non-determinism can be due to the interleaving of concurrently running threads, or to unknown assignments to variables, program inputs, to explicit choice points imposed by the programmer, or to abstractions of deterministic programs.

For program model checking, the source code has to be parsed. As the programming language C++ is rather complex [51], we adapted the tool `JavaCC` by Sreenivasa Viswanadha that was published in 1997 to parse the input. As an unfortunate consequence, recent developments of C++ like STL are not covered by our research. The parser yields an abstract syntax tree, which we present as a navigational aid to the programmer, and which is used for further processing for the model checker. Inspired by an existing interface the different program model checkers including StEAM for the controlled execution of the verification process, the source code can be annotated with the following commands:

- `VLOCK(<variable>)` restricts the access to the variable `<variable>` in the currently invoked thread. All upcoming locks to the same variable are blocked.

---

[6] `http://nusmv.fbk.eu`
[7] `http://jabc.cs.tu-dortmund.de/modelchecking`
[8] `http://www.informatik.uni-hamburg.de/TGI/PetriNets/tools`
[9] `http://groove.cs.utwente.nl`
[10] The application domain has been part of international knowledge engineering competitions.

- VUNLOCK(<variable>) releases the lock to the variable <variable>.
- BEGINATOMIC() dictates that the current thread cannot be suspended.
- ENDATOMIC() terminates the atomic block selection within a thread.
- VASSERT(<condition>) tracks assertion violations in the model checker, s.t. <condition> has to be satisfied each time the program reaches VASSERT.
- RANGE(<variable>,<low>,<high>) offers non-deterministic choices to a program. At this program counter position the variable <variable> is assigned to a value in between <low> and <high>.

By the current limitation of PDDL, states are fixed-sized variable assignment vectors and do not allow dynamic creation of domain objects.

6   Generation of the Dependency Graph

A program consists of a hierarchy of variables, methods and classes. This object-oriented structure represents the scopes of a program and is exploited for constructing a *dependency graph*. The graph has nodes for representing a *class*, a *method*, or a *statement*, and edges for representing *member*, *data*, *control*, *method call*, *use*, or *define* dependencies. An example is shown in Fig. 1 together with parts of the parse tree to its left.

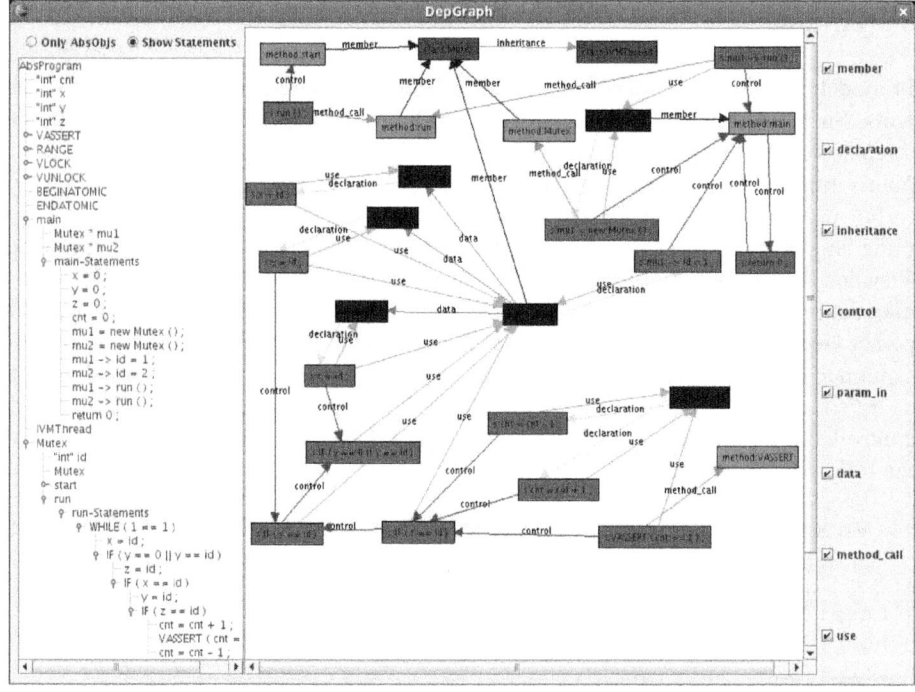

Fig. 1. Parse tree and dependency graph of a sample C++ program in our tool

The *state* of a program includes information like assignments to global and local variables, as well as stack and dynamic memory contents. We distinguish binary, integer- or real-valued variables. The situation before the execution of a program is called *initial state*, and the state of a program at its termination is called (valid) end state. Additionally to the variable assignments, a state contains information about the program counter, denoting which transition has been or will be executed. If the program is multi-threaded, a program counter is maintained for every running thread including the thread for *main*. For the conversion, we assume that a static analysis, applied after parsing the code, can detect the number of threads running concurrently.

7 Translation into PDDL

As indicated above, the core motivation of translating C++ sources of a program into PDDL is the exploitation of planner in-built heuristics to drive the exploration process towards falsifying a property, e.g., in form of a deadlock, a failed assertion, a global invariance, or an array access violation. After parsing we can assume the input has been parsed into some form of internal dictionary, while the output has to please (one of the first two levels of) PDDL [27]. In the following, we explain the transformation using a simple example.

7.1 Fluents

For a variable *declaration*, like int a, we reserve a PDDL fluent int_a. Since a program can contain several variables with name *a*, every PDDL fluent is suffixed with an additional id, such that for our case we infer int_a_1, as it is the first (and only) appearance of *a* that is converted. As *a* can appear in different threads, we provide an additional parameter to the PDDL predicate, yielding the expression (int_a_1 ?t – thread) to represent the variable declaration of *a*. For variable int b the conversion is analogous. In short, variable conversion is a mapping that assigns a fluent to each program variable.

7.2 Propositions

In addition to fluents to represent numbers the following (specialized) propositions are used in the preconditions and effects of the actions as well as in the goal (condition).

```
(atomic) (is-atomic ?t - thread)
(thread-run ?t - thread) (thread-ended ?t - thread)
(array-index-calculated ?t -thread ?n1 - number)
(array-index-converted ?t - thread ?n1 - number)
(index ?t - thread ?n1 ?n2 - number)
(calculating-index ?t - thread)
(method-call-done ?t - thread ?n - number)
(no-error) (assertion-violation)
(deadlock) (blocked ?t - thread)
```

For example, given that three threads t_1, t_2 and t_3 are blocked based on accessing already locked variables, a deadlock is declared in PDDL as follows.

```
(:action detect-deadlock
 :precondition (and (blocked t1) (blocked t2) (blocked t3))
 :effect (deadlock))
```

7.3 Expressions

The conversion of Boolean and numerical expressions, which appear in both conditions and assignments, from infix notation (as used in C++) to prefix notation (as used in PDDL) is realized by traversing the parse tree and using a stack data structure.

7.4 Assignments

One of the simplest operation in a program is the *assignment* of a value to a variable. For translating it into PDDL, we construct actions, which convert the state in the planning model in the same way it does within the program.

PDDL actions consist of three major parts: the parameter list, the precondition and the effect lists. If we ignore the working of the program counter, the parameter is selected by the thread, while the effect changes the planning state equivalent to the assignment (see Fig. 2 for an example).

```
(:action SimpleAssignment
:parameters (?t - thread)
:precondition (<predecessor has finished>)
:effect (and (assign (int_a_1 ?t) 1000 )
     (<this action has finished>)
     (not (<predecessor has finished>)))))
```

Fig. 2. PDDL action for a=1000;

7.5 Program Counter

The *program counter* to monitor the flow of control in the program is the most important aspect to be modeled. For each action we usually have one predecessors action. Several predecessors are available only for the special case of a RANGE-statement, where different value assignments are made available.

7.6 Control Flow

We use predicates to model line numbers. Every action includes as a precondition that the predecessor (line) has finished its execution. For example, in a sequential execution line 20 has to finish before line 21 is processed. To avoid ambiguities, every line number is attached to the file in which the line is contained. It is also parameterized with the thread that is invoked. Since in PDDL every possible action is checked for execution, the list of preconditions for every action has been enlarged to allow selecting the actions that are currently active wrt. the flow of the program.

The action for the first line in the main program includes (start T0) as a precondition triggered by the initial state, since it does not have a direct predecessor. The first instruction of a method also contains a label that it has been called.

Consider the example program in Fig. 3. After calling the *run* method, we have two running concurrent threads, the *main* method (thread t_0), and the thread (t_1) that has been invoked. If we omit the details for calling the thread, the remaining program logic has to include the variables a and b, their order and the constraints imposed. The PDDL result for the assignment a=1000; and b=20; is shown in Fig. 4.

```
#include "Thread.h"
[...]
class SimpleExample:public Thread {
public:
 SimpleExample();
 void run();
};
SimpleExample::SimpleExample(){}
  void SimpleExample::run(){
    int a;
    int b;
    a=1000;
    b=20;
    VASSERT(a < b);
}
```

Fig. 3. Example program

```
(:action SimpleExample_cpp_Line_20
:parameters (?t - thread)
:precondition (SimpleExample_cpp_Line_19 ?t)
:effect (and (assign (int_a_1 ?t) 1000 )
    (SimpleExample_cpp_Line_20 ?t)
    (not (SimpleExample_cpp_Line_19 ?t))))

(:action SimpleExample_cpp_Line_21
:parameters (?t - thread)
:precondition (SimpleExample_cpp_Line_20 ?t)
:effect (and (assign (int_b_2 ?t) 20)
    (SimpleExample_cpp_Line_21 ?t)
    (not (SimpleExample_cpp_Line_20 ?t))))
```

Fig. 4. PDDL actions for a=1000; and b=20;

7.7 Conditional Branches

An `if` statement exists in two different variants (with or without else block). A model without an else-branch is not directly convertible in PDDL, as failing the `if` condition would not increase the program counter. We observe that every action has access to its immediate predecessor, and every action has at most two successors in case of a branch and two predecessors in case of a join. A `while` statement is an `if` statement featuring a backward jump.

For `if` statements we introduce a virtual-else branch, short VELSE. The `if` statement itself would vanish as the conditions are imposed as additional preconditions to the actions. But without modeling the `if` statements explicitly, there is a subtle problem in modeling nested `if` statements. Consider the small extension of the running example in Fig. 5. If one uses one action per instruction, then implementing correct precedences among the if statements is tricky, i.e., to connect an else-branch to the corresponding if. Therefore, we decided to include an additional flag and an additional action for starting and ending an `if` or `else` part.

```
void SimpleExample::run(){
    int a;
    int b;
    a=1000;
    b=20;
    if (a > b) {
        if (a > 20) {
            a=20;
        } else {
            a=0;
        }
    } else {
        a=1000;
    }
    VASSERT(a < b);
}
```

Fig. 5. A nested `if` statement and induced control flow for the PDDL model

Fig. 6 relates the source of a simple `while` statement to the according automaton, that is used to monitor the flow of control in the PDDL code.

7.8 Model Checking Statements

A VASSERT statement is dealt with similarly to an `if` statement, and, hence, split into two parts. One branch considers the violation of the assertion, in which case the predicate `assertion-violation` is set, the other branch continues with the flow of instructions. When searching for the violation of safety properties, this predicate is included as a precondition of one goal-achieving action. For a RANGE statement we adapt the increase of the program counter, such that only one action can be executed at a time.

```
void SimpleExample::run(){

    int a;
    int b;

    a=1000;
    b=20;

    while (a > b) {
        a=20;
        b=1000;
    }
    VASSERT(a < b);
}
```

Fig. 6. A while program and induced control flow for the PDDL model

The VLOCK statement denotes that a thread requires exclusive access to a variable. The first thread that locks the variable has top priority, such that all upcoming accesses to the same variable are rejected. The PDDL model is extended in the sense that the actions include another precondition, denoting that the variable is not locked. As one subtle issue, we further have to avoid multiple locks on one variable.

A proper locking mechanism yields the implementation for the check of invalid end states (deadlocks). A supplementary action wait is generated, that indicates that a thread waits for a resource. If all threads are blocked, a deadlock has occurred, an a goal achieving flag is triggered. Note that waiting does not increase the program counter to allow continuation of the program, once the lock is released.

Unlocking via VUNLOCK is converted into an action that increases the program counter and that deletes the predicate for locking the variable.

For *atomic blocks* within BEGINATOMIC and ENDATOMIC, in the PDDL model two new predicates are inserted; atomic, that denotes that the execution is atomic mode and is-atomic ?t - thread that denotes which thread is actually atomic. Most ordinary actions are extended by the precondition atomic ⇒ (is-atomic ?t). The end of the block generates an action without further specialized preconditions that deletes atomic and (is-atomic ?t).

7.9 Complex Statements

Arrays allow direct access to a vector of variables, like the one illustrated in Fig. 7. In PDDL2 such *indexed variable access* to variables is performed in two steps. In the first step the index is determined, which corresponds to evaluating an expression. In the second step the access to the array is executed. As PDDL does not provide a mechanism to index variables with numbers, we urge the user to provide array bounds to the parser. For an array of size k, $k + 1$ actions are generated, one for the evaluation of the index and one for the instruction itself. Given that fluents cannot be used directly for array-access, we introduce additional *compare-actions* that compare the index with the available constants and include the appropriate object to the parameters. For an

```
int c[1];
int c[0]=2;  // direct addressing + value direct
int a[3];
int b=0;
a[b] = c[0]; // indirect addressing + value indirect
```

Fig. 7. Different forms of array addressing

example we first compute the index of the array index like 3, converted to a constant PDDL object like $n3$, and use it to access the array like (a n3).

Under certain assumptions the conversion of *C++-objects* into PDDL is possible, if the initialization uses the new-operator and gets assigned to a unique name. The *new-statement* induces the reservation of a PDDL object with a reference to this object; the variables of the class contain an additional parameter, whose type is the class name.

7.10 Methods

PDDL models cannot generate objects dynamically. The only *methods* that can be processed are those that have integer* → integer or integer* → void in their signature. *Methods* are converted in actions that wait for being invoked by setting a predicate for the call of the method. The parameters are found on the method-stack, and the solutions are found in a special solution register, accessible from the calling action, similar to what is done in an ordinary executable. The actions are indexed such that more than one call is possible.

The running time of the conversion is comparable to the running time of a compiler, as they both satisfy similar requirements. The compiler, however, produces object code, while the approach presented here generated a PDDL model.

8 Data Abstraction

Arithmetics on integer variables suggest a conversion of the C++ program into PDDL2, level 2, for which inferences can become rather complex. In fact, such metric planning is undecidable in general [35], while propositional planning is known to be PSPACE-complete [7]. Abstraction [13] is a simplification of the problem that finds traces to target states faster, but may introduce spurious counterexample paths. If the abstract model can be proven correct, however, the original one is correct as well.

We support different forms of abstraction, mainly data abstraction similar to [49]. If a state s is represented as a state vector $(s_1, \ldots, s_k)$ with variables s_i in some finite domains, then data abstraction is established by a projection, reducing the domains of some s_i, $i \in \{1, \ldots, k\}$. In the extreme, the domain is reduced to the empty set, which entails ignoring the value of the variable, matching with pattern abstraction needed for constructing database heuristics [16]. In model checking this corresponds to a form of data abstraction, which exploits the fact that specifications for software models usually consider fairly simple relationships among the data values in the system. In such cases, one can map the domain of the actual data values into a smaller domain of abstract data values. Such mapping induces a mapping of the states of the system, which in turn induces an abstract system. In many cases the abstract system simulates the original one, by means that each behavior in the original model is present in the abstracted one.

```
;constants
neg,zero,pos
;constant definitions
:neg: ( x < 0 )
:pos: ( x > 0 )
:zero: ( x == 0 )
;operation definitions
:add:dadd:
(neg,zero,neg)
(zero,neg,neg)
(neg,pos,*)
(pos,neg,*)
...
```

Fig. 8. Data abstraction library definition

Data abstraction, however, is not the only approach. With predicate abstraction the concrete states of a system are mapped to abstract states according to their evaluation under a finite set of predicates [30]. Automatic predicate abstraction approaches have been designed and implemented for finite and infinite state systems. Both data and predicate abstraction induce abstract systems that simulate the original one. We call such an abstraction a simulation abstraction. A refined planning heuristic based on abstraction has been contributed by [38].

We look at abstractions for the arithmetics with numbers. It is evident that abstractions introduce additional branching to the search. In the *neg-pos-zero* abstraction, for example, integers are projected to three values of being either positive negative, or equal to zero. If two negative or two positive values are multiplied, the result is determined, while for mixed multiplication, different options are possible. An alternative is an *odd-even* abstraction with obvious semantics.

Numerical abstraction in C++ can be implemented elegantly using the operator overloading mechanism. Following the purpose of this paper, however, we propose to build abstraction libraries on the planning level. For the example of the *neg-pos-zero* abstraction we store an convenient PDDL-like interface for the library that is shown in Fig. 8. The interface serves a macro that is automatically extended to enrich the initial state and the PDDL operators to realize abstraction.

The dependency graph helps to deduce the set of all variables that are affected if one is abstracted.

9   Results

The Eclipse plugin that has been developed[11] enables software developers to discover bugs during the process of writing code. Detected errors are presented interactively as a highlighted sequence of source code. The implementation itself includes the following

---

[11] Available at www.tzi.de/~edelkamp/AbsPlugin. The repository contains data abstraction definition files, the models that were analyzed, models to verify features of the plugin (such as method call, array access, etc.), planners compiled for *x86*, and the plugin as *jar* package (ready to be used with Eclipse).

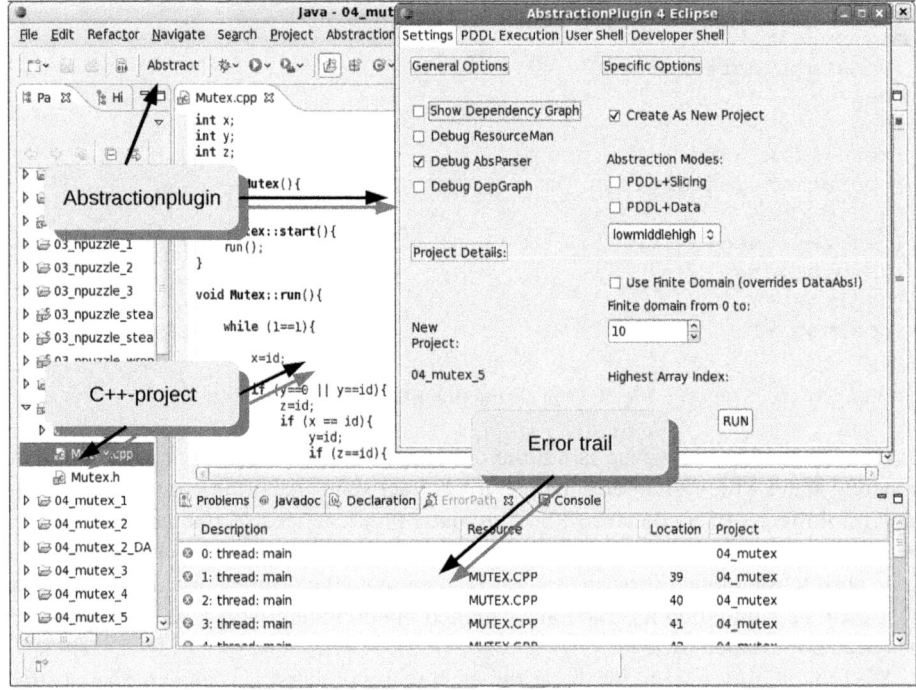

Fig. 9. Eclipse SDK with (abstraction) plugin and error trailer

components: Eclipse + CDT, (besides others planners like MIPS and SGPLAN) the planners FF/Metric-FF [39], and the Java SDK. The plugin consists of the GUI for parameterizing the algorithms, the parser, the generator for the dependency graph data structure and the PDDL output, and and the error trailer.

Fig. 10 cross-compares[12] the performance with our C++ program model checker StEAM [48][13][14].

Recall that StEAM has the same in- and output behavior, systematically analyzes a program as an executable in object code and can apply different search heuristics. The C++ source code examples we considered include:

- *Mutex* is a flawed version of a solution to a mutual exclusion problem as considered in [42].
- *Producer-Consumer* is an implementation of a distributed queue, chosen to test a concurrent program for a assertion.

---

[12] We use a Laptop computer running one core of the Intel(R) Core(TM) 2 CPU with 1.66 GHz and 1GB RAM for the experiments.

[13] Available at http://steam.cs.uni-dortmund.de

[14] In our tables l denotes the length of the counterexample, s denotes the number of states, t denotes the CPU time, DA denotes Data Abstraction, and EHC denotes enforced hill climbing as applied in MetricFF. A dash (–) denotes that the program model checker ran out of memory.

Checker	Mutex			Producer-Consumer			BubbleSort10		
	l	s	t	t	s	t	l	s	t
StEAM DFS	66	742	90	122	353	59	594	1184	124
StEAM Best-First	30	1630	198	29	4383	690	594	1774	88
MetricFF EHC	27	747	6	20	23	2	-	-	-
MetricFF Best-First	27	251	4	20	3405	10	-	-	-
FF DA EHC	28	39	28	20	33	2	661	670	1312
MetricFF DA EHC	28	39	108	20	34	56	661	670	8938
MetricFF DA Best-First	27	922	877	20	3405	1609	661	73294	79674

Checker	8-Puzzle			3-Philosophers		
	l	s	t	l	s	t
STEAM DFS	36096	70366	6.5s	33	46	0.05s
STEAM Best-First	86	7836	0.26s	33	707	0.13s
MetricFF EHC	-	-	-	42	0.21s	0.003s
MetricFF Best-First	-	-	-	41	3270	0.01s
FF DA EHC	115	932	2585	42	209	0.002s
MetricFF DA EHC	361	56257	1177572	42	212	0.004s
MetricFF DA Best-First	99	4113	96291	41	212	0.01s

Fig. 10. Results for benchmarks domains

Program	Metric-FF EHC			Metric-FF Best-First		
	l	s	t	l	s	t
4-Philosophers	45	0.05	0.05s	45	139	0.01s
5-Philosophers	51	22092	2.23s	61	224	0.03s
8-Philosophers	–	–	–	79	337	0.12s
8-Philosophers	–	–	–	121	663	0.24s
16-Philosophers	–	–	–	369	3887	8.89s
24-Philosophers	–	–	–	745	11719	98.07s
32-Philosophers	–	–	–	–	–	–

Fig. 11. Results for program model checking with a rising number of dining philosophers

- *Bubblesort* is a deterministic program with one thread that sorts 10 numbers. The error specification is chosen in such a way that the sorted sequence throws an exception.
- *8-Puzzle* is the implementation of a sliding-tile puzzle on a 3 times 3 board. The puzzle is described using an integer array $\langle 1, 4, 2, 3, 7, 5, 6, 0, 8 \rangle$, with value 0 denoting the blank. Moves are implemented using Range.
- *Philosophers* is a standard deadlock example. The solution is buggy, as the selection of forks can be interleaved, and correct if taking the two forks is contained in an atomic region. Therefore, with this example we tested the correct working of VLOCK, VUNLOCK, BEGINATOMIC and ENDATOMIC.

Between the two there is no clear-cut winner. In the rather artificial examples for verification, namely BubbleSort and 8-Puzzle, the program model checker is faster, and only planning with data abstraction solves the problem. In the three concurrent model checking examples of communication protocols, the analysis via PDDL is superior. In *Producer-Consumer* the planner does find the shortest path independent to the use of breadth-first search. More examples are needed to provide more insights, when and why general planning heuristics pay off.

In Fig. 11 we increase the number of philosophers. According to [1] nuSMV and according to [24] SPIN both have severe problems in proper scaling for this domain (when given a formal model of the program). The reason is the lack of a proper search heuristic that guides the exploration towards an error state. Directed model checkers like HSF-SPIN overcome the problem and scale to a very large number of philosophers. Compared to a recent paper on bounded model checking multi-threaded programs with SMT solvers [15], however, the number of philosophers was at most 7. Therefore, by program model checking with over 24 philosophers the presented approach is competitive.

10   Conclusion and Discussion

This work addresses the automated transformation of C++ program source code into PDDL for a planner to find plans that serve as counterexamples. Using PDDL, the generic approach adapts to almost all current deterministic planners (including non-heuristic search planners like SAT- or BDD-based planners). In our example setting we applied the so-called relaxed planning heuristic as implemented in FF, but the emphasize is not to experiment with any available heuristics. There are several related directed model checking approaches, but none of them directly applies heuristic search planning to program model checking.

Our program model checker prototype is capable of parsing a sizable but small fragment of multi-threaded C++ programs that include non-determinism in form of range statements and threads. The latter is of increasing importance for validating software developed for multi-core architectures.

The prototype touches most aspects of a modern program model checking tool: parsing the sources, generating the dependency graph, slicing the program, specifying the error type as well as generating and presenting the output in an SDK for debugging. Additionally, different options for data abstractions that determine the planning level and the complexity of finding a plan are discussed. The core technical contribution is the representation of the program flow in form of PDDL actions via explicitly modeling the program counter, and using the schematic representation of such actions with parameters for representing threads and finite domain numbers.

In some cases, the results compare well with a program model checker that executes the program on the object code level. At least for some domains advanced planner-inherent estimates can compete with simpler ones implemented in a directed model checker. This indicates that existing heuristic search planning technology may have impact for the formal verification of programs.

As current PDDL is inherently static, besides the restriction due to the chosen parsing tool that cannot handle STL, there are additional restrictions to the expressiveness of program sources that can be processed. For example, PDDL does not allow the dynamic creation of objects, which induces a fixed-sized state vector. This implies that dynamic data structures cannot be checked. Moreover, we have to depend on static bounds for modeling array access, and more complex features of C++, e.g., multiple inheritance, exceptions, etc. are also not yet supported. So far out approach only illustrates the potential of efficiency advantages, and suggests program checking via PDDL as an exciting research avenue to the community. On the other hand, as we have concentrated on the imperative kernel of C++, the approach likely extends to other programming languages.

Acknowledgments. Thanks to the critical reviewers that beside observing traditional techniques and smaller-sized examples saw pioneering aspects in the interconnection of planning and program verification, and honored the efforts to design and implement a novel C++ program model checking approach. We thank DFG for grants in the area of directed model checking.

References

1. Albarghouthi, A., Baier, J., McIlraith, S.A.: On the use of planning technology for verification. In: Workshop on ICAPS 2009 (2009)
2. Andrews, T., Qadeer, S., Rajamani, S.K., Rehof, J., Xie, Y.: Zing: Exploiting program structure for model checking concurrent software. In: Gardner, P., Yoshida, N. (eds.) CONCUR 2004. LNCS, vol. 3170, pp. 1–15. Springer, Heidelberg (2004)
3. Bakera, M., Edelkamp, S., Kissmann, P., Renner, C.D.: Solving μ-calculus parity games by symbolic planning. In: Peled, D.A., Wooldridge, M.J. (eds.) MoChArt 2008. LNCS, vol. 5348, pp. 15–33. Springer, Heidelberg (2009)
4. Biere, A., Cimatti, A., Clarke, E., Zhu, Y.: Symbolic model checking without bDDs. In: Cleaveland, W.R. (ed.) TACAS 1999. LNCS, vol. 1579, pp. 193–207. Springer, Heidelberg (1999)
5. Bonet, B., Haslum, P., Hickmott, S.L., Thiébaux, S.: Directed unfolding of Petri nets. T. Petri Nets and Other Models of Concurrency 1, 172–198 (2008)
6. Bryant, R.E.: Symbolic boolean manipulation with ordered binary-decision diagrams. ACM Computing Surveys 24(3), 142–170 (1992)
7. Bylander, T.: The computational complexity of propositional STRIPS planning. Artificial Intelligence, 165–204 (1994)
8. Cimatti, A., Giunchiglia, E., Giunchiglia, F., Traverso, P.: Planning via model checking: A decision procedure for AR. In: Steel, S. (ed.) ECP 1997. LNCS, vol. 1348, pp. 130–142. Springer, Heidelberg (1997)
9. Cimatti, A., Pistore, M., Roveri, M., Traverso, P.: Weak, strong, and strong cyclic planning via symbolic model checking. Artif. Intell. 147(1-2), 35–84 (2003)
10. Cimatti, A., Roveri, M., Bertoli, P.: Conformant planning via symbolic model checking and heuristic search. Artif. Intell. 159(1-2), 127–206 (2004)
11. Clarke, E., Kröning, D., Lerda, F.: A tool for checking ANSI-C programs. In: Jensen, K., Podelski, A. (eds.) TACAS 2004. LNCS, vol. 2988, pp. 168–176. Springer, Heidelberg (2004)
12. Clarke, E., Kröning, D., Sharygina, N., Yorav, K.: SATABS: SAT-based predicate abstraction for ANSI-C. In: Halbwachs, N., Zuck, L.D. (eds.) TACAS 2005. LNCS, vol. 3440, pp. 570–574. Springer, Heidelberg (2005)
13. Clarke, E.M., Grumberg, O., Long, D.: Model checking and abstraction. ACM Transactions on Programming Languages and Systems 16(5), 1512–1542 (1994)
14. Clarke, E.M., Grumberg, O., Peled, D.A.: Model checking. MIT Press, Cambridge (1999)
15. Cordeiro, L., Fischer, B.: Bounded model checking of multi-threaded software using smt solvers, vol. abs/1003.3830 (2010)

16. Culberson, J.C., Schaeffer, J.: Pattern databases. Computational Intelligence 14(4), 318–334 (1998)
17. Dams, D., Namjoshi, K.S.: Orion: High-precision methods for static error analysis of C and C++ programs. In: de Boer, F.S., Bonsangue, M.M., Graf, S., de Roever, W.-P. (eds.) FMCO 2005. LNCS, vol. 4111, pp. 138–160. Springer, Heidelberg (2006)
18. Aan de Brugh, N.H.M., Nguyen, V.Y., Ruys, T.C.: MOONWALKER: Verification of .NET programs. In: Kowalewski, S., Philippou, A. (eds.) TACAS 2009. LNCS, vol. 5505, pp. 170–173. Springer, Heidelberg (2009)
19. Edelkamp, S.: Promela planning. In: Ball, T., Rajamani, S.K. (eds.) SPIN 2003. LNCS, vol. 2648, pp. 197–212. Springer, Heidelberg (2003)
20. Edelkamp, S., Jabbar, S.: Action planning for directed model checking of Petri nets. Electronic Notes in Theoretical Computer Science (ENTCS) 149(2), 3–18 (2006)
21. Edelkamp, S., Jabbar, S., Lluch-Lafuente, A.: Action planning for graph transition systems. In: ICAPS 2005-Workshop on Verification and Validation of Model-Based Planning and Scheduling Systems (2005)
22. Edelkamp, S., Jabbar, S., Midzic, D., Rikowski, D., Sulewski, D.: External memory search for verification of multi-threaded C++ programs. KI 22(2), 44–50 (2008)
23. Edelkamp, S., Jabbar, S., Sulewski, D.: Distributed verification of multi-threaded C++ programs, vol. 198, pp. 33–46 (2008)
24. Edelkamp, S., Leue, S., Lluch-Lafuente, A.: Directed explicit-state model checking in the validation of communication protocols. STTT 5(2-3), 247–267 (2004)
25. Edelkamp, S., Rensink, A.: Graph transformation and AI planning. In: ICAPS 2007-Workshop on the Knowledge Engineering Competition (2007)
26. Edelkamp, S., Schuppan, V., Bošnački, D., Wijs, A., Fehnker, A., Aljazzar, H.: Survey on directed model checking. In: Peled, D.A., Wooldridge, M.J. (eds.) MoChArt 2008. LNCS, vol. 5348, pp. 65–89. Springer, Heidelberg (2009)
27. Fox, M., Long, D.: PDDL2.1: An extension of pddl for expressing temporal planning domains. JAIR 20, 61–124 (2003)
28. Gerevini, A., Haslum, P., Long, D., Saetti, A., Dimopoulos, Y.: Deterministic planning in the fifth international planning competition: 7pddl3
29. Gleick, J.: Little bug, big bang. New York Times vom 1 (Dezember 1996)
30. Graf, S., Saidi, H.: Construction of abstract state graphs with PVS. In: Grumberg, O. (ed.) CAV 1997. LNCS, vol. 1254, pp. 72–83. Springer, Heidelberg (1997)
31. Groce, A., Visser, W.: Heuristics for model checking java programs. STTT 6(4), 260–276 (2004)
32. Haslum, P., Bonet, B., Geffner, H.: New admissible heuristics for domain-independent planning. In: AAAI, pp. 1163–1168 (2005)
33. Havelund, K., Pressburger, T.: Model checking java programs using JAVA pathfinder. STTT 2(4), 366–381 (2000)
34. Havelund, K., Visser, W.: Program model checking as a new trend. STTT 4(1), 8–20 (2002)
35. Helmert, M.: Decidability and undecidability results for planning with numerical state variables. In: AIPS, pp. 303–312 (2002)
36. Helmert, M.: A planning heuristic based on causal graph analysis. In: ICAPS, pp. 161–170 (2004)
37. Helmert, M., Domshlak, C.: Landmarks, critical paths and abstractions: What's the difference anyway? In: ICAPS (2009)
38. Helmert, M., Haslum, P., Hoffmann, J.: Flexible abstraction heuristics for optimal sequential planning. In: ICAPS, pp. 176–183 (2007)
39. Hoffmann, J.: The Metric-FF planning system: Translating ignoring delete lists to numeric state variables. JAIR 20, 291–341 (2003)

40. Hoffmann, J., Edelkamp, S.: The deterministic part of ipc-4: An overview, vol. 24, pp. 519–579 (2005)
41. Hoffmann, J., Edelkamp, S., Thiebaux, S., Englert, R., Liporace, F., Trueg, S.: Engineering benchmarks for planning: the domains used in the deterministic part of IPC-4. JAIR 26(2), 453–541 (2006)
42. Holzmann, G.J.: The Spin Model Checker: Primer and Reference Manual. Addison-Wesley, Reading (2004)
43. Kautz, H.A., Selman, B.: Pushing the envelope: Planning, propositional logic, and stochastic search. In: AAAI, pp. 1194–1201 (1996)
44. König, B., Kozioura, V.: Augur - a tool for the analysis of graph transformation systems. Bulletin of the EATCS 87, 126–137 (2005)
45. Kupferschmid, S., Hoffmann, J., Larsen, K.G.: Fast directed model checking via russian doll abstraction. In: Ramakrishnan, C.R., Rehof, J. (eds.) TACAS 2008. LNCS, vol. 4963, pp. 203–217. Springer, Heidelberg (2008)
46. Leven, P., Mehler, T., Edelkamp, S.: Directed error detection in C++ with the assembly-level model checker stEAM. In: Graf, S., Mounier, L. (eds.) SPIN 2004. LNCS, vol. 2989, pp. 39–56. Springer, Heidelberg (2004)
47. McDermott, D.: The 1998 AI Planning Competition. AI Magazine 21(2) (2000)
48. Mehler, T.: Challenges and Applications of Assembly-Level Software Model Checking. PhD thesis, Dortmund University of Technology (2006)
49. Merino, P., del Mar Gallardo, M., Martinez, J., Pimentel, E.: αSPIN: Extending SPIN with abstraction. In: Bošnački, D., Leue, S. (eds.) SPIN 2002. LNCS, vol. 2318, pp. 254–258. Springer, Heidelberg (2002)
50. Rabinovitz, I., Grumberg, O.: Bounded model checking of concurrent programs. In: Etessami, K., Rajamani, S.K. (eds.) CAV 2005. LNCS, vol. 3576, pp. 82–97. Springer, Heidelberg (2005)
51. Stroustrup, B.: The C++ Programming Language, 2nd edn. Addison-Wesley Publishing Company, Reading (1994)
52. Visser, W., Havelund, K., Brat, G., Park, S., Lerda, F.: Model checking programs. Automated Software Engineering Journal 10(2), 203–232 (2003)
53. Visser, W., Mehlitz, P.C.: Model checking programs with Java PathFinder. In: Godefroid, P. (ed.) SPIN 2005. LNCS, vol. 3639, p. 27. Springer, Heidelberg (2005)
54. Wehrle, M., Helmert, M.: The causal graph revisited for directed model checking. In: Palsberg, J., Su, Z. (eds.) SAS 2009. LNCS, vol. 5673, pp. 86–101. Springer, Heidelberg (2009)

Automatic Data-Abstraction in Model Checking Multi-Agent Systems

Alessio Lomuscio[1], Hongyang Qu[2], and Francesco Russo[1]

[1] Department of Computing, Imperial College London, London, UK
[2] Computing Laboratory, Oxford University, Oxford, UK

Abstract. We present an automatic data-abstraction technique for the verification of the universal fragment of the temporal-epistemic logic CTLK. We show the correctness of the methodology and present an implementation operating on ISPL models, the input files for MCMAS, a model checker for multi-agent systems. The experimental results point to the attractiveness of the technique in a number of examples in the multi-agent systems domain.

1 Introduction

Over the past few years model checking techniques [3] have been extended to temporal-epistemic logics [11]. Several model checkers, including MCMAS [15], McK [12] and Verics [14], are now available supporting this and other extended functionalities. Expressive specification languages find a natural application in the area of multi-agent systems [18]. Because of their autonomous nature multi-agent systems (MAS) naturally generate very large state spaces. Therefore, being able to tackle the state-space explosion remains of fundamental importance if we are to develop model checking techniques for the verification of MAS. While a number of abstraction-based techniques have been put forward for plain temporal logic, e.g., [2,6], little attention has gone so far towards developing efficient state-reduction methodologies preserving the validity of temporal-epistemic specifications. Crucially, there is no automatic implementation enabling the user to perform automatic abstraction directly on the program. This paper aims to make a first attempt at filling this gap.

In line with much of the literature we represent MAS as interpreted systems. In this paradigm we model agents by programming the local evolution of the agents' data in their local states. We use ISPL, the input language of MCMAS, to program interpreted systems. In this paper we show that data-abstraction notions can be defined on interpreted systems semantics and automatic reduction can be performed directly on ISPL programs. We illustrate the technique on two scenarios inspired by popular examples in the MAS literature: card games [9], and the bit transmission problem [11]. Both the scenarios we consider have over 10^{10} reachable states so are too large to be checked by MCMAS directly, but can be verified effectively by model checking the reduced program.

R. van der Meyden and J.-G. Smaus (Eds.): MoChArt 2010, LNAI 6572, pp. 52–68, 2011.
© Springer-Verlag Berlin Heidelberg 2011

Related work. Abstraction for epistemic specifications was defined on Kripke models in [7,10]. However, given these structures are computationally ungrounded [17], it is difficult to apply these results to MAS descriptions. Previous work by some of the authors of this paper [5] established the basic theoretical framework for abstraction on interpreted systems, but the results were not applied to data-abstraction specifically, nor to concrete ISPL programs, the basis for this investigation.

More broadly, three main approaches are prominent in abstraction techniques for temporal logic. The first focuses on studying partial symmetries of the system under investigation [4]. In the second, predicate abstraction, introduced in [13], the system is described by a set of logical formulas; a finite set of local state predicates are selected, and any two local states satisfying exactly the same predicates are collapsed. Finally, the third technique, introduced by Cousot [6] and further developed by Clarke at al. [2,1] involves automatically reducing local states by collapsing the data values they are built from. This is the basis for the technique presented here.

Outline of the paper. The rest of the paper is organised as follows. Section 2 describes the interpreted system framework, the temporal epistemic specification logic ACTLK, the model checker MCMAS, and abstraction of interpreted systems. Section 3 reports the theoretical basis of this investigation, namely that ACTLK properties are preserved under abstraction, as well as details of the implementation. Section 4 presents experimental results. We conclude in Section 5.

2   Interpreted Systems, ACTLK and Abstraction

We use interpreted systems [11] as a semantic model for multi-agent systems. In this formalism a system is composed of n agents and an environment. Each agent and the environment are associated with a set of *local states* and a set of *actions*. The local states are private to the agent and the environment. *Local protocols* define the actions that may be executed at a given local state. The *local evolution function* of the agent defines the transition relation among the local states. The environment has the same structure as the agents. The formal definition of an interpreted system is given as follows.

Definition 1 (Interpreted system). *An interpreted system over a set $Ag = \{1, \ldots, n\}$ of agents and an environment e is a tuple*

$$\mathcal{I} = \langle \{L_i\}_{i \in Ag} \cup \{L_e\}, \{ACT_i\}_{i \in Ag} \cup \{ACT_e\}, \{P_i\}_{i \in Ag} \cup \{P_e\}, \{t_i\}_{i \in Ag} \cup \{t_e\}, I_0, V \rangle$$

where:

- L_i *(L_e, respectively) is a non-empty set of possible local states for agent $i \in Ag$ (the environment, respectively). The set of possible global states is denoted by $S = L_1 \times \cdots \times L_n \times L_e$. For any global state $g \in S$, we write g_i for the i-th component in g, i.e., the local state of agent i in g. Similarly, g_e represents the local state of e in g.*

- ACT_i (ACT_e, respectively) is a non-empty set of possible actions for agent $i \in Ag$ (the environment, respectively). The set of possible joint actions is denoted by $ACT = ACT_1 \times \cdots \times ACT_n \times ACT_e$.
- $P_i : L_i \longrightarrow 2^{ACT_i}$ is the local protocol for agent i and $P_e : L_e \longrightarrow 2^{ACT_e}$ is the local protocol for the environment.
- $t_i : L_i \times ACT \longrightarrow 2^{L_i}$ is the local evolution function for agent i, and $t_e : L_e \times ACT \longrightarrow 2^{L_e}$ for the environment.
- $I_0 \subseteq S$ is a non-empty set of initial states.
- $V : S \longrightarrow 2^{AP}$ is the evaluation function for the set AP of atomic propositions.

The Cartesian product of the local evolution functions denotes the global evolution function that describes how the system evolves from a global state to the next one. Let $\bar{a} \in ACT$ be a joint action and a_i the action of agent i ($i \in Ag$) in $\bar{a}$, as well as a_e for the environment.

Definition 2 (Global transition relation). *Given an interpreted system $\mathcal{I}$, the global transition relation $T \subseteq S \times ACT \times 2^S$ is such that $\langle g, \bar{a}, S' \rangle \in T$ (where $S' \subseteq S$) if and only if:*

$$\big(\forall i \in Ag : \langle g_i, \bar{a}, S'_i \rangle \in t_i \wedge \langle g_i, a_i \rangle \in P_i\big) \wedge \langle g_e, \bar{a}, S'_e \rangle \in t_e \wedge \langle g_e, a_e \rangle \in P_e$$

where $S'_i \subseteq L_i$ and $S'_e \subseteq L_e$. In the following we assume that the global transition relation T is total, i.e., for every $g \in S$, there is $S' \subseteq S$ such that gTS' and $S' \neq \emptyset$.

Definition 3 (Path). *A path π in $\mathcal{I}$ is an infinite sequence $g^0 g^1 \ldots$ of global states in S such that every pair of adjacent states forms a transition, i.e., $g^k T g^{k+1}$ for all $k \geq 0$. Let $\pi(k)$ be the kth global state in π, i.e., g^k.*

As standard [11] the knowledge of an agent is defined by means of relations over global states defined as follows.

Definition 4 (Epistemic indistinguishability relation). *The epistemic indistinguishability relation for agent i in system $\mathcal{I}$ is:*

$$\sim_i = \{\langle g, g' \rangle \in S \times S \mid g_i = g'_i\}$$

ACTLK logic. We consider specifications expressed in the logic ACTLK [16], which adds epistemic modalities to the temporal logic ACTL, the universal fragment of Computation Tree Logic [8].

Definition 5 (ACTLK). *ACTLK formulae over a set Ag of agents and a set AP of propositions are defined by:*

$$\phi ::= \alpha \mid \neg\alpha \mid \phi \wedge \phi \mid K_i\phi \mid AX\phi \mid A(\phi U \phi) \mid A(\phi R \phi)$$

where $\alpha \in AP$ and $i \in Ag$.

As customary, a formulas $K_i\phi$ is read as "Agent i knows ϕ". The formula $AX\phi$ specifies that "for all paths ϕ holds in the next state of the path"; the formula $A(\phi U\psi)$ specifies that "along all paths ϕ holds until ψ holds"; the formula $A(\phi R\phi')$ specifies that "along all paths, ϕ releases ϕ'". Other universal temporal operators AF and AG can be equivalently expressed as $AF\phi = A(trueU\phi)$ and $AG\phi = A(falseR\phi)$.

The combination of temporal and epistemic modalities allows us to specify how agents' knowledge evolves over time. For example, $AG(\alpha \rightarrow AF(K_iK_j\psi))$ expresses that whenever α holds, eventually agent i will know that agent j knows ψ.

Given an interpreted system $\mathcal{I}$, the ACTL modalities are interpreted via the global transition relation $\mathcal{T}$, while the epistemic modality K_i is interpreted by the epistemic relation $\sim_i$ for agent i:

Definition 6 (Satisfaction). *Let $\mathcal{I}$ be an interpreted system over the set Ag of agents and the set AP of propositions, let ϕ be an ACTLK formula over Ag and AP, and let $g \in G$ be a reachable state. Truth of ϕ at g in $\mathcal{I}$, written $(\mathcal{I}, g) \models \phi$, is defined inductively by the following conditions:*

- *$(\mathcal{I}, g) \models \alpha$ iff $\alpha \in V(g)$, for $\alpha \in AP$;*
- *$(\mathcal{I}, g) \models \neg\phi$ iff $(\mathcal{I}, g) \not\models \phi$;*
- *$(\mathcal{I}, g) \models \phi \wedge \psi$ iff $(\mathcal{I}, g) \models \phi$ and $(\mathcal{I}, g) \models \psi$;*
- *$(\mathcal{I}, g) \models K_i\phi$ iff $(\mathcal{I}, g') \models \phi$ for all $g' \in G$ such that $g \sim_i g'$;*
- *$(\mathcal{I}, g) \models AX\phi$ iff for every path $\pi = g^0g^1 \ldots$ in $\mathcal{I}$ such that $g = g^0$, we have $(\mathcal{I}, \pi(1)) \models \phi$;*
- *$(\mathcal{I}, g) \models A(\phi U\psi)$ iff for every path $\pi = g^0g^1 \ldots$ in $\mathcal{I}$ such that $g = g^0$, there exists $k \geq 0$ such that $(\mathcal{I}, \pi(k)) \models \psi$ and $(\mathcal{I}, \pi(j)) \models \phi$ for all $0 \leq j < k$;*
- *$(\mathcal{I}, g) \models A(\phi R\phi')$ iff for every i and every path $g^0, g^1, \ldots$ in $\mathcal{I}$ such that $g = g^0$, if for all $0 \leq j < i$, $(\mathcal{I}, \pi(j)) \not\models \phi$ then $(\mathcal{I}, \pi(i)) \models \phi'$.*

Formula ϕ is true in $\mathcal{I}$, denoted by $\mathcal{I} \models \phi$, iff $(\mathcal{I}, g) \models \phi$ for all $g \in I_0$.

The abstraction technique [2] involves converting a ground, or *concrete* system, into an *abstract* system, typically smaller than the original. The abstract system is obtained by partitioning the system states into equivalence classes. Each equivalence class is represented by an *abstract state* in the abstract system. Every transition in the concrete system has a corresponding one in the abstract system; so every behavior of the concrete system is also a behavior of the abstract system. In [5] a quotient construction was defined.

Definition 7 (Quotient of interpreted system [5]). *Assume an interpreted system $\mathcal{I}$ over the set Ag of agents, the environment e, and the set AP of atomic propositions. For each $i \in Ag$, assume an equivalence $\equiv_i \subseteq L_i \times L_i$ and an equivalence $\equiv_i^a \subseteq ACT_i \times ACT_i$. For $l \in L_i$, we write $[l]$ for the equivalence class of l with respect to $\equiv_i$. Similarly, we write $[a_i]$ for the equivalence class of $a_i \in ACT_i$ with respect to $\equiv_i^a$. Likewise we define $\equiv_e$, $\equiv_e^a$, and equivalence classes on L_e and ACT_e. We write $[g]$ for $\langle [g_1], \ldots, [g_n], [g_e] \rangle$ and write $[\bar{a}]$ for $\langle [a_1], \ldots, [a_n], [a_e] \rangle$. Let $AP' \subseteq AP$ consist of all propositions of AP that do* not distinguish between equivalent local states, i.e., all $\alpha \in AP$ such that for all $g, g' \in S$: if $\alpha \in V(g)$ and $g_i \equiv g_i'$ for all $i \in Ag$, as well as $g_e \equiv g_e'$, then $\alpha \in V(g')$. The quotient system of $\mathcal{I}$ is the interpreted system $\mathcal{I}'$ over the set Ag of agents, the environment e and the set AP' of proposition such that:

- $L_i' = \{[l] \mid l \in L_i\}$ for all $i \in Ag$, and $L_e' = \{[l] \mid l \in L_e\}$.
- $ACT_i' = \{[a] \mid a \in ACT_i\}$ for all $i \in Ag$, and $ACT_e' = \{[a] \mid a \in ACT_e\}$.
- $P_i' = \{\langle [l], [a] \rangle \mid \langle l, a \rangle \in P_i\}$ for all $i \in Ag$, and $P_e' = \{\langle [l], [a] \rangle \mid \langle l, a \rangle \in P_e\}$.
- $t_i' = \{\langle [l], [\overline{a}], [l'] \rangle \mid \langle l, \overline{a}, l' \rangle \in t_i\}$ for all $i \in Ag$, and $t_e' = \{\langle [l], [\overline{a}], [l'] \rangle \mid \langle l, \overline{a}, l' \rangle \in t_e\}$.
- $I_0' = \{[g] \mid g \in I_0\}$.
- $V'([g]) = V(g) \cap AP'$.

It has been proved in [5] that the construction above preserves satisfaction from abstract to concrete models.

Theorem 1 (Preservation [5]). *Let $\mathcal{I}'$ be a quotient of interpreted system $\mathcal{I}$. For any ACTLK formula ϕ over AP', if $\mathcal{I}' \models \phi$, then $\mathcal{I} \models \phi$.*

3   Implementation and Data Abstraction Theorem

Definition 7 and Theorem 1 do not give a constructive way for building the abstract model. For any implementation purposes we need to give an algorithm for defining appropriate equivalence relations. In the following we give such procedure in the case of ISPL files, the input to the model checker MCMAS [15]. We operate on ISPL files as they provide a natural operational correspondence to interpreted systems.

In a nutshell an ISPL program P defines local states, actions, protocols, and local transition for agents and environment corresponding to a given interpreted system. Local states for the agents are defined by means of a finite set $V = \{v_1, \ldots, v_m\}$ of variables. Each variable $v_k \in V$ has an associated finite domain D_k. We consider the set $\{+, -, \div, \cdot\}$ denoting standard arithmetic operations. We also use *binary relation symbols* from the set $\{<, >, =, \leq, \geq\}$. An *arithmetic expression* is built from variables in V, constants in D_k and arithmetic operations; for instance, $v_2 - 5$ is an arithmetic expression. A *logic expression* p is built from arithmetic expressions and relation symbols as natural; for instance, $v_2 - 5 > 4$ is a logic expression. A *Boolean expression* ψ is composed from logic expressions p using negation $\neg$, conjunction $\wedge$ and disjunction $\vee$. Any global state g can be seen as an evaluation over V, i.e., $g = (d_1, \ldots, d_m) \in D = D_1 \times \cdots \times D_m$. Similarly, the local states of an agent can be seen as evaluations over a subset of V, named *local variables* of the agent. We proceed by giving an example to explain the details of the abstraction procedure on the data of the program.

Card Game Example [9,5]. *The system has two agents Player1 and Player2 and an environment e. There is a deck of $2N$ cards. Each player receives $N - 1$ cards. Two cards are put aside. Higher index cards beat lower index cards. In each round of the game, each player plays a card from his or her hand. The player playing* *the stronger card wins the round. The game continues until all cards have been played. The player who won the most number of rounds wins the game.*

An ISPL program for this example is described as follows. Let $C = \{1, \ldots, 2N\}$ represent the set of $2N$ cards. We call *red cards* the subset $\{N+1, \ldots, 2N\}$ and the remaining cards *black cards*. A player $i \in \{1, 2\}$ can either play a card or do nothing: $ACT_i = \{playcard\ c_i^k \mid c_i^k \in C\} \cup \{nothing\}$. The environment either calculates who wins the current round or does nothing: $ACT_e = \{eval, nothing\}$. The local state of an agent describes what cards he or she holds and how many rounds he has played so far, as well as the outcome of the game: $L_i = \{(\mathcal{H}_i, k, a, b) \mid |\mathcal{H}_i| + 1 = |\mathcal{N}|\}$, where $\mathcal{H}_i \subset C$ represents the cards held by the agent i and $\mathcal{N} = \{1, \ldots, N\}$ represents the game rounds. The environment records the current score in its local state, whose domain is $L_e = \{(\mathcal{H}_1, \mathcal{H}_2, a, b) \mid a + b \leq N - 1\}$ where a and b encode the number of deals won by player 1 and 2, respectively. The local protocols are defined as follows.

$$P_i(\mathcal{H}_i, k, a, b) = \{playcard\ c_i^k \mid c_i^k \in \mathcal{H}_i \text{ and } k \in \mathcal{N}\}, \text{ if } k < N;$$
$$P_i(\mathcal{H}_i, k, a, b) = \{nothing\}, \text{ if } k = N;$$
$$P_e(\mathcal{H}_1, \mathcal{H}_2, a, b) = \{eval\}, \text{ if } a + b < N - 1;$$
$$P_e(\mathcal{H}_1, \mathcal{H}_2, a, b) = \{nothing\}, \text{ if } a + b = N - 1.$$

The local evolution functions have the form:

$$t_i((\mathcal{H}_i, k, a, b), \langle nothing \rangle) = (\mathcal{H}_i, k, a, b); \qquad (1)$$
$$t_i((\mathcal{H}_i, k, a, b), \langle playcard\ c_i^k \rangle) = (\mathcal{H}_i, k+1, a', b'), \qquad (2)$$
$$t_e((\mathcal{H}_1, \mathcal{H}_2, a, b), \langle playcard\ c_1^k, playcard\ c_2^k, eval \rangle) = (a+1, b), \text{ if } c_1^k > c_2^k; (3)$$
$$t_e((\mathcal{H}_1, \mathcal{H}_2, a, b), \langle playcard\ c_1^k, playcard\ c_2^k, eval \rangle) = (a, b+1), \text{ if } c_1^k < c_2^k; (4)$$
$$t_e((\mathcal{H}_1, \mathcal{H}_2, a, b), \langle nothing \rangle) = (a, b). \qquad (5)$$

where a' and b' in (2) are the new updated values of a and b, according to (3) and (4).

The set of initial states is: $I_0 = \{(\mathcal{H}_1, 0, 0, 0), (\mathcal{H}_2, 0, 0, 0), (\mathcal{H}_1, \mathcal{H}_2, 0, 0)\}$. The atomic propositions we consider are $allred_i$ ("Player i holds only red cards."), win_i ("Player i has won the game."), $topred_i$ and $lowred_i$ for $i \in \{1, 2\}$.

$$allred_i \text{ holds where } \mathcal{H}_i \subset \{N+1, \ldots, 2N\};$$
$$win_1 \text{ holds where } a > b \text{ and } a + b = N - 1;$$
$$win_2 \text{ holds where } b > a \text{ and } a + b = N - 1;$$
$$topred_i \text{ holds where } \mathcal{H}_i = \{N+2, \ldots, 2N\};$$
$$lowred_i \text{ holds where } \mathcal{H}_i \subset \{N, \ldots, 2N\}.$$

Fig 1 shows an ISPL program encoding the example above in the case of $N = 3$, where $\mathcal{H}_1$ is described by the variables c11 and c12, and $\mathcal{H}_2$ by c21 and c22. In this case, $L_e = \{(\mathcal{H}_1, \mathcal{H}_2, a, b) \mid a + b \leq 2\}$, i.e., there are just two rounds. In the first round, the players play the cards c11, c21; in the second round, they play

```
Agent Environment                       n=1: { playcard1 };
Obsvars:                                n=2: { playcard2 };
  a: 0 .. 2;                            n=3: { null };
  b: 0 .. 2;                          end Protocol
end Obsvars                          Evolution:
Vars:                                   n = 2  if n=1;
  c11: 1 .. 6;                          n = 3  if n=2;
  c12: 1 .. 6;                        end Evolution
  c21: 1 .. 6;                      end Agent
  c22: 1 .. 6;
end Vars                             -- Agent Player2 omitted
--Actions and Protocol are omitted
Evolution                            Evaluation
  a=a+1 if c11>c21 and ...             lowred1  if (c11>2 and c12>2);
  b=b+1 if c11<c21 and ...             topred1  if (c11>4 and c12>4);
--the rest of the Evolution is omitted allred1  if (c11>3 and c12>3);
end Agent                              win1 if (a>b and a+b=2);
                                       --The same properties
Agent Player1                          --for Player2 are omitted
Lobsvars={c11,c12};                  end Evaluation
Vars:
  n: 1 .. 3;                         --InitStates omitted
end Vars
Actions = {null,playcard1,playcard2}; Formulae
Protocol:                              (AG(allred1->K(Player1,(AF win1))));
                                     end Formulae
```

Fig. 1. Sketch of an ISPL program for the *Card Game* with 6 cards ($N = 3$)

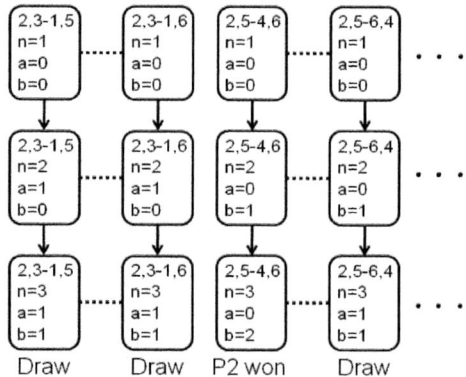

Fig. 2. Sketch of the global transition relation for the concrete *Card Game Example* with 6 cards. The dashed line represents the epistemic relation $\sim_1$.

$c21$, $c22$. Note from Fig 1 that *Player1* has a special set called *Lobsvars*. This represents the environment variables accessible, i.e., visible, to the agent. This makes the program more succinct.

Fig 2 illustrates four possible paths in the model representing a run of the game. The notation "$i, j - k, t$" in Fig 2 means: $c11 = i$, $c12 = j$, $c21 = k$, $c22 = t$ for $i, j, k, y \in \{1, 2, 3, 4, 5, 6\}$.

Implementation. We now describe the procedure of the tool performing data abstraction on ISPL programs by partitioning the domain of variables. This extension takes an ISPL program for an interpreted system $\mathcal{I}$ as input and returns an ISPL program denoting a quotient interpreted system $\mathcal{I}'$ for $\mathcal{I}$ according to Definition 7. Briefly, the tool builds a new set of abstract reachable states G' from G by constructing new domains for the variables in $\mathcal{I}$. The procedure consists of four key steps. All steps are executed automatically.

Algorithm 1. The generation of the Boolean four-dimension Q.

1: **for all** $i \in Ag$ **do**
2:     **for all** $\alpha \in AP$ **do**
3:         **for all** p in precondition of α **do**
4:             **if** $var(p) \in i$ **then** $LE_i \Leftarrow LE_i \cup p$; **end if**
5:         **end for**
6:     **end for**
7: **end for**
8: $Q(i, v, p, d_t) \Leftarrow 0$;
9: **for all** $i \in Ag$ **do**
10:     **for all** local variable v of agent i **do**
11:         **for all** $p \in LE_i$ **do**
12:             **for all** $d_t \in D_v$ **do**
13:                 **if** $d_t \models p$ **then** $Q(i, v, p, d_t) \Leftarrow True$; **else** $Q(i, v, p, d_t) \Leftarrow False$; **end if**
14:             **end for**
15:         **end for**
16:     **end for**
17: **end for**

1: Building the set LE$_i$. In an ISPL program P each atomic proposition $\alpha \in AP$ is defined by a boolean expression over variables defining on which global states α holds, thereby implementing the evaluation V. For each agent i, the tool builds a set LE_i of logic expressions containing local variables for agent i that appear in the definition of any $\alpha \in AP$. In the end, the tool builds LE by the union of all LE_i for all $i \in Ag$.

For example, for the card game reported in Fig 1, we have: $D_{c11} = D_{c12} = D_{c21} = D_{c22} = \{1, 2, 3, 4, 5, 6\}$, $V_e = \{c11, c12, c21, c22, a, b\}$, $V_{P_1} = \{n\}$, $V_{P_2} = \{n\}$. Notice that in V_{P_1} and V_{P_2} the other four variables are not present: $c11$, $c12$, a, b for P_1 and $c21$, $c22$, a, b for P_2. Those variable are not inserted in V_{P_1} and V_{P_2} by the procedure since all cij are local observable variables (*Lobsvars*) and a, b are global observable variables (*Obsvars*). Local observable variables of an agent i are those variables belonging to the environment agent that can be "seen" by the agent i. Therefore, the agent i knows the values of those variables at every moment and those variables contribute to form the local state of the agent i. However, the agent i cannot change the value of a local observable variable. Observable variables have the same characteristics of the local observable ones, but they can be seen by all agents indifferently.

Now, the abstraction tool automatically builds the sets $LE_e = \{c11 > 2,$ $c12 > 2, c21 > 2, c22 > 2, c11 > 3, c12 > 3, c21 > 3, c22 > 3, c11 > 4, c12 > 4,$ $c21 > 4, c22 > 4\}$, $LE_{P_1} = \emptyset$ and $LE_{P_2} = \emptyset$ from the logic expressions found in the *Evaluation* section of the ISPL-file. Note the following.

- Local variables from different agents cannot appear in the same logic expression.
- If a logic expression contains more than one variable, we rewrite it as a Boolean expression where each logic expression contains exactly one variable.
- If a logic expression contains the "not" connective, we rewrite it as an equivalent Boolean expression where the "not" connective does not appear.
- We cannot collapse values for variables that are updated by an arithmetic expression. This is because we may have transitions that are present in the original model but not present in the abstract one. Therefore, for the card game we cannot collapse a and b as they are updated in the Evolution by the arithmetic expressions $a = a + 1$ and $b = b + 1$ respectively (see Fig.1).

2: Generating the four-dimension vector Q. The tool automatically builds a four-dimension vector Q of Boolean values. The first dimension, i, of Q represents the agents; the second dimension, j, encodes the variables of a given agent; the third one, k, represents all logic expressions in which the current variable appears; the last one, t, represents the values d_t of the current variables. The vector Q encodes whether a logic expression p is evaluated to true when all free occurrences of the current variables are replaced by d_t, denoted by $d_t \models p$. From the vector Q we build new domains of abstract variables by collapsing values of every concrete variable that satisfies the same set of logic expressions. Algorithm 1 presents the generation of Q, where *var* is a function that returns the variable contained in the given logic expression.

3: Generating the abstraction functions by defining value clusters. The tool automatically builds a set of abstraction functions $\rho_1, \ldots, \rho_n$, where each ρ_i is defined on D_i, the domain of variable v_i. Given two local states $\bar{d} = (d_1, \ldots, d_m)$ and $\bar{e} = (e_1, \ldots, e_m)$ of agent i, we define the component abstraction functions ρ_i in the same way as defined in [2], i.e.:

$$\rho_i(d_1, \ldots, d_m) = \rho_i(e_1, \ldots, e_m) \quad \text{iff} \quad \bigwedge_{p \in LE_i} (d_1, \ldots, d_m) \models p \Leftrightarrow (e_1, \ldots, e_m) \models p \quad (6)$$

In other words, two tuples of values $\bar{e}, \bar{d}$ are in the same equivalence class if they cannot be distinguished by the same subset of logic expressions. Therefore, the particular $\equiv_i$ is automatically chosen according to formula (6).

The new values for the card game example (shown in bold fonts) are reported in Fig 3. Some instances of variables $c11$, $c12$, $c21$, $c22$ are collapsed into new values in the following way: $\mathbf{1} = \{1, 2\}$, $\mathbf{2} = \{3\}$, $\mathbf{3} = \{4\}$, $\mathbf{4} = \{5, 6\}$, because of $1, 2 \models \{\emptyset\}$, $3 \models \{cij > 2\}$, $4 \models \{cij > 2, cij > 3\}$, $5, 6 \models \{cij > 2, cij > 3, cij > 4\}$, where $i, j \in \{1, 2\}$. The partitioning of variable domains is done automatically.

4: Generating new domains for the abstract ispl-file P'. New values of the variables for the ISPL-file P' representing the abstract model are calculated from

Algorithm 2. The generation of new Domains. Line 8 shows how the partitioning of variable domains is calculated.

```
 1: for all i ∈ Ag do
 2:     for all local variable v of agent i do
 3:         for all dₜ ∈ Dᵥ do
 4:             indxₚ ⇐ 0; newval ⇐ 0;
 5:             for all p ∈ LEᵢ do
 6:                 if var(p) ∈ i then
 7:                     if Q(i, v, dₜ, p) = true then newval ⇐ newval + 2^{indxₚ}; end if
 8:                 end if
 9:                 indxₚ ⇐ indxₚ + 1;
10:             end for
11:             D'ᵥ ⇐ D'ᵥ ∪ {newval};
12:         end for
13:     end for
14: end for
```

the old ones by taking into account what formulas the old values satisfy. Each formula is identified by an index $(indx_p)$. These indexes are used to calculate an integer number (see line 8 of Algorithm 2) that will be the corresponding new value. Line 8 of Algorithm 2 shows how the partitioning of values is calculated. Values that satisfy the same set of formulas will get the same integer. The abstract ISPL-file P' is generated by substituting in every logic expression $p \in P$ the corresponding new value in D'. Notice from Fig 3 that the new domains of the abstract model in the example become $D'_{cij} = \{\mathbf{0, 1, 3, 7}\}$. The concrete values 1 and 2 are collapsed into the abstract value **0** as they do not satisfy any atomic proposition in LE_e. The concrete value 3 becames the abstract value $\mathbf{1} = 2^0$ since it satisfies formula $cij > 2$ and this formula gets the index 0. This index is used in the power 2^0 to calculates the new value **1**. The concrete value 4 becomes **3** since it satisfies formulas $cij > 2$ and $cij > 3$. Those formulas have the index 0 and 1 respectively. Therefore, the abstract value **3** is the result of the following calculation: $3 = 2^0 + 2^1$. Finally, the abstract value **7** represents the concrete values 5 and 6 that satify formulas $cij > 2$, $cij > 3$ and $cij > 4$. Those formulas have index 0, 1 and 2 respectively, therefore: $2^0 + 2^1 + 2^2 = 7$. The new abstract domain $D'_{cij} = \{\mathbf{0, 1, 3, 7}\}$ is "flattened" by an extra procedure that transforms D'_{cij} into $D''_{cij} = \{\mathbf{1, 2, 3, 4}\}$, where **0, 1, 3, 7** of D'_{cij} correspond to **1, 2, 3, 4** of D''_{cij} respectively.

In this case, the abstraction process has reduced the number of reachable states from $\frac{6!}{2!} = 360$ different initial card combinations to $4! = 24$ in the new program.

As expected, the abstraction process might synthesise behaviours not present in the original model. For instance, let us analyse the following program lines describing part of the environment's evolution.

```
a=a+1 if c11>c21
b=b+1 if c11<c21
```

```
Agent Environment                          Evolution:
 --Obsvars are not changed                   n = 2  if n=1;
 Vars:                                        n = 3  if n=2;
  c11: 1 .. 4;                              end Evolution
  c12: 1 .. 4;                            end Agent
  c21: 1 .. 4;
  c22: 1 .. 4;                            -- Agent Player2 omitted
 end Vars
 --Actions,Protocol and Evolution omitted  Evaluation
end Agent                                    lowred1  if (c11>1 and c12>1);
                                             topred1  if (c11>3 and c12>3);
Agent Player1                                allred1 if (c11>2 and c12>2);
 Lobsvars={c11,c12};                         win1 if (a>b and a+b=2);
 Vars:                                        --The same properties
  n: 1 .. 3;                                  --for Player2 are omitted
 end Vars                                    end Evaluation
 Actions = {null,playcard1,playcard2};
 Protocol:                                  --InitStates omitted
  n=1: { playcard1 };
  n=2: { playcard2 };                       Formulae
  n=3: { null };                             (AG(allred1->K(Player1,(AF win1))));
 end Protocol                              end Formulae
```

Fig. 3. Sketch of an ISPL-file for the abstract *Card Game* with 6 cards

Those lines are transformed in the following:

```
a=a+1  if (c11=6  and  c21=5)  or  (c11=6  and  c21=4)  or ...
b=b+1  if (c11=5  and  c21=6)  or  (c11=4  and  c21=6)  or ...
```

Following the abstraction process, the program for the abstract model includes the following non-determinism:

```
a=a+1 if (c11=4 and c11=4)  or ...
b=b+1 if (c11=4 and c21=4)  or ...
```

Fig 4 illustrates execution branches not existing in the original model. This phenomenon can cause *false negatives*, i.e., the property checked results to be false in the abstract model while it is true in the original one.

Still, it can be checked that validity is preserved under the construction above.

Theorem 2 (Data Abstraction Theorem). *Given an ISPL-program P describing an interpreted system $\mathcal{I}$ and given a specification ϕ of the logic ACTLK, let P' be the ISPL program, generated from P by the procedure presented above. P' describes an interpreted system $\mathcal{I}'$. We have that specification ϕ holds in $\mathcal{I}$ if ϕ holds in $\mathcal{I}'$, i.e.,*

$$\mathcal{I}' \models \phi \implies \mathcal{I} \models \phi.$$

Proof. We have to show that abstraction algorithm generates an ISPL-code P' that describes an interpreted system $\mathcal{I}'$ that is a quotient one of the interpreted system $\mathcal{I}$ described by the original ISPL-code P

By Theorem 1, we only need to prove that $\mathcal{I}'$ is a quotient of $\mathcal{I}$ according to Definition 7.

1. L'_i is generated by the abstraction function ρ_i such that $L'_i = \{[l] \mid l \in L_i\}$, which is a partition of the set L_i. So, we have proved point 1 of the definition 7.

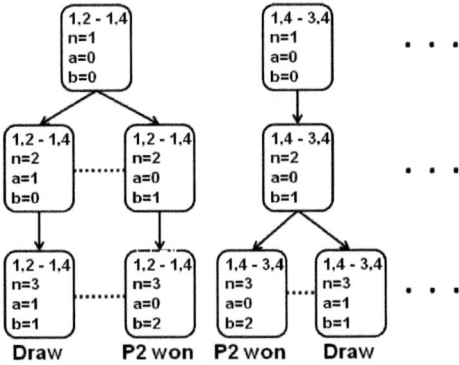

Fig. 4. Sketch of the global transition relation for the abstract *Card Game Example* with 6 cards. Notice how some paths split. This splitting causes new behaviours in the abstract model.

2. $ACT'_i = ACT_i$ *(i.e., $[a] \equiv a$) because ρ_i does not partition the set of actions.*
3. $P' = \{\langle[l], a\rangle \mid \langle l, a\rangle \in P\}$ *because the abstraction technique simply replaces the old values of a variable with the new ones.*
4. *Note that $[l] \neq [l']$ ($[l], [l'] \in L'_i$) if and only if there is at least one $l \in [l]$ and one $l' \in [l']$ in L_i such that $l \neq l'$.*

   Now, we have to show that if they are connected in the concrete system, then they are also connected in the abstract one. Formally, we have to show the following condition holds:

   $$\forall l, l'(\, \rho(l) = [l] \wedge \rho(l') = [l'] \wedge lRl' \;\Rightarrow\; [l]\hat{R}[l']\,)$$

   Suppose $\rho(l) = [l] \wedge \rho(l') = [l'] \wedge lRl'$, we show $[l]\hat{R}[l']$. By assuming lRl', we know $\exists \bar{a} \in Act\ \forall i \in Ag : \langle l, \bar{a}, l'\rangle \in t_i$ and $\langle l, a\rangle \in P_i$ by definition. Since the abstraction technique performs a partition of states, we have, for all agents $i \in Ag$ and for all local states, $[l] \neq [l']$. As actions are not modified, we have $\langle[l], [a]\rangle \in P'_i$, where $l \in [l]$ and $a \equiv [a]$. Moreover, Since the local evolution function is rebuilt by substituting l_i, such that $l \in [l]$, with $[l]$, we have $\langle[l], \bar{a}, [l']\rangle \in t'_i$ iff $l, \bar{a}, l' \in t_i$. Therefore, we have $\langle[l], \bar{a}, [l']\rangle \in t'_i$ and $\langle[l], [a]\rangle \in P'_i$, but that means $[l]\hat{R}[l']$.
5. *Point 5 and 6 in Definition 7 can be proved trivially.*   □

4 Experimental Results

We now report on the experimental results obtained by the implementation described in the previous section. Specifically, we comment on our findings for the card game example and a variant of the bit transmission problem. These scenarios are to be considered as a sanity check of the technique and not as real applications. We leave these for further work.

Number Transmission Protocol. This scenario is an extension of the well known *bit transmission problem* described in [11]. Let $Ag = \{S, R\}$ be the set of agents where S, R represent the *sender* and the *receiver* respectively. Moreover, there is the *environment* agent labelled with the letter E.

In this scenario, a number is sent from the sender to the receiver via a an unreliable channel modelled by the environment. Note that in the known bit transmission problem only one bit is sent. In this case the sender sends a number ranging from 1 to N. In the experiments below we used N in the set $D = \{0.5 \cdot 10^4,$ $10^4, 2 \cdot 10^4, 2.5 \cdot 10^4, 3 \cdot 10^4\}$.

We describe below the interpreted system for the protocol above. The Environment is described by the set of local states $L_E = \{S, R, RS, none\}$. The local state S represents the channel reliably sending messages from sender to receiver and dropping messages from receiver to sender. Conversely, R represents a situation where messages only travel from receiver to sender. RS encodes a situation where the channel is transmitting both directions, whereas when in *none* the channel loses all messages. The set of local states for the sender is $L_S = D \times \{true, false\}$ where $D = \{1, \ldots, N\}$ represents the domain of the integer that can be sent and $\{true, false\}$ is the domain of the variable *ack* keeping track of whether an acknowledgement has been received from the sender. We model the receiver by considering the set $L_R = \{received, notrec\}$; *notrec* represents a situation where the receiver has not yet received any message, while *received* encodes the fact that the receiver got a message. The environment can perform four actions: $ACT_E = \{S, SR, R, none\}$ representing which direction, if any, it is letting messages flow. The sender can either send the intended message or do nothing (*null*) $ACT_S = \{send\,N \mid N \in D\} \cup \{nothing\}$. Similarly, the receiver can either send an acknowledgement or remain silent: $ACT_R = \{sendack, nothing\}$. As in the original bit transmission problem we assume the sender keeps sending the same message until he or she receives an acknowledgement; the receiver remains silent before receiving the message from the sender; after that he repeatedly sends acknowledgements back to the sender. Consequently the protocols can be defined as follows.

$$P_E(S) = \{S\}; \qquad P_E(R) = \{R\};$$
$$P_E(SR) = \{SR\}; \qquad P_E(none) = \{none\};$$
$$P_S(N, false) = \{send\,N\}; \quad P_S(N, true) = \{nothing\};$$
$$P_R(notrec) = \{nothing\}; \quad P_R(received) = \{sendack\}.$$

Local evolution functions are defined as follow:

$$t_E(state, \langle a_E, a_S, a_R \rangle) = state'; \tag{7}$$
$$t_S((N, false), \langle SR, a_S, sendack \rangle) = (N, true); \tag{8}$$
$$t_S((N, false), \langle R, a_S, sendack \rangle) = (N, true); \tag{9}$$
$$t_R(notrec, \langle SR, send\,N, a_R \rangle) = received; \tag{10}$$
$$t_R(notrec, \langle S, send\,N, a_R \rangle) = received. \tag{11}$$

Where $state, state' \in L_E$ and $a_k \in ACT_k$, for $k \in Ag$. Note that by (7) the channel moves non-deterministically. In (8) and (9) the sender receives an acknowledgement from the receiver as the channel transmits messages from the receiver to the sender in both cases. Similarly, in (10) and (11) the receiver receives the number.

The set of initial states I_0 is as follows: $I_0 = \{(E.state, (N, false), notrec) \mid E.state \in L_E\}$. The evaluation for the proposition $numberN, recack, recNumber$ is the obvious one. Fig 5 represents a sketch of an ISPL-file corresponding to the interpreted system defined above for $N = 10000$. From Fig 5, in the *Evaluation* section, we want to know if the number sent was either exactly 1 or it was greater than 2500, 5000 or 7500. By running the abstraction toolkit to this file we obtain an abstract Number Transmission ISPL-file in which the Sender can only send 5 possible digits. This is of course the result we would expect. The system in Fig 5 corresponds to the second one listed in Table 2.

We tested both examples above on the abstraction toolkit paired with MC-MAS against known specifications for the protocols. In particular we verified $AG(allred_1 \rightarrow K_{Player1}(AFwin1))$ in the case of the card game example (specifying that if player one has only red cards he knows he will win the game), and $AG((numberN \wedge recack) \rightarrow (K_S K_R number = N))$ for the number transmission protocol (specifying that once an ack has been received the sender knows that the receiver knows the value of the number transmitted).

```
Agent Environment                      Agent Receiver
Vars:                                  Vars:
  state : {S,R,SR,none};                 state : boolean;
end Vars                               end Vars
Actions = {S,SR,R,none};               Actions = {nothing,sendack};
Protocol:                              Protocol:
  state=S: {S,SR,R,none};                state=false : {nothing};
  state=R: {S,SR,R,none};                state=true : {sendack};
  state=SR: {S,SR,R,none};             end Protocol
  state=none: {S,SR,R,none};           Evolution:
end Protocol                             state=true if (Sender.Action=send)
-- Evolution Omitted                     and (state=false)
end Agent                                and ((Environment.Action=SR)
                                         or (Environment.Action=S));
Agent Sender                           end Evolution
Vars:                                  end Agent
  number : 0..10000;
  ack : boolean;
end Vars                               Evaluation
Actions = { send,nothing };             recNumber if ( (Receiver.state=true);
Protocol:                               recack if ( ( Sender.ack = true ) );
  ack=false : {send};                   N1 if ( (Sender.number=1));
  ack=true : {nothing};                 N2500 if ( (Sender.number>2500) );
end Protocol                            N5000 if ( (Sender.number>5000) );
Evolution:                              N7500 if ( (Sender.number>7500) );
  (ack=true) if (ack=false)            end Evaluation
  and (Receiver.Action=sendack)        InitStates
  and ((Environment.Action=SR)          !Sender.Number=0 and Receiver.state=false
  or (Environment.Action=R));           and Sender.ack=false and (Environment.state=S)
end Evolution                           or Environment.state=R or Environment.state=SR
end Agent                               or Environment.state=none ;
                                       end InitStates
```

Fig. 5. Sketch of an ISPL-file for the number transmission protocol for $N = 10000$

Table 1. Verification results for the *Card Game*

Number of cards	With reduction			Without reduction		
	States	Time (s)	BDD (MB)	States	Time (s)	BDD (MB)
6	138	0	4.70	11316	0	4.67
8	22528	2	6.67	80640	4	15.27
10	135866	4	9.59	$2,167 \times 10^9$	867	66.71
12	762812	26	31.87	?	> 86400	?
14	3.877×10^6	106	41.68	?	> 86400	?

Table 2. Verification results for the *Number Transmission Problem*

Maximum number N	With reduction			Without reduction		
	States	Time (s)	BDD (MB)	States	Time (s)	BDD (MB)
5000	48	0	4.55	98292	11	5.72
10000	60	0	4.59	196596	47	6.58
15000	84	1	4.67	196596	118	7.12
20000	108	1	4.64	393204	216	8.24
25000	132	1	4.82	393204	350	8.62
30000	156	1	5.64	393204	485	8.56

The experiments were executed on a machine running Ubuntu 9.10 on an Intel Core 2 1.86GHz with 1GB memory. The results are reported in Table 1 and Table 2.

From Table 1 we can notice that as expected the implementation drastically reduces both memory and time for the verification process. In the case of 12 and 14 cards, MCMAS could not verify the specification in over 24hrs, while the abstract systems could be verified in seconds. It is perhaps less obvious that, from Table 2, in the transmission problem for the case of $N = 10000$ and $N = 15000$ the two systems have the same number of reachable states. This is because MCMAS uses 14 BDD variables to encode both 10000 and 15000 states and MCMAS does not remove redundant states, using 2^{14} BDD states in both cases. The same phenomenon occurs for $N = 20000$, $N = 25000$ and $N = 30000$. In this case, MCMAS uses 15 BDD variables.

5   Conclusions

In this paper we began to explore fully automatic abstraction techniques for multi-agent systems. The technique abstracts a multi-agent system, described by an ISPL program, by collapsing the local states for the agents. We showed that our technique builds an abstract system that simulates the concrete thereby guaranteeing the methodology is sound. We evaluated the technique on a card game example for several numbers of cards and on the number transmission protocol. The results produced point to a considerable, although expected, reduction in the verification time and memory.

In the future we intend to test the methodology on more complex cases and to implement a refinement procedure that can be used to refine the model upon receiving false negatives from MCMAS.

Acknowledgements. This research was partially funded by EPSRC under grant EP/E035655 "Verification of security protocols: a multi-agent systems approach".

References

1. Clarke, E.M., Grumberg, O., Jha, S., Lu, Y., Veith, H.: Counterexample-guided abstraction refinement. In: Emerson, E.A., Sistla, A.P. (eds.) CAV 2000. LNCS, vol. 1855, pp. 154–169. Springer, Heidelberg (2000)
2. Clarke, E.M., Grumberg, O., Long, D.E.: Model checking and abstraction. ACM Trans. Program. Lang. Syst. 16(5), 1512–1542 (1994)
3. Clarke, E.M., Grumberg, O., Peled, D.A.: Model Checking. The MIT Press, Cambridge (1999)
4. Cohen, M., Dam, M., Lomuscio, A., Qu, H.: A data symmetry reduction technique for temporal-epistemic logic. In: Liu, Z., Ravn, A.P. (eds.) ATVA 2009. LNCS, vol. 5799, pp. 69–83. Springer, Heidelberg (2009)
5. Cohen, M., Dam, M., Lomuscio, A., Russo, F.: Abstraction in model checking multi-agent systems. In: AAMAS 2009 (2009)
6. Cousot, P., Cousot, R.: Abstract interpretation: A unified lattice model for static analysis of programs by construction or approximation of fixpoints. In: POPL, pp. 238–252 (1977)
7. Dechesne, F., Orzan, S., Wang, Y.: Refinement of kripke models for dynamics. In: Fitzgerald, J.S., Haxthausen, A.E., Yenigun, H. (eds.) ICTAC 2008. LNCS, vol. 5160, pp. 111–125. Springer, Heidelberg (2008)
8. Emerson, E.A., Clarke, E.M.: Using branching time temporal logic to synthesize synchronization skeletons. Science of Computer Programming 2(3), 241–266 (1982)
9. van Ditmarsch, H., van der Hoek, W., van der Meyden, R., Ruan, J.: Model Checking Russian Cards. Electr. Notes Theor. Comput. Sci. 149(2), 105–123 (2006)
10. Enea, C., Dima, C.: Abstractions of multi-agent systems. In: Burkhard, H., Lindemann, G., Verbrugge, R., Varga, L.Z. (eds.) CEEMAS 2007. LNCS (LNAI), vol. 4696, pp. 11–21. Springer, Heidelberg (2007)
11. Fagin, R., Halpern, J.Y., Moses, Y., Vardi, M.Y.: Reasoning about Knowledge. MIT Press, Cambridge (1995)
12. Gammie, P., van der Meyden, R.: MCK: Model checking the logic of knowledge. In: Alur, R., Peled, D.A. (eds.) CAV 2004. LNCS, vol. 3114, pp. 479–483. Springer, Heidelberg (2004)
13. Graf, S., Saïdi, H.: Construction of abstract state graphs with pvs. In: Grumberg, O. (ed.) CAV 1997. LNCS, vol. 1254, pp. 72–83. Springer, Heidelberg (1997)
14. Kacprzak, M., Nabialek, W., Niewiadomski, A., Penczek, W., Pólrola, A., Szreter, M., Wozna, B., Zbrzezny, A.: Verics 2007 - a model checker for knowledge and real-time. Fundamenta Informaticae 85(1-4), 313–328 (2008)

15. Lomuscio, A., Qu, H., Raimondi, F.: Mcmas: A model checker for the verification of multi-agent systems. In: Bouajjani, A., Maler, O. (eds.) CAV 2009. LNCS, vol. 5643, pp. 682–688. Springer, Heidelberg (2009)
16. Penczek, W., Lomuscio, A.: Verifying epistemic properties of multi-agent systems via bounded model checking. Fundamenta Informaticae 55(2), 167–185 (2003)
17. Wooldridge, M.: Computationally grounded theories of agency. In: Durfee, E. (ed.) ICMAS, pp. 13–22. IEEE Press, Los Alamitos (2000)
18. Wooldridge, M.: An introduction to MultiAgent systems, 2nd edn. Wiley, Chichester (2009)

Automated Verification of Resource Requirements in Multi-Agent Systems Using Abstraction*

Natasha Alechina, Brian Logan, Hoang Nga Nguyen, and Abdur Rakib

University of Nottingham, UK
{nza,bsl,hnn,rza}@cs.nott.ac.uk

Abstract. We describe a framework for the automated verification of multi-agent systems which do distributed problem solving, e.g., query answering. Each reasoner uses facts, messages and Horn clause rules to derive new information. We show how to verify correctness of distributed problem solving under resource constraints, such as the time required to answer queries and the number of messages exchanged by the agents. The framework allows the use of abstract specifications consisting of Linear Time Temporal Logic (LTL) formulas to specify some of the agents in the system. We illustrate the use of the framework on a simple example.

1   Introduction

Much current work in multi-agent systems (MAS) development relies on the developer specifying agent behaviour in terms of pre-defined plans [1]. While the use of pre-defined plans makes it easier to guarantee the behaviour of the multi-agent system, e.g., [2], it can make it harder for the system to solve novel problems not anticipated by the system designers. As a result, there has recently been increasing interest in providing general reasoning capabilities to agents in multi-agent systems (see, for example, [3,4]). However, while the incorporation of reasoning abilities into agents brings great benefits in terms of flexibility and ease of development, these approaches also raise new challenges for the agent developer, namely, how to ensure correctness (will an agent produce the correct output for all legal inputs), termination (will an agent produce an output at all), and response time (how much computation will an agent have to do before it generates an output). For example, when developing a distributed problem solving system which provides subway routes to users of the London Underground, a developer may wish to verify that the system does not provide invalid routes (e.g., that it takes current service disruptions into account), and that it provides bounded response times under expected system loads (e.g., asynchronous queries from multiple simultaneous users). Proving correctness or resource bounds for such large complex reasoning systems is infeasible with current verification technologies.

In [5], an approach to verifying resource requirements in systems of communicating rule-based reasoners was proposed. The main emphasis of that paper was on modelling

---

* This work was supported by the UK Engineering and Physical Sciences Research Council [grant EP/E031226/1].

R. van der Meyden and J.-G. Smaus (Eds.): MoChArt 2010, LNAI 6572, pp. 69–84, 2011.

systems of communicating reasoners as state transition systems, where states correspond to beliefs of the agents and transitions correspond to the application of a rule of inference or sending a message. Properties of the system, for example, that a system of two agents will be able to produce an answer to a query after exchanging at most one message and applying 4 rules, were specified in modal logic, and proof-of-concept verification experiments using Mocha model-checker [6] reported. However, the encoding of the system in the Mocha specification language had to be handcrafted, rules had to be propositionalised using all possible substitutions for variables, and scalability of the verification approach was not explored.

In this paper we describe an automated verification framework for resource-bounded reasoners, which takes rules specified in Hornlog RuleML with negation as failure [7] augmented with communication primitives, and automatically produces a Maude [8] specification of the system which can be efficiently verified. The properties that we wish to verify are response-time guarantees of the form: if the system receives a query, then a response will be produced within n timesteps. To allow larger systems to be verified, *abstract specifications* can be used to model some agents in the system. Abstract specifications are given as LTL formulas which describe the external behaviour of agents, and allow their temporal behaviour (the response time behaviour of the agent), to be compactly modelled. We illustrate the scalability of our approach by comparing it to results presented in [9] for a synthetic distributed reasoning problem, and presenting results for a more complex multi-agent reasoning example.

The remainder of the paper is organised as follows. In section 2 we describe our model of communicating rule-based reasoners. In section 3 we describe the basic components and ideas behind the verification framework, including our approach to producing abstractions of agents. In section 4 we briefly describe a tool for translating rule-based specification of the agents into Maude, and in section 5 we evaluate its performance. We discuss related work and open problems in section 6 and conclude in section 7.

2   Communicating Reasoners

We adopt a general model of distributed reasoners. A distributed reasoning system consists of n (≥ 1) individual reasoners or *agents*. Each agent is identified by a value in $\{1, 2, \ldots, n\}$ and we use variables i and j over $\{1, 2, \ldots, n\}$ to refer to agents. Each agent i has a program, consisting of first-order Horn clause rules with negation-as-failure allowed in the premises[1], and a working memory, which contains facts (ground atomic formulas) representing the initial state of the system. The agents execute synchronously. At each cycle, each agent matches (unifies) the conditions of its rules against the contents of its working memory. The conditions of a rule are evaluated using the closed world assumption (i.e., $not\ P$ evaluates to true if P is not in working memory). A match for every condition of a rule constitutes an instance of that rule (a rule may have more than one instance). The set of all rule instances for an agent form the agent's *conflict set*. Each agent then chooses a subset of rule instances from the conflict

---

[1]   Rules are of the form $P_1 \wedge \ldots \wedge P_n \rightarrow P$ where P is an atomic formula and P_i are atomic formulas or atomic formulas preceded by the negation as failure operator.

set to be applied. Applying a rule adds the consequent of the rule as a new fact to the agent's working memory. The cycle begins again with the match phase and the process continues until no more rules can be matched and all agents have an empty conflict set.[2]

We assume that each reasoner has a *reasoning strategy* (or conflict resolution strategy) which determines the order in which rules are applied when more than one rule matches the contents of the agent's working memory. The choice of reasoning strategy is important in determining the capabilities of the agent. For example, different reasoning strategies may determine how quickly/efficiently an answer to a query can be derived, or even whether an answer can be produced at all. The reasoning strategy is also important in determining trade-offs between the resources required to process a query. For example, if multiple queries arrive at about the same time, processing them sequentially may reduce the memory required at the cost of increasing the worst case response time for queries. Conversely, processing the queries in parallel may reduce the worst case response time at the cost of increasing the peak memory usage.

We assume that each reasoner executes in a separate process and that reasoners communicate via message passing. For concreteness, we assume a simple query-response scheme based on asynchronous message passing. Each agent's rules may contain two distinguished communication primitives: $ASK(i, j, P)$, and $TELL(i, j, P)$, where i and j are agents and P is an atomic formula not containing an ASK or a $TELL$. $ASK(i, j, P)$ means 'i asks j whether P is the case' and $TELL(i, j, P)$ means 'i tells j that P ($i \neq j$). The positions in which the ASK and $TELL$ primitives may appear in a rule depends on which agent's program the rule belongs to. Agent i may have an ASK or a $TELL$ with arguments (i, j, P) in the consequent of a rule, e.g.,

$$P_1 \wedge P_2 \wedge \ldots \wedge P_n \implies ASK(i, j, P)$$

Agent j may have the same expressions in the antecedent of the rule, e.g.,

$$TELL(i, j, P) \implies P$$

is a well-formed rule for agent j, that causes it to believe i when i informs it that P is the case. No other occurrences of ASK or $TELL$ are allowed. For simplicity, we assume that communication is error-free and takes one tick of time.

3   Verification Framework

We would like to be able to verify properties of systems consisting of arbitrary numbers of complex communicating reasoners. However verifying such large, complex reasoning systems is infeasible with current verification technologies.

The most straightforward approach to defining the global state of a multi-agent system is as a (parallel) composition of the local states of the agents. At each step in the evolution of the system, each agent chooses from a set of possible actions (we assume that an agent can always perform an 'idle' action which does not change its state). The

---

[2] Note that, although execution is synchronous, agents can return a 'null action' at any given cycle, allowing the modelling of multi-agent systems in which each agent deliberates at a rate which is a multiple of the cycle time of the fastest agent.

actions selected by the agents are then performed in parallel and the system advances to the next state. In a multi-agent system composed of n (≥ 1) agents, if each agent i can choose between performing at most m (≥ 1) actions, then the system as a whole can move in m^n different ways from a given state at a given point in time. Along with state space size, model checking performance is heavily dependent on the branching factor of states in the reachable state space and the solution depth of a given problem. In general, the model checking algorithm for reachability analysis performs a breadth-first exploration of the state transition graph. When checking invariant (safety) properties, the model-checker will either determine that no states violate the invariant by exploring the entire state space, or will find a state violating the invariant and produce a counter-example.[3] However, even with state-of-the-art BDD-based model-checkers, memory exhaustion can occur when computing the reachable state space due to the large size of the intermediate BDDs (because of the high branching factor).

To overcome this problem, our modelling approach abstracts from some aspects of system behaviour to obtain a system model that is tractable for a standard model-checker. Our use of abstraction is however different from classic approaches in model-checking, such as [11,12]. We assume that, at any given point in the design of the overall system, the detailed behaviour of only a small number of agents (perhaps only a single agent) is of interest to the system designer, and the remaining agents in the system can be considered at a high level of abstraction. When verifying response time guarantees of the 'focal' agent(s), the concrete representation of 'peripheral' agents can be replaced by an abstract specification of their external (communication) behaviour, so long as the abstract specification results in behaviour that is indistinguishable from the original concrete representation for the purposes of verification, i.e., it produces queries and responds to queries within specified bounds. All other details of an abstract agent's internal behaviour are omitted.

The decision regarding which agents to abstract and how their external behaviour should be specified rests with the modeller/system designer. Specifications of the external (observable) behaviour of abstract agents may be derived from, e.g., assumed characteristics of as-yet-unimplemented parts of the system, assumptions regarding the behaviour of parts of the overall system the designer does not control (e.g., quality of service guarantees offered by an existing web service) or from the prior verification of the behaviour of other (concrete) agents in the system. The behaviour of abstract agents is specified using the language of the temporal logic LTL containing epistemic operators. The general form of the formulas which can be used to represent the external behaviour of abstract agents is given below, where X is the next step temporal operator, X^n is a sequence of n X operators, G is the temporal 'in all future states' operator, and B_i for each agent i is a syntactic epistemic operator used to specify agent i's 'beliefs' or the contents of its working memory.

$$\rho :: X^n \phi_1 \mid G(\phi_2 \rightarrow \phi_3)$$
$$\phi_1 :: B_i \, ASK(i, j, P)$$

---

[3] Even with on-the-fly model-checking [10], the model checker has to explore the state space at least until the solution depth.

$$|B_i\,TELL(i,j,P)$$
$$|B_i\,ASK(j,i,P)$$
$$|B_i\,TELL(j,i,P)$$
$$|B_i\,P$$
$$\phi_2 :: Bj\,ASK(i,j,P)$$
$$\phi_3 :: X^n\,B_i\,TELL(j,i,P)$$

Formulas of the form $X^n\phi_1$ describe agents which produce a certain message or input to the system within n time steps. The $G(\phi_2 \rightarrow \phi_3)$ formulas describe agents which are always guaranteed to reply to a request for information within n timesteps. Note that we do not need the full language of LTL (for example, the Until operator) in order to specify abstract agents. The verification language of Maude contains full LTL, but abstract specifications and the response-time guarantee properties we wish to verify can be expressed in the fragment above.

Formulas expressing abstract specifications are translated into the specification language of the model checker. This is a kind of backward modeling, which basically imposes a restrictions on possible runs of a model. The multi-agent system is then simply a parallel composition of both the concrete and abstract agents in the system.

4   Automated Verification Tool

In this section, we describe a tool based on the Maude [8] rewriting system which implements the approach to verification described above. The tool generates an encoding of a distributed system of reasoning agents for the Maude LTL model checker, which is then used to verify the desired properties of the system. We chose the Maude LTL model checker because it can model check systems whose states involve arbitrary algebraic data types. The only assumption is that the set of states reachable from a given initial state is finite. This simplifies modelling of the agents' (first-order) rules and reasoning strategies. For example, a rule used by a route planning agent such as

$$Connected(station1, station2, line1) \wedge Reachable(station2, station3, [route])$$
$$\rightarrow Reachable(station1, station3, [station2|route])$$

where $station1$, $station2$, $station3$, $line1$ and $route$ are variables, can be represented directly in the Maude encoding, without having to generate all ground instances resulting from possible variable substitutions.

The tool consists of three main components: the user interface, the encoding generator and the system verifier. The tool takes as input: (a) a set of concrete agent descriptions, each comprising a set of rules, a set of initial working memory facts, and a control strategy, (b) a set of abstract agent descriptions specified by a set of temporal epistemic logic formulas, and (c) the properties of the system to be verified specified in temporal epistemic logic. Rules and facts can be expressed in RuleML or in a simplified ASCII syntax e.g., $< n{:}P_1 \,\&\ldots\&\, P_n => P >$, P_k . The general XML syntax of rules accepted by the framework corresponds to Hornlog RuleML with negation as failure, and is shown below.

```
<!- -Representation of rules - ->
<Implies>
  <head>
    <Atom>
      <Rel>Predicate< /Rel>
      <Var>variable< /Var>
                  ⋮
      <Ind>constant< /Ind>
                  ⋮
    < /Atom>
  < /head>
  <body>
    <And>
      <Atom>
        <Rel>Predicate< /Rel>
        <Var>variable< /Var>
                    ⋮
        <Ind>constant< /Ind>
                    ⋮
      < /Atom>
                 ⋮
      <Naf>
        <Atom>
          <Rel>Predicate< /Rel>
          <Var>variable< /Var>
                      ⋮
          <Ind>constant< /Ind>
                      ⋮
        < /Atom>
      < /Naf>
    < /And>
  < /body>
< /Implies>
         ⋮
<!- -Representation of facts - ->
<Atom>
  <Rel>Predicate< /Rel>
  <Ind>constant< /Ind>
         ⋮
< /Atom>
         ⋮
```

Rules are translated internally into the simplified ASCII syntax. Once translated, they can be annotated by the user with rule priorities, and these annotated rules are then used to produce Maude specification. Rule priorities are required by some of the supported inference (conflict resolution) strategies. The tool supports a wide range of inference strategies including those provided by the CLIPS expert system shell [13], the Jess rule engine [14], and others [15]. Different agents in the system may use different strategies. The LTL specification of the behaviour of abstract agents and properties to be verified are given in a simplified ASCII notation.

4.1 Maude Implementation

The overall structure of the implementation is shown in Figure 1. Each agent has a configuration (local state) and the composition of all these (local state) configurations make the (global state) configuration of the multi-agent system.

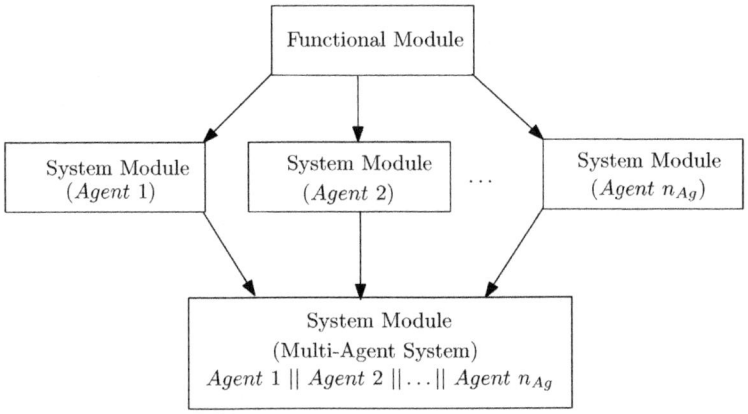

Fig. 1. Structure of the Maude implementation

The types necessary to implement the local state of an agent (working memory, program, control strategy, message counters, timestep etc.) are declared in a generic Maude functional module. The local configuration of each agent is represented as a tuple $Si[a : Agenda, a' : Agenda, tw : TimeWM, w : WM, t : Nat, t' : Nat, mc : Nat, b : Bool]iS$, where t represents the system cycle time, mc is the message counter, and b is a Boolean flag which is used for synchronisation. The rules of each agent are defined using an operator which takes as arguments a set of patterns (of sort $TimeWM$) specifying the antecedents of the rule and a single patten (of sort $TimeP$) specifying the consequent, and returns an element of sort $Rule$. In the case of concrete agents, each of the agent's Horn clause rules is represented by an element of sort $Rule$. As an example, a rule (expressed in the ASCII syntax) $\langle 1:Father(x, y) \Rightarrow Male(x)\rangle$ is represented as follows

$ceq\ rule\text{-}ins(A, [t1 : Father(x, y)]\ TM, M)\ =\ Rl\langle 1 : [t1 : Father(x, y)]\ -\ >>$
$[0 : Male(x)]\rangle lR\ rule\text{-}ins(Rl\langle 1 : [t1 : Father(x, y)]\ -\ >>\ [0 : Male(x)]\rangle lR\ A, [t1 :$
$Father(x, y)]\ TM, M)\ if\ (not\ inAgenda(Rl\langle 1 : [t1 : Father(x, y)]\ -\ >>\ [0 :$
$Male(x)]\rangle lR, A))\ \wedge\ (not\ inWorkingMemory(Male(x), M)).$

Note that the rule is translated using the corresponding time pattern for efficiency purposes. In the rule the number 1 represents rule salience and the placeholder $t1$ represents time stamp of the corresponding pattern. Each equation may give rise to more than one rule instance depending on the elements in working memory. To prevent the regeneration of the same rule instance, the conditional equation checks whether the rule instance and its consequent are already present in the agenda and working memory. A sort $Agenda$ is declared as a supersort of $Rule$. These data types are manipulated by a set of equations, e.g., to check whether or not a given pattern (used to represent fact) is already in the agent's working memory, whether or not a rule instance is already in the agenda etc. Additional equations are used to implement control strategies, e.g., to determine the highest priority rule instance in the agenda, or the pattern with highest time stamp in working memory etc.

We model each (concrete and abstract) agent using a Maude system module which imports the generic functional module. System modules contain both functions and rewrite rules which are used to implement the dynamic behaviour of the system. For concrete agents, the agent's inference cycle is implemented using three Maude rules:

$rl[match] : [A\,|\,RL\,|\,TM\,|\,M\,|\,t\,|\,msg\,|\,1\,|\,true] => [rule\text{-}ins(A, TM, M)A\,|\,RL\,|$
$TM\,|\,M\,|\,t\,|\,msg\,|\,2\,|\,false].$

$rl[select] : [A\,|\,RL\,|\,TM\,|\,M\,|\,t\,|\,msg\,|\,2\,|\,true] => [del(strategy(A, A), A)\,|$
$strategy(A, A)\ RL\,|\,TM\,|\,M\,|\,t\,|\,msg\,|\,3\,|\,false].$

$crl[execute] : [A\,|\,Rl\langle n : Ant\ -\ >>\ Cons\rangle lR\ RL\,|\,Ant\ TM\,|\,M\,|\,t\,|\,msg\,|\,3\,|$
$true] => [A\,|\,RL\,|\,Ant\ time(Cons, t + 1)TM\,|\,pattern(Cons)\ M\,|\,t + 1\,|\,msg\,|\,1\,|$
$false]\ if\ (not\ inWorkingMemory(pattern(Cons), M)).$

The *match* phase is implemented by the *match* rule, which generates a set of rule instances based on the elements of $TimeWM$. The *conflict resolution* phase is implemented using the *select* rule, which selects a subset of rule instances from the agenda for execution based on the agent's control strategy. Finally, the *execute* phase is implemented using the *execute* rule, which executes the rule instances selected for execution. These three Maude rules are controlled using a flag which ensures that only one rule is applied at each system cycle. When the *match* and *select* rules execute, the time counter in the agent's configuration remain unchanged. However, the time counter is increased by one when the *execute* executes. All three phases, *match*, *select* and *execute*, therefore happen in one timestep.

The external behaviour of abstract agents are represented by means of temporal epistemic formulas. These formulas are translated into Maude agent specifications. For example, the formula $G(B_j ASK(i, j, P) \rightarrow X^n B_i TELL(j, i, P)))$ which states that if the abstract agent j believes that (concrete or abstract) agent i asks whether P is the case, then j should respond to agent i within n time steps, is translated as

$op\ halt\text{-}condition : TimeWM\ Nat\ WM\ -\ >\ Bool.$

eq $halt$-$condition([t':ASK(i,j,p)]TM,t,M) = if ((t == t' + m)$ and $(not$ $inWorkingMemory(p,M)))$ $then$ $true$ $else$ $halt$-$condition(TM,t,M)$ $fi.$

eq $halt$-$condition(TM,t,M) = false$ $[owise].$

crl $[reply] : Sj[A \mid RL \mid [t':ASK(1,2,P)]TM \mid M \mid t \mid msg \mid 3 \mid true]jS => Sj[A \mid RL \mid [t':ASK(1,2,P)][t+1:P]TM \mid P\,M \mid t+1 \mid msg \mid 1 \mid false]jS$ if $(not$ $inWorkingMemory(P,M)) \wedge t < t' + m.$

crl $[idle] : S2[A \mid RL \mid TM \mid M \mid t \mid msg \mid 3 \mid true]2S => S2[A \mid RL \mid TM \mid M \mid t+1 \mid msg \mid 1 \mid false]2S$ if $(not$ $halt$-$condition(TM,t,M)).$

where t is the current cycle time, t' is the time stamp when agent j came to believe that agent i asked for P and m is the bound defined above. The two Maude rules *reply* and *idle* execute non-deterministically when $t < t' + m$, but the *idle* rule cannot be applied when $t = t' + m$, forcing the agent to reply at $t' + m$ if it has not already done so.

Once all the agents of the system have been defined using system modules, we import them all into a single MAS system module. The MAS module defines two Maude rules, *parallel-comp*, which implements the parallel composition of agent configurations in the system, and *sync-rule*, which is used to synchronise the time cycle of the global system.

op $\_||\_ : Config$ $Config$ $-> Config$ $[comm$ $assoc].$

crl $[parallel$-$comp] : C1{:}Config \parallel C2{:}Config => C1'{:}Config \parallel C2'{:}Config$ if $C1{:}$ $Config => C1 : Config \wedge C2{:}Config => C2' : Config \wedge C1'{:}Config \neq C1{:}$ $Config \wedge C2'{:}Config \neq C2{:}Config.$

rl $[sync$-$rule] : S1[A1 \mid RL1 \mid TM1 \mid M1 \mid t1 \mid msg1 \mid rc1 \mid false]1S \parallel \ldots \parallel Sn[An \mid RLn \mid TMn \mid Mn \mid tn \mid msgn \mid rcn \mid false]nS \Rightarrow S1[A1 \mid RL1 \mid TM1 \mid M1 \mid t1 \mid msg1 \mid rc1 \mid true]1S \parallel \ldots \parallel Sn[An \mid RLn \mid TMn \mid Mn \mid tn \mid msgn \mid rcn \mid true]nS.$

Communication between agents is also implemented using rules in the MAS module. For example, if agent i fires a communication rule of the form $< n{:}P_1 \& \ldots \& P_n => ASK(i,j,P) >$ which adds a fact $ASK(i,j,P)$ to its working memory, this fact is communicated to agent j using the following Maude rule

crl $[comm]$:

$S1[A1 \mid RL1 \mid TM1 \mid M1 \mid t1 \mid msg1 \mid 3 \mid true]1S$

$\vdots$

$\parallel Si[Ai \mid RLi \mid TMi \mid ASK(i,j,P)\,Mi \mid ti \mid msgi \mid 3 \mid true]iS$

$\vdots$

$\parallel Sj[Aj \mid RLj \mid TMj \mid Mj \mid tj \mid msgj \mid 3 \mid true]jS$

$\vdots$

$\parallel Sn[An \mid RLn \mid TMn \mid Mn \mid tn \mid msgn \mid 3 \mid true]nS$
$=>$
$C1' : Config$

$\vdots$

$\parallel Si[Ai \mid RLi \mid TMi \mid ASK(i,j,P)\,Mi \mid ti+1 \mid msgi+1 \mid 1 \mid false]iS$

$\vdots$

$\|Sj[Aj \mid RLj \mid [tj+1:ASK(i,j,P)]TMj \mid ASK(i,j,P) \; Mj \mid tj+1 \mid msgj+1 \mid 1 \mid false]jS$

$\vdots$

$\| \; Cn'{:}Config$
$if \; (not \; inWorkingMemory(ASK(i,j,P),Mj))$
$\wedge \; S1[A1 \mid RL1 \mid TM1 \mid M1 \mid t1 \mid msg1 \mid 3 \mid true]1S => C1'{:}Config$

$\vdots$

$\bigwedge \; Sn[An \mid RLn \mid TMn \mid Mn \mid tn \mid msgn \mid 3 \mid true]nS => Cn'{:}Config$
$\bigwedge \; C1'{:}Config \neq S1[A1 \mid RL1 \mid TM1 \mid M1 \mid t1 \mid msg1 \mid 3 \mid true]1S$

$\vdots$

$\bigwedge \; Cn'{:}Config \neq Sn[An \mid RLn \mid TMn \mid Mn \mid tn \mid msgn \mid 3 \mid true]nS.$

When $ASK(i,j,P)$ is added to agent j's working memory, j may perform some computation if it does not know whether P is the case. In this model, communication requires a single timestep, i.e., when agent i asks agent j whether P is the case at time step t, agent j will receive the request at time cycle $t + 1$. However the time agent i has to wait for a response to its query depends on the reasoning j must (or chooses) to do (if j is concrete), or j's specification (if j is abstract). A similar approach is used when j tells i that P.

5 Experimental Evaluation

In this section we report experiments designed to illustrate the scalability and expressiveness of our approach. All the experiments reported here were performed on an Intel Pentium 4 CPU 3.20GHz with 2GB of RAM under CentOS release 4.8.

5.1 Scalability

To illustrate the scalability of our approach we implemented an example scenario reported in [9]. In this scenario, a system of communicating reasoners attempt to solve a (synthetic) distributed reasoning problem in which the set of rules and facts that describes agents' knowledge base are constructed from a complete binary tree. For example, a complete binary tree with 8 leaf facts has the following set of rules

RuleB1 $A_1(x) \wedge A_2(x) \to B_1(x)$ **RuleB2** $A_3(x) \wedge A_4(x) \to B_2(x)$

RuleB3 $A_5(x) \wedge A_6(x) \to B_3(x)$ **RuleB4** $A_7(x) \wedge A_8(x) \to B_4(x)$

RuleC1 $B_1(x) \wedge B_2(x) \to C_1(x)$ **RuleC2** $B_3(x) \wedge B_4(x) \to C_2(x)$

RuleD1 $C_1(x) \wedge C_2(x) \to D_1(x)$

For compatibility with the propositional example considered in [9], we assume that the variable x is substituted by a single constant value 'a', and the goal is to derive $D_1(a)$. One can easily see that a larger system can be generated using 16 'leaf' facts $A_1(x), \ldots, A_{16}(x)$, adding extra rules to derive $B_5(x)$ from $A_9(x)$ and $A_{10}(x)$, etc., and a new goal $E_1(x)$ derivable from $D_1(x)$ and $D_2(x)$ to give a '16 leaf example'. Similarly, we can consider systems with 32, 64, 128,. . .,2048 etc. leaf facts. Such generic distributed reasoning problems can be easily parameterised by the number of leaf facts and the distribution of facts and rules among the agents.

In [9], the results of experiments on such problems using the Mocha model-checker [6] are reported. In the simplest case of a single agent, the largest problem that could be verified using Mocha had 128 leaf facts. However, using our tool we are able to verify a system with 2048 leaf facts. The experimental results are summarised in Table 1.

Table 1. Resource requirements for a single agent

		CPU Time	
# leaves	# steps	Mocha	Maude
128	127	1:47:52	0:0:1
512	511	—	0:1:37
1024	1023	—	0:15:03
2048	2047	—	3:40:52

In case of a multi-agent systems, the exchange of information between agents was modelled as an abstract Copy operation in [9]. Each copy operation takes one tick of system time and does not require any special communication rules. As an example, to verify a multi-agent system consisting of two agents with 16 leaf facts, the Mocha encoding requires 1 hour and 36 minutes of CPU time. In our framework, communication between agents is achieved using *ASK* and *TELL* actions. The results presented in [9] and those for our tool are therefore not directly comparable in the multi-agent case. Nevertheless, we can show that much larger multi-agent systems can be modelled using our approach.

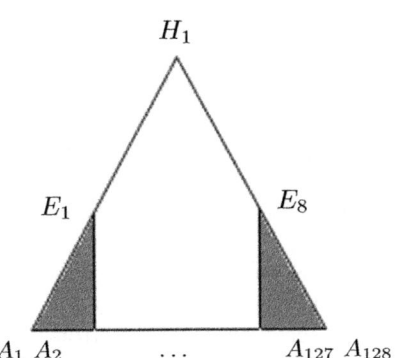

Fig. 2. Binary tree

Consider a multi-agent system consisting of two agents each with a knowledge base of facts and rules for the 128 leaf example (i.e., both agents have all the rules and leaf facts). Agent1 uses a reasoning strategy which assigns lower priority to rules in the right-hand shaded triangular region depicted in Fig. 2. In contrast, agent2 uses a rea-soning strategy which assigns lower priority to rules in the left-hand shaded triangular region of Figure 2. Suppose agent1 asks agent2 if $E_8(a)$ is the case. If agent1 receives the fact $E_8(a)$ from agent2 before deriving $E_8(a)$ itself, it can avoid firing 15 rules, and the agents are able to derive the goal $H_1(a)$ in 115 steps while exchanging two messages.

Similarly, consider the scenario in which there are three agents, each with a knowl-edge base of facts and rules for the 128 leaf example. Assume agent1 asks agent2 if $E_1(a)$ is the case and also that agent1 asks agent3 if $E_8(a)$ is the case. Suppose the agents utilise reasoning strategies similar to the previous case where the set of rules in the unshaded region have higher priority for agent1, the rules in left hand shaded region have higher priority for agent2, and the rules in the right hand shaded region have higher priority for agent3. Then the agents can derive the goal $H_1(a)$ in 103 steps while ex-changing four messages. The experimental results are summarised in Table 2. Although these examples are very simple, they point to the possibility of complex trade-offs be-tween time and communication bounds in systems of reasoning agents.

Table 2. Resource requirements for multiple agents

# agents	# leaves	# steps	#msgs	CPU Time
2	128	115	2	0:0:7
3	128	103	4	0:0:18

5.2   A More Complex Example

To illustrate the application of the framework on a more complex example we con-sider the following scenario. The system consists of several agents representing users who have queries about possible subway routes on the London Underground denoted by u_i, and two agents that provide travel advice: a 'route planning' agent, p, which computes routes between stations and an 'engineering work' agent, e, which has infor-mation about line closures and other service disruptions. The user agents ask for route information to the route planning agent, that is, they generate queries of the form:

$$ASK(u_i, p, Route(start\_station, destination\_station)).$$

The route planning agent has a set of facts corresponding to connections between sta-tions, and a set of rules for finding a path between stations which returns a route (a list of intermediate stations). Upon receiving a request from the user agent, the route plan-ning agent tries to find a route from the $start\_station$ to the $destination\_station$ by firing a sequence of rules based on the facts in its working memory. To ensure a route is valid, the planner must check that it is not affected by service disruptions caused by engineering work, which it does by querying the engineering work agent. If the route is open, the planner returns the route from $source\_station$ to the $destination\_station$ to the user agent.

The user agents are modelled as abstract agents, which generate a query at a nonde-terministically chosen timestep within a specified interval, e.g.:

$$X^5 B_{u_i} ASK(u_i, p, Route(MarbleArch, Victoria))$$

The engineering work agent is also modelled as an abstract agent which is assumed to respond to a query within some bounded number of timesteps, e.g., n timesteps:

$$G(B_e ASK(p, e, RouteList(start\_station, destination\_station,$$
$$[station_1 \mid station_2 \mid \ldots \mid station_n])) \rightarrow$$
$$X^n B_e TELL(e, p, RouteList(start\_station, destination\_station,$$
$$[station_1 \mid station_2 \mid \ldots \mid station_n]))$$

where $[station_1 \mid station_2 \mid \ldots \mid station_n]$ is a list of intermediate stations from the $start\_station$ to the $destination\_station$, and the response from the engineering agent indicates that the route from the $start\_station$ to the $destination\_station$ via $station_1, station_2, \ldots, station_n$ is open.

The system designer may wish to verify that the proposed design of the route planning agent, together with the assumed or known properties of the engineering work agent, is able to respond to a given number of user queries arriving within a specified interval, within a specified period of time. For a typical routing query, e.g., for an abstract user agent u_i asking for a route between station1 and station2, we can verify that response is received within n timesteps:

$$G(B_{u_i} ASK(u_i, p, Route(s1, s2)) \rightarrow$$
$$X^n B_{u_i} TELL(p, u_i, RouteList(s1, s2, [t_1 \mid t_2 \mid \ldots \mid t_n])))$$

Table 3. Resource requirements for the route planning example

# user agents	# timesteps	CPU Time
2	21	00:00:39
4	29	00:03:56
5	33	00:08:50

Table 3 reports experimental results for a multi-agent system consisting of a planner agent, an engineering agent and varying number of user agents. In this experiment, we have used 6 stations connected by 3 different lines (a total of 7 facts) and the planner can derive 8 different routes. Different user agents in the system make queries about different routes at different times in the interval $[1, 10]$. For example, the user agent u_i may request a route between *Marble Arch* and *Victoria*:

$$ASK(u_i, p, Route(MarbleArch, Victoria))$$

and receive the reply

$$TELL(p, u_i, RouteList(MarbleArch, Victoria, [BondStreet \mid GreenPark]))$$

The *timesteps* value in Table 3 gives the maximum number of timesteps necessary to return a route to a user agent under the specified system load.

6   Related Work

There has been considerable work on the execution properties of rule-based systems, both in AI and in the active database community. In AI, perhaps the most relevant is that of Chen and Cheng on predicting the response time of OPS5-style production systems. In [16], they show how to compute the response time of a rule-based program in terms of the maximum number of rule firings and the maximum number of basic comparisons made by the Rete network. In [17], Cheng and Tsai describe a tool for detecting the worst-case response time of an OPS5 program by generating inputs which are guaranteed to force the system into worst-case behaviour, and timing the program with those inputs. However, the results obtained using these approaches are specific to a particular rule-based system (OPS5 in this case), and cannot easily be extended to systems with different rule formats or rule execution strategies. Nor are they capable of dealing with the asynchronous inputs found in communicating rule-based systems. The problem of termination and query boundedness has also been studied in deductive databases [18]. However, again this work considers a special (and rather restricted with respect to rule format and execution strategy) class of rule-based systems.

In [19] the Datalaude system is presented, which essentially implements a Datalog interpreter in Maude. However the encoding of rules and rule execution strategy is very different from that proposed in this paper, in using functional modules and implementing a backward chaining rule execution strategy. The aim of the Datalaude project is not to analyse Datalog programs as such, but to provide a fast and 'declarative' (in the sense of functional programming) specification of memory management in Java programs (the example application in [19] uses Datalog facts represent information about references, and some simple rules ensure transitivity of the reference relation).

There has been considerable work on the use of abstraction in model-checking, e.g., [11,12]. These approaches use a mapping between an abstract transition system and a concrete program. Depending on this mapping, verification results may be correct but not complete. In contrast, our approach uses a very specific kind of abstraction, which replaces a concrete agent with an abstract one that implements guarantees of its response time behaviour. If those guarantees are correct, then our approach gives both correct and complete results. Agents can be modelled as abstract if their response time guarantees have already been verified or the system designer is prepared to assume them.

7   Conclusion

We described an automated verification framework for communicating resource-bounded reasoners which takes a set of agents specified in terms of facts and Horn clause rules and automatically produces a Maude [8] specification of the system which can be efficiently verified. We illustrated the scalability of our approach by comparing it to results presented in [9] for a synthetic distributed reasoning problem. We also showed how to further improve scalability by using abstract agents specified in terms of temporal epistemic formulas.

The tool described in the paper is a simple prototype. In future work, we plan to extend the language for specifying the rules of concrete agents to include function terms, and introduce a language for specifying reasoning strategies.

References

1. Bordini, R.H., Hübner, J.F., Vieira, R.: *Jason* and the Golden Fleece of agent-oriented programming. In: Bordini, R.H., Dastani, M., Dix, J., El Fallah Seghrouchni, A. (eds.) Multi-Agent Programming: Languages, Platforms and Applications. Springer, Heidelberg (2005)
2. Bordini, R., Fisher, M., Visser, W., Wooldridge, M.: State-space reduction techniques in agent verification. In: Jennings, N.R., Sierra, C., Sonenberg, L., Tambe, M. (eds.) Proceedings of the Third International Joint Conference on Autonomous Agents and Multi-Agent Systems (AAMAS 2004), pp. 896–903. ACM Press, New York (2004)
3. Adjiman, P., Chatalic, P., Goasdoué, F., Rousset, M.C., Simon, L.: Distributed reasoning in a peer-to-peer setting. In: López de Mántaras, R., Saitta, L. (eds.) Proceedings of the Sixteenth European Conference on Artificial Intelligence (ECAI 2004), Valencia, Spain, pp. 945–946. IOS Press, Amsterdam (2004)
4. Claßen, J., Eyerich, P., Lakemeyer, G., Nebel, B.: Towards an integration of Golog and planning. In: Proceedings of the 20th International Joint Conference on Artifical Intelligence (IJCAI 2007), pp. 1846–1851. Morgan Kaufmann Publishers Inc., San Francisco (2007)
5. Alechina, N., Jago, M., Logan, B.: Modal logics for communicating rule-based agents. In: Brewka, G., Coradeschi, S., Perini, A., Traverso, P. (eds.) Proceedings of the 17th European Conference on Artificial Intelligence (ECAI 2006), pp. 322–326. IOS Press, Amsterdam (2006)
6. Alur, R., Henzinger, T.A., Mang, F.Y.C., Qadeer, S., Rajamani, S.K., Tasiran, S.: MOCHA: Modularity in model checking. In: Y. Vardi, M. (ed.) CAV 1998. LNCS, vol. 1427, pp. 521–525. Springer, Heidelberg (1998)
7. Hirtle, D., Boley, H., Grosof, B., Kifer, M., Sintek, M., Tabet, S., Wagner, G.: Schema Specification of RuleML 0.91 (2006), http://ruleml.org/0.91/
8. Clavel, M., Eker, S., Lincoln, P., Meseguer, J.: Principles of maude. Electr. Notes Theor. Comput. Sci. 4 (1996)
9. Alechina, N., Logan, B., Nga, N.H., Rakib, A.: Verifying time and communication costs of rule-based reasoners. In: Peled, D., Wooldridge, M. (eds.) MoChArt 2008. LNCS, vol. 5348, pp. 1–14. Springer, Heidelberg (2009)
10. Holzmann, G.J.: On-the-fly model checking. ACM Computing Surveys 28(4) (1996)
11. Clarke, E.M., Grumberg, O., Long, D.E.: Model checking and abstraction. In: Proceedings of the 19th Annual ACM SIGPLAN-SIGACT Symposium on Principles of Programming Languages, pp. 342–354 (1992)
12. Cousot, P., Cousot, R.: Abstract interpretation: A unified lattice model for static analysis of programs by construction or approximation of fixpoints. In: Proceedings of the 4th Annual ACM Symposium on Principles of Programming Languages, pp. 238–252 (1977)
13. Culbert., C.: CLIPS reference manual. NASA (2007)
14. Friedman-Hill., E.J.: Jess, The Rule Engine for the Java Platform. Sandia National Laboratories (2008)
15. Tzafestas, S., Ata-Doss, S., Papakonstantinou., G.: Knowledge-Base System Diagnosis, Supervision and Control. Plenum Press, New York (1989)

16. Chen, J.R., Cheng, A.M.K.: Predicting the response time of OPS5-style production systems. In: Proceedings of the 11th Conference on Artificial Intelligence for Applications, p. 203. IEEE Computer Society, Los Alamitos (1995)
17. Cheng, A.M.K., yen Tsai, H.: A graph-based approach for timing analysis and refinement of OPS5 knowledge-based systems. IEEE Transactions on Knowledge and Data Engineering 16(2), 271–288 (2004)
18. Brodsky, A., Sagiv, Y.: On termination of Datalog programs. In: International Conference on Deductive and Object-Oriented Databases (DOOD), pp. 47–64 (1989)
19. Alpuente, M., Feliu, M.A., Joubert, C., Villanueva, A.: Defining datalog in rewriting logic. In: De Schreye, D. (ed.) LOPSTR 2009. LNCS, vol. 6037, pp. 188–204. Springer, Heidelberg (2010)

The Blow-Up in Translating LTL to Deterministic Automata

Orna Kupferman and Adin Rosenberg

School of Computer Science and Engineering,
Hebrew University, Jerusalem 91904, Israel
{orna,adinr}@cs.huji.ac.il

Abstract. The translation of LTL formulas to nondeterministic automata involves an exponential blow-up, and so does the translation of nondeterministic automata to deterministic ones. This yields a $2^{2^{O(n)}}$ upper bound for the translation of LTL to deterministic automata. A lower bound for the translation was studied in [KV05a], which describes a $2^{2^{\Omega(\sqrt{n})}}$ lower bound, leaving the problem of the exact blow-up open. In this paper we solve this problem and tighten the lower bound to $2^{2^{\Omega(n)}}$.

1 Introduction

The logic LTL (linear temporal logic) [Pnu81] is used for the specification of on-going behaviors of reactive systems. Such behaviors can be specified also using highly expressive second-order logics, but LTL offers two important advantages. First, writing formulas in temporal logic is simpler. Second, decision procedures for temporal logic are of elementary complexity. These advantages have made temporal logic, and in particular LTL, useful in practice.

The key to the elementary complexity of the decision procedures for temporal logics is their elementary translation to automata on infinite objects. In contrast, the translation of monadic second order logic formulas to automata is nonelementary [Büc62, Rab69]. In particular, given an LTL formula ψ of length n, it is possible to translate ψ to a nondeterministic Büchi word automaton (NBW, for short) with at most $2^{O(n)}$ states [VW94]. The translation of LTL to NBW has been a subject of extensive research, studying its theoretical complexity, optimizations, and performance in practice (c.f., [GPVW95, EH00, SB00, GO01]).

NBWs are strictly more expressive than deterministic Büchi word automata (DBWs, for short): a language $L \subseteq \Sigma^\omega$ can be recognized by a DBW iff there is a language $R \subseteq \Sigma^*$ such that for every word $w \in \Sigma^\omega$, we have that $w \in L$ iff w has infinitely many prefixes in R [Lan69]. All ω-regular languages, however, and therefore also all LTL formulas, can be translated to deterministic word automata with richer acceptance conditions, like Rabin or parity [Saf88, Pit06]. Such a translation is part of several decision procedures for LTL (e.g., synthesis and control [PR89]), algorithms for translating LTL to other logics (e.g., LTL to alternation-free μ-calculus [KV05a] and to general μ-calculus [Dam94]), as well as decision procedures for other logics (e.g., satisfiability for CTL* [ES84]). The

R. van der Meyden and J.-G. Smaus (Eds.): MoChArt 2010, LNAI 6572, pp. 85–94, 2011.
© Springer-Verlag Berlin Heidelberg 2011

blow-up that the translation involves plays a role even in algorithms that avoid determinization [KV05b, Kup06].

Recall that the translation of LTL to NBW involves an exponential blow-up. Determinization of NBWs also involves an exponential blow-up [Saf88, Pit06], yielding a doubly-exponential upper bound for the translation of LTL to deterministic automata. The doubly-exponential upper bound holds both for deterministic automata with rich acceptance conditions as well as for DBWs. We note, however, that the translation of LTL to DBW, when it exists, can avoid Safra's determinization and is much simpler [BK09]. In [KV05a], Kupferman and Vardi studied a lower bound for the translation. They described a family of languages $L_1, L_2, \ldots$ such that L_n is can be specified by an LTL formula of length $O(n^2)$ yet the smallest DBW for it needs at least 2^{2^n} states. This implies a $2^{2^{\Omega(\sqrt{n})}}$ lower bound for the translation, leaving the problem of the exact tight bound open.

In this paper we solve this problem. We first describe a family of languages $L_1, L_2, \ldots$ such that L_n can be specified by an LTL formula of length $O(n \log n)$ yet the smallest DBW for it needs at least 2^{2^n} states. The languages L_n are defined with respect to an alphabet of a constant size (6 letters). We then show that moving to an alphabet of size $O(n)$ we can tighten the lower bound further and describe a family $L_1, L_2, \ldots$ such that L_n can be specified by an LTL formula of length $O(n)$ yet the smallest DBW for it needs at least 2^{2^n} states. This implies a $2^{2^{\Omega(n)}}$ lower bound for the translation, matching the known upper bound. As in [KV05a], the languages we use are DBW-recognizable. By [KPB94], if a deterministic Rabin automaton (DRW, for short) recognizes a language that is DBW-recognizable, then a DBW for it can be defined on top of the same structure. It follows that our results imply a tight $2^{2^{\Theta(n)}}$ bound for the translation of LTL to both DBW and DRW.

2   Preliminaries

2.1   Linear Temporal Logic

The logic *LTL* is a linear temporal logic [Pnu81]. Formulas of LTL are constructed from a set AP of atomic propositions using the usual Boolean operators and the temporal operators X ("next time") and U ("until"). Formally, an LTL formula over AP is defined as follows:

- *true, false*, or p, for $p \in AP$.
- $\neg \psi_1$, $\psi_1 \wedge \psi_2$, $X\psi_1$, or $\psi_1 U \psi_2$, where ψ_1 and ψ_2 are LTL formulas.

The logic LTL is used for specifying on-going behaviors of reactive systems. Consider a computation $\pi = \pi_0, \pi_1, \pi_2, \ldots$, where for every $j \geq 0$, the set $\pi_j \subseteq AP$ is the set of atomic propositions that hold in the j-th position of π. We denote the suffix $\pi_j, \pi_{j+1}, \ldots$ of π by π^j. We use $\pi \models \psi$ to indicate that an LTL formula ψ holds in the computation π. The relation $\models$ is inductively defined as follows:

- For all π, we have that $\pi \models true$ and $\pi \not\models false$.
- For an atomic proposition $p \in AP$, we have that $\pi \models p$ iff $p \in \pi_0$.
- $\pi \models \neg\psi_1$ iff $\pi \not\models \psi_1$.
- $\pi \models \psi_1 \wedge \psi_2$ iff $\pi \models \psi_1$ and $\pi \models \psi_2$.
- $\pi \models X\psi_1$ iff $\pi^1 \models \psi_1$.
- $\pi \models \psi_1 U \psi_2$ iff there exists $k \geq 0$ such that $\pi^k \models \psi_2$ and $\pi^i \models \psi_1$ for all $0 \leq i < k$.

Each LTL formula ψ over AP defines a language $L(\psi) \subseteq (2^{AP})^\omega$ of the computations that satisfy ψ. Formally, $L(\psi) = \{\pi \in (2^{AP})^\omega | \pi \models \psi\}$.

We denote the size of an LTL formula φ by $|\varphi|$ and we use the following abbreviations in writing formulas:

- $\vee, \rightarrow$, and $\leftrightarrow$, interpreted in the usual way.
- $F\psi = true U \psi$ ("eventually").
- $G\psi = \neg F \neg \psi$ ("always").

2.2 Automata over Infinite Words

For a finite alphabet Σ, an infinite word $w = \sigma_1 \cdot \sigma_2 \cdots$ is an infinite sequence of letters from Σ. A property of a system with a set AP of atomic propositions can be viewed as a language over the alphabet 2^{AP}. We have seen in Section 2.1 that LTL can be used in order to define properties. Another way to define properties is using automata.

A *nondeterministic Büchi automaton* over infinite words is a tuple $\mathcal{A} = \langle \Sigma, Q, Q_0, \delta, \alpha \rangle$, where Σ is a finite nonempty alphabet, Q is a finite nonempty set of states, $Q_0 \subseteq Q$ is a nonempty set of initial states, $\delta : Q \times \Sigma \rightarrow 2^Q$ is a transition function, and $\alpha \subseteq Q$ is an acceptance condition. Intuitively, when an automaton $\mathcal{A}$ runs on an input word over Σ, it starts in one of the initial states, and it proceeds along the word according the transition function. Thus, $\delta(q, \sigma)$ is the set of states that $\mathcal{A}$ can move into when it is in state q and it reads the letter σ. Note that the automaton may be *nondeterministic*, since it may have many initial states and the transition function may specify many possible transitions for each state and letter. The automaton $\mathcal{A}$ is *deterministic* if $|Q_0| = 1$ and $|\delta(q, \sigma)| \leq 1$ for all states $q \in Q$ and letters $\sigma \in \Sigma$.

Formally, a *run* r of $\mathcal{A}$ on an infinite word $w = \sigma_1 \cdot \sigma_2 \cdots \in \Sigma^\omega$ is an infinite sequence $q_0, q_1, \ldots$ of states in Q such that $q_0 \in Q_0$, and for all $i \geq 0$, we have $q_{i+1} \in \delta(q_i, \sigma_{i+1})$. Note that a nondeterministic automaton can have many runs on a given input word. In contrast, a deterministic automaton can have at most one run on a given input word. The acceptance condition α determines which runs are accepting. A run r is accepting if it visits some state in α infinitely often. Formally, let $inf(r) = \{q : q_i = q \text{ for infinitely many } i\text{'s }\}$. Then, r is accepting iff $inf(r) \cap \alpha \neq \emptyset$. This is called the Büchi acceptance condition.

We also refer here to the Rabin acceptance condition. The Rabin acceptance condition is richer than the Büchi acceptance condition: $\alpha \subseteq 2^Q \times 2^Q$ is a set of pairs of subsets of states, and a run r satisfies a condition $\alpha =$

$\{\langle G_1, B_1 \rangle, \ldots, \langle G_k, B_k \rangle\}$ iff there is $1 \le i \le k$ such that $inf(r) \cap G_i \ne \emptyset$ and $inf(r) \cap B_i = \emptyset$. We are not going to use the Rabin condition and only refer to known results about it. We use NBW, DBW, and DRW to denote nondeterministic Büchi automata, deterministic Büchi automata, and deterministic Rabin automata, respectively.

3   From LTL to DBW

It is shown in [VW94] that every LTL formula ψ can be translated to an NBW $\mathcal{A}_\psi$ of size $2^{O(|\psi|)}$ such that $L(\mathcal{A}_\psi) = L(\psi)$. It is shown in [Saf88] that every NBW with n states can be translated to a deterministic Rabin automaton with $2^{O(n \log n)}$ states. It follows that every LTL formula ψ can be translated to a DRW $\mathcal{A}_\psi$ of size $2^{2^{O(|\psi|)}}$ such that $L(\mathcal{A}_\psi) = L(\psi)$. Moreover, it is shown in [KPB94] that DRWs are *Büchi type*: if a DRW recognizes a language that is DBW-recognizable, then an equivalent DBW can be defined on the same structure. It follows that if $L(\psi)$ is DBW-recognizable, then there is a DBW $\mathcal{A}_\psi$ of size $2^{2^{O(|\psi|)}}$ such that $L(\mathcal{A}_\psi) = L(\psi)$.

3.1   The Known Lower Bound: From $O(n^2)$ to 2^{2^n}

In [KV05a], Kupferman and Vardi studied a lower bound for the translation of LTL to DBW. By the Büchi-typeness of DRWs, the same bound applies for the translation of LTL to DRW. We review their result below.

Theorem 1. *[KV05a] There exists an infinite family of DBW-recognizable languages $L_1, L_2, \ldots$ such that for every $n \ge 1$, the language L_n can be specified by an LTL formula of length $O(n^2)$, and every DBW that recognizes L_n has at least 2^{2^n} states.*

Proof: Let $\Sigma = \{a, b, \#, \$\}$. We define the family of languages as follows:

$$L_n = \{(a + b + \#)^* \cdot \# \cdot w \cdot \# \cdot (a + b + \#)^* \cdot \$ \cdot w \cdot \#^\omega \mid w \in \{a, b\}^n\}.$$

For $n \ge 1$, we use the term n-block to refer to a word in $(a + b)^n$. It is not hard to see that L_n contains exactly all words in which some n-block w appears both after the single $\$$, with a $\#^\omega$ tail after it, and before the $\$$, where it is surrounded by $\#$'s.

For every n, the language L_n can be specified by the LTL formula

$$\psi_n = \quad [(\neg \$) U (\$ \wedge \overbrace{X((a \vee b) \wedge X((a \vee b) \wedge \ldots X((a \vee b) \wedge X G \#}^{n}) \ldots)))] \wedge$$
$$F[\# \wedge \bigwedge_{1 \le i \le n} ((X^i a \wedge G(\$ \to X^i a)) \vee (X^i b \wedge G(\$ \to X^i b))) \wedge X^{n+1} \#].$$

The first clause of the formula asserts that there is exactly one $\$$ in the word, followed by an n-block and an infinite tail of $\#$'s. The second clause asserts that there exists a position in which $\#$ is true and the i-th letter from this position, for $1 \leq i \leq n$, agrees with the i-th letter after the \$. Also, the $(n + 1)$-th letter from this position is #. Clearly, the length of ψ_n is quadratic in n. Note that the quadratic blow-up arises from the need to repeat n checks, where the check for the i-th letter requires a subformula of length $O(i)$.

By [CKS81], the smallest deterministic automaton on finite words that accepts L_n (omitting the $\#^\omega$ suffix) has at least 2^{2^n} states. The same argument can be used to prove that the smallest DBW that accepts L_n has at least 2^{2^n} states: reaching the \$, the DBW should remember the set of n-blocks that have appeared, surrounded by #'s, before. $\square$

Note that, for simplicity, [KV05a] assumes that the atomic propositions over which the LTL formulas are defined are mutually exclusive (that is, at each moment, exactly one proposition holds). Since the number of atomic propositions is fixed, this can be achieved by adding a conjunction of a fixed size that enforces it.

3.2   Improvement # 1: From $O(n \log n)$ to 2^{2^n} with a Fixed Alphabet

In the proof above, the LTL formula checks that for some n-block w appearing before the \$, the i-th letter after the \$ matches the i-th letter of w. Each of these checks is done using a subformula of length $O(i)$, and a check is required for all $1 \leq i \leq n$, leading to an overall formula of a quadratic length. In this section we consider a variant of L_n in which each letter in the n-blocks is prefixed by the binary encoding of its position in the block. This enables each of the checks to be specified by an LTL formula of length $O(\log n)$, resulting in a formula of length $O(n \log n)$ for all positions. The formulas should also assert that each letter is indeed prefixed by the encoding of its position, but this can be done by a conjunction of length $O(n \log n)$, leading to an entire formula of length $O(n \log n)$. Formally, we have the following.

Theorem 2. *There exists a family of DBW-recognizable languages $L_1, L_2, \ldots$ over a 6-letter alphabet, such that for every n, the language L_n can be defined by an LTL formula of length $O(n \log n)$, and every DBW that recognizes L_n has at least 2^{2^n} states.*

Proof: Let $\Sigma = \{a, b, \#, \$, 0, 1\}$. We first introduce some notations.

- For $n \geq 1$ and $1 \leq i \leq n$, let $k = \lceil \log n \rceil$ and $b_{n,i}$ be the k-bit binary encoding of $i - 1$. For example, $b_{8,4} = 011$ and $b_{12,11} = 1010$.
- Let $b_{n,i}[j]$ denote the j-th bit in $b_{n,i}$.

We are going to define L_n as the language of words consisting of a sequence of n-blocks, separated by #, followed by a \$, a copy of some n-block, and an infinite tail of #'s. Each n-block must be well-formatted; that is, rather than being a simple word in $(a + b)^n$, it is now a subword of length $n(k + 1)$, consisting of n letters in $\{a, b\}$, with the i-th letter, for $1 \leq i \leq n$, being prefixed by $b_{n,i}$. Thus, each bit in the n-block is "labeled" by its position in the block. These labels allow an LTL formula to efficiently verify that the n-block following the letter $\$$ is indeed a copy of one of the n-blocks appearing before the letter $\$$.

We define L_n as an intersection of two languages, S_n and R_n. The language S_n contains all words that have the proper format; i.e., the word is a sequence of n-blocks, separated by $\#$'s, followed by $\$$, another n-block, and an infinite tail of $\#$'s. The language R_n contains all words in which some n-block surrounded by $\#$'s appear before and after a single $\$$. Formally, let $r_n = b_{n,1} \cdot (a+b) \cdot b_{n,2} \cdot (a+b) \cdots b_{n,n} \cdot (a+b)$. Then,

$$S_n = \# \cdot (r_n \cdot \#)^* \cdot \$ \cdot r_n \cdot \#^\omega$$
$$R_n = \bigcup_{w \in r_n} \Sigma^* \cdot \# \cdot w \cdot \# \cdot \Sigma^* \cdot \$ \cdot \Sigma^* \cdot w \cdot \Sigma^\omega$$
$$L_n = S_n \cap R_n.$$

We now turn to define the LTL formula ψ_n that specifies L_n. As in [KV05a], we assume that the atomic propositions are mutually exclusive. As there, since the number of atomic propositions is fixed, this can be enforced by a fixed-length subformula. For $1 \leq i \leq n$, we let $\varphi_{n,i}$ assert that the current position starts with $b_{n,i}$. Formally,

$$\varphi_{n,i} = b_{n,i}[1] \wedge X(b_{n,i}[2] \wedge X(b_{n,i}[3] \wedge \ldots \wedge X(b_{n,i}[k]) \ldots)).$$

We now define the LTL formula ψ_n as the conjunction of the following clauses:

$$\# \wedge X(\varphi_{n,1}) \tag{1}$$

$$\wedge \ G(\bigwedge_{i=1}^{n-1} (\varphi_{n,i} \to X((a \vee b) \wedge X\varphi_{n,i+1}))) \tag{2}$$

$$\wedge \ G(\varphi_{n,n} \to X((a \vee b) \wedge X(\# \wedge X(\varphi_{n,1} \vee \$ \vee G\#)))) \tag{3}$$

$$\wedge \ (\neg\$)U(\$ \wedge X^{n \cdot (k+1)}G\#) \tag{4}$$

$$\wedge \ F(\# \wedge (\bigwedge_{i=1}^{n} (\varphi_{n,i} \to X^k \bigvee_{\sigma \in \{a,b\}} (\sigma \wedge F(\$ \wedge F(\varphi_{n,i} \wedge X^k\sigma))))))U\#). \tag{5}$$

Clause (1) asserts that the word begins correctly. Clause (2) asserts that the n-blocks are well formed. Clause (3) asserts that the n-blocks are separated by $\#$'s, and right after them starts a new n-block, or there is a $\$$, or a $\#^\omega$ tail. Clause (4) asserts that the first $\$$ symbol is followed by a subword of length $n(k+1)$ after which a $\#^\omega$ tail starts. Clause (5) asserts that there exists a string w, surrounded by $\#$'s, with each letter appearing again after a $\$$ symbol. Note that Clauses (1) through (4) assert that the word is in S_n, while Clause (5), given that Clauses (1)-(4) hold, adds the requirement that the input is in R_n.

Since $|\varphi_{n,i}| = O(k)$ and $k = \lceil \log n \rceil$, it follows that $|\psi_n| = O(n \log n)$.

Since L_n is of the form $L'_n \cdot \#^\omega$ for a regular language L'_n, a DBW recognizing it can easily be constructed by adding a transition from the accepting state of a DFW accepting L'_n to a one state DBW that accepts the $\#^\omega$ tail.

It is left to prove that every DBW that recognizes L_n must have at least 2^{2^n} states. Assume by contradiction that there exists a DBW $\mathcal{A}$ that recognizes L_n and has less than 2^{2^n} states. For $0 \leq i \leq 2^n - 1$, let w_i be the n-block that corresponds to the the i-th word in $(a+b)^n$, say, according to a lexicographic order. For every $S = \{i_1, i_2, \ldots, i_k\} \subseteq \{0, 1, \ldots, 2^n - 1\}$, let $p_S = \#w_{i_1}\#w_{i_2}\#\cdots\#w_{i_k}\#\$$. Let q_S be the state that $\mathcal{A}$ visits after reading p_S. Since $\mathcal{A}$ has less than 2^{2^n} states, there must be two distinct sets $S, S' \subseteq \{0, 1, \ldots, 2^n - 1\}$ such that $q_S = q_{S'}$. Since $S \neq S'$, there must be $0 \leq i \leq 2^n - 1$ that distinguishes them. Without loss of generality, assume that $i \in S \setminus S'$. Since $i \in S$, it follows that $p_S \cdot w_i\#^\omega \in L_n$, and the run of $\mathcal{A}$ on $p_S \cdot w_i\#^\omega$ is accepting. Therefore, the run on $p_{S'} \cdot w_i\#^\omega$ is accepting as well. However, $i \notin S'$, so $p_{S'} \cdot w_i\#^\omega \notin L_n$, which leads to a contradiction. □

3.3 Improvement #2: from $O(n)$ to 2^{2^n} with a Linear Alphabet

In the proof above, in a well-formatted n-block, each letter a or b was prefixed by the binary encoding of its position, which is of length $\lceil \log n \rceil$. By using an alphabet of linear size, we can use the alphabet in order to encode the position of the a's and the b's. This will allow the LTL formula to check the matching of each letter in the n-block by a formula of a fixed length. Checking for all letters can then be done by a formula of a linear length. In addition, we have to check that the letters we use indeed encode the positions, which again can be done by a formula of a linear length. Formally, we have the following.

Theorem 3. *There exists a family of DBW-recognizable languages $L_1, L_2, \ldots$ such that for every n, the language L_n can be specified by an LTL formula of length $O(n)$, and every DBW that recognizes L_n has at least 2^{2^n} states.*

Proof: First we define the alphabet Σ_n. Let $\Sigma'_n = \{1, 2, \ldots, n\} \times \{a, b\}$, and $\Sigma_n = \Sigma'_n \cup \{\#, \$\}$. For clarity, we use the symbols a_i and b_i for $\langle i, a \rangle$ and $\langle i, b \rangle$, respectively.

Next, we define L_n. Intuitively, L_n is again the language of words consisting of n-blocks, separated by $\#$'s, followed by a $\$$ symbol, a copy of some n-block, and an infinite $\#^\omega$ tail. Now however, the n-blocks are well-formatted in a different way: for each $1 \leq i \leq n$, the i-th letter is a_i or b_i. Thus, again each occurrence of a and b is "labeled" by its position in the n-block. These labels allow an LTL formula to efficiently check that the n-block following the $\$$ symbol is indeed a copy of one of the n-blocks appearing before the $\$$.

Again, we define L_n as an intersection of S_n and R_n, which are defined exactly as in the proof of Theorem 2, only with $r_n = (a_1 + b_1) \cdot (a_2 + b_2) \cdots (a_n + b_n)$. Thus,

$$S_n = \# \cdot (r_n \cdot \#)^* \cdot \$ \cdot r_n \cdot \#^\omega$$
$$R_n = \bigcup_{w \in r_n} \Sigma_n^* \cdot \# \cdot w \cdot \# \cdot \Sigma_n^* \cdot \$ \cdot \Sigma_n^* \cdot w \cdot \#^\omega$$
$$L_n = S_n \cap R_n$$

Finally, we define an LTL formula ψ_n that recognizes L_n. Again, we assume that the atomic propositions are mutually exclusive. A naive way to enforce this is by a conjunction disabling all pairs of atomic propositions to hold simultaneously. This, however, would result in a formula quadratic in n, and is thus too long. As we shall see below, the fact the formula ψ_n forces the letters # or $ to appear between n-block can be used in order to specify mutual exclusiveness with a formula of linear length. Now, ψ_n is a conjunction of the following clauses.

$$\# \wedge X(a_1 \vee b_1 \vee \$)$$

$$\wedge G(\bigwedge_{i=1}^{n-1} ((a_i \vee b_i) \rightarrow X(a_{i+1} \vee b_{i+1})))$$

$$\wedge G((a_n \vee b_n) \rightarrow X(\# \wedge X(a_1 \vee b_1 \vee \$ \vee G\#)))$$

$$\wedge (\neg\$)U(\$ \wedge X((a_1 \vee b_1) \wedge X^n G\#))$$

$$\wedge F(\# \wedge X(((\bigwedge_{i=1}^{n} (a_i \wedge F(\$ \wedge Fa_i)) \vee (b_i \wedge F(\$ \wedge Fb_i))))U\#))$$

The structure of the clauses is similar to these used in the proof of Theorem 2. Clearly, $|\psi_n| = O(n)$. Also, the language L_n is DBW-recognizable, and the proof that the minimal DBW that recognizes L_n has at least 2^{2^n} states is identical to the previous one, with the present format of n-blocks.

It is left to show that we can enforce mutual exclusion using a formula of linear size. We use the following formula:

$$G((\# \vee \$) \rightarrow \neg \bigvee_{i=1}^{n} (a_i \vee b_i))$$

$$\wedge G((\# \rightarrow \neg\$))$$

$$\wedge G(\bigwedge_{i=1}^{n} (a_i \rightarrow \neg b_i)).$$

The formula guarantees that the atomic propositions # and $ are mutually exclusive to all other atomic propositions, and that for all $1 \leq i \leq n$, the atomic propositions a_i and b_i are mutually exclusive. We claim that this, together with ψ_n, implies that x_i and y_j are also mutually exclusive, for all $x, y \in \{a, b\}$ and $1 \leq i < j \leq n$. Assume by contradiction that there is some n-block such that both x_i and y_j hold in a position k in the n-block. By the formula ψ_n, the fact that y_j holds in position k implies that # holds in position $k+n-j+1$. Also, the fact that x_i holds in position k and $i < j$ implies that $a_{i+n-j+1} \vee b_{i+n-j+1}$ also holds in position $k+n-j+1$. This, however, contradicts the mutual exclusiveness of # with $a_{i+n-j+1}$ and $b_{i+n-j+1}$, so we are done.   □

4   Discussion

We tightened the lower bound in the blow-up involved in the translation of LTL formulas to deterministic Büchi automata from $2^{2^{\Omega(\sqrt{n})}}$ to $2^{2^{\Omega(n)}}$. Interestingly, we had to distinguish between the case the set of atomic propositions is fixed and the case it is not. This is interesting, as the known translations with which the upper bound for the blow-up is proven do not try to take advantage of a fixed alphabet. Indeed, given an LTL formula ψ of length n, its translation goes through a nondeterministic Büchi automaton with $2^{O(n)}$ states, which is then determinized to a Büchi automaton with $2^{2^{O(n)}}$ states. A more careful analysis of the constants hiding in the $O()$ notations reveals that one can actually take advantage of the fixed alphabet.

In [BKR10], the authors define the class of *ordered alternating automata*. In ordered automata, the non-accepting states of the automaton are ordered, and transitions between non-accepting states must respect the order. LTL formulas can be translated to ordered alternating automata. Unlike general alternating automata, for which removal of alternation involves that break-point construction and a 3^n blow up [MH84], alternation of ordered automata (as well as very weak alternating automata, which are a special case of ordered automata [GO01]) can be removed with only an $n2^n$ blow-up. Moreover, it is shown in [BKR10] that for ordered automata with m letters, alternation can be removed with a 2^{m+n} blow-up, in a construction that makes use of the fact that the break-point construction can be based on subsets of letters rather than subsets of states. Our results here motivate further study of constructions that explicitly refer to the set of letters. It may well be that the lower bound described here for the case of an alphabet of a constant size is tight, and that efforts should now be directed at improving the upper bound for this setting.

Acknowledgement. We thank the anonymous reviewers for helpful comments.

References

[BK09]   Boker, U., Kupferman, O.: Co-ing Büchi made tight and helpful. In: Proc. 24th IEEE Symp. on Logic in Computer Science, pp. 245–254 (2009)

[BKR10]   Boker, U., Kupferman, O., Rosenberg, A.: Alternation Removal in Büchi Automata. In: Abramsky, S., Gavoille, C., Kirchner, C., Meyer auf der Heide, F., Spirakis, P.G. (eds.) ICALP 2010. LNCS, vol. 6199, pp. 76–87. Springer, Heidelberg (2010)

[Büc62]   Büchi, J.R.: On a decision method in restricted second order arithmetic. In: Proc. Int. Congress on Logic, Method, and Philosophy of Science. 1960, pp. 1–12. Stanford University Press, Standford (1962)

[CKS81]   Chandra, A.K., Kozen, D.C., Stockmeyer, L.J.: Alternation. Journal of the Association for Computing Machinery 28(1), 114–133 (1981)

[Dam94]   Dam, M.: CTL* and ECTL* as fragments of the modal μ-calculus. Theoretical Computer Science 126, 77–96 (1994)

[EH00]   Etessami, K., Holzmann, G.J.: Optimizing büchi automata. In: Palamidessi, C. (ed.) CONCUR 2000. LNCS, vol. 1877, pp. 153–167. Springer, Heidelberg (2000)

[ES84]   Emerson, E.A., Sistla, A.P.: Deciding branching time logic. In: Proc. 16th ACM Symp. on Theory of Computing, pp. 14–24 (1984)

[GO01]   Gastin, P., Oddoux, D.: Fast LTL to Büchi automata translation. In: Berry, G., Comon, H., Finkel, A. (eds.) CAV 2001. LNCS, vol. 2102, pp. 53–65. Springer, Heidelberg (2001)

[GPVW95]   Gerth, R., Peled, D., Vardi, M.Y., Wolper, P.: Simple on-the-fly automatic verification of linear temporal logic. In: Dembiski, P., Sredniawa, M. (eds.) Protocol Specification, Testing, and Verification, pp. 3–18. Chapman and Hall, Boca Raton (1995)

[KPB94]   Krishnan, S.C., Puri, A., Brayton, R.K.: Deterministic ω-automata vis-a-vis deterministic Büchi automata. In: Du, D.-Z., Zhang, X.-S. (eds.) ISAAC 1994. LNCS, vol. 834, pp. 378–386. Springer, Heidelberg (1994)

[Kup06]   Kupferman, O.: Avoiding determinization. In: Proc. 21st IEEE Symp. on Logic in Computer Science, pp. 243–254 (2006)

[KV05a]   Kupferman, O., Vardi, M.Y.: From linear time to branching time. ACM Transactions on Computational Logic 6(2), 273–294 (2005)

[KV05b]   Kupferman, O., Vardi, M.Y.: Safraless decision procedures. In: Proc. 46th IEEE Symp. on Foundations of Computer Science, pp. 531–540 (2005)

[Lan69]

[MH84]   Miyano, S., Hayashi, T.: Alternating nite automata on!-words. Theoretical Computer Science 32, 321–330 (1984)

[Pit06]   Piterman, N.: From nondeterministic Büchi and Streett automata to deterministic parity automata. In: Proc. 21st IEEE Symp. on Logic in Computer Science, pp. 255–264. IEEE Press, Los Alamitos (2006)

[Pnu81]   Pnueli, A.: The temporal semantics of concurrent programs. Theoretical Computer Science 13, 45–60 (1981)

[PR89]   Pnueli, A., Rosner, R.: On the synthesis of a reactive module. In: Proc. 16th ACM Symp. on Principles of Programming Languages, pp. 179–190 (1989)

[Rab69]   Rabin, M.O.: Decidability of second order theories and automata on infinite trees. Transaction of the AMS 141, 1–35 (1969)

[Saf88]   Safra, S.: On the complexity of ω-automata. In: Proc. 29th IEEE Symp. on Foundations of Computer Science, pp. 319–327 (1988)

[SB00]   Somenzi, F., Bloem, R.: Efficient Büchi automata from LTL formulae. In: Emerson, E.A., Sistla, A.P. (eds.) CAV 2000. LNCS, vol. 1855, pp. 248–263. Springer, Heidelberg (2000)

[VW94]   Vardi, M.Y., Wolper, P.: Reasoning about infinite computations. Information and Computation 115(1), 1–37 (1994)

Improved Bounded Model Checking for a Fair Branching-Time Temporal Epistemic Logic⋆

Xiaowei Huang, Cheng Luo, and Ron van der Meyden

The University of New South Wales, Australia
{xiaoweih,luoc,meyden}@cse.unsw.edu.au

Abstract. Bounded model checking is a verification technique based on searching for counter-examples to the validity of the specification using an encoding to propositional sastisfiability. The paper identifies a number of inefficiencies in prior encodings for bounded model checking for a logic of knowledge and branching time. An alternate encoding is developed, and theoretical and experimental results are presented that show this leads to improved performance of bounded model checking for a range of examples.

1 Introduction

In the context of distributed and multi-agent systems, as well as autonomous systems that must operate in an uncertain environment, it has been argued that *epistemic* logics, i.e., logics of *knowledge*, provide a useful expressiveness for dealing with agents' need to relate their actions to their state of information [5]. This has led to the study of model checking for temporal epistemic logics [6,10]. There exist a variety of approaches to model checking. Binary Decision Diagram (BDD) techniques use a graph-based encoding to efficiently represent boolean functions and computes the set of states satisfying the specification in this encoding. A more recent approach is Bounded Model Checking (BMC) [1], which works by representing the statement that there exists a counter-example to the specification, of a particular structure and finite size k, as a propositional logic formula, and then using SAT-solving to determine the satisfiability of this formula.

Bounded model checking was first proposed in the context of linear-time temporal logic, where the structure of the counter-examples can be taken to be a run, a linear sequence of states, with the final one equal to one of the intermediate states to represent cyclical behaviour. There have subsequently been proposals to apply BMC to branching-time temporal logics, and to logics combining temporal and epistemic logic. A BMC encoding for ACTL, the universal fragment of the branching time logic CTL, has been proposed in [14], and extended to the richer logic ACTL* (which combines elements of linear- and branching-time logics) in [16]. The encoding for ACTL has been extended to a logic ACTLK$_n$, which also contains epistemic operators, in [13].

We show in this paper that it is possible to significantly improve upon the efficiency of BMC for temporal epistemic logic by means of an improved encoding. We develop

⋆ Work supported by Australian Research Council Linkage Grant LP0882961 and Defence Research and Development Canada (Valcartier) contract W7701-082453. An abstract of this paper also appears in the AAMAS 2010 proceedings.

R. van der Meyden and J.-G. Smaus (Eds.): MoChArt 2010, LNAI 6572, pp. 95–111, 2011.
© Springer-Verlag Berlin Heidelberg 2011

an efficient encoding for fair $ACTLK_n$ logic, which extends $ACTLK_n$ with a generalized Büchi fairness condition. Two main ideas underly the efficiency of our encoding. First, we sharpen the relationship between the formula and the runs in the counter-example: rather than simply evaluating the semantics of the formula over the counter-example, so that any run could be a candidate for the witness required for an existential claim, our encoding identifies a particular run as providing the required witness. Secondly, we associate particular subformulas with particular points in the counter-example structure, and use atomic propositions to represent the satisfaction of these subformulas in a way that eliminates exponential blowups in previous encodings by means of structure-sharing. Additionally, we use a number of optimizations that enable the number of runs required in the search for a counter-example to be reduced, and the shape of these runs to be simplified in a number of cases.

We show by both theoretical arguments and experimental results that our encoding yields an improved performance of BMC on a range of examples. Theoretically, we present examples where the size of the encoding is reduced from exponential to quadratic. One such example is the "nested knowledge" formula $(K_a K_b)^n p$ expressing that two agents a, b have degree n mutual knowledge of the proposition p.

Such improvements in encoding size are shown to have a significant impact on the runtimes required to find counter-examples in practice. In our experimental results, we have implemented three BMC encodings (that of [13], an earlier improvement [17] and our new encoding) in the epistemic model checker MCK [6]. MCK already supported a range of BDD-based model checking algorithms. We report the results of experiments on several protocols, including Dining Cryptographers [3], Byzantine Generals [9] and a simple Pursuit-Evasion Game. For each example, we consider a number of specification formulas. Both the systems description and the specification formulas involve a numerical parameter, and we show how the run-time of model checking scales with this parameter in each experiment, comparing the BMC techniques and a BDD-based technique. The experimental results show that our new BMC encoding often yields a much better performance than the previous BMC encodings. On the other hand, which of our new BMC encoding and BDD-based model checking is more efficient depends on the example.

The structure of the paper is as follows. Section 2 defines the logic of knowledge and time $ACTLK_n$ that we study, and defines the model checking problem for this logic. Previous bounded model checking approaches for this and related logics are reviewed in Section 3. We describe our new encoding in Section 4, where we also motivate on theoretical grounds why we expect this encoding to yield improved model checking performance. This is followed in Section 5 by a discussion of experimental results which validate and quantify the improved performance. Section 6 discusses related work, and Section 7 concludes with a discussion of future work.

2   Preliminaries

We work with a logic $ACTLK_n$ that combines the branching time logic ACTL (i.e., the universal fragment of the branching time temporal logic CTL) and the logic of knowledge and common knowledge for n agents, as well as its dual $ECTLK_n$. Dually, the logic $ECTLK_n$ can be defined as $\{\neg\psi \mid \psi \in ACTLK_n\}$; we give an expressively equivalent syntax for this logic below. In model checking these logics, we are interested in verifying that an $ACTLK_n$ formula is valid in a model. To find a counterexample for a specification ψ in the logic $ACTLK_n$ is the same as to find a witness for $\phi = \neg\psi$ in the logic $ECTLK_n$. Since BMC works by searching for such witnesses, we concentrate on the $ECTLK_n$ syntax in what follows.

Let *Prop* be a set of atomic propositions and $Ags = \{1, \ldots, n\}$ be a set of n agents. $\mathbb{T}$ and $\mathbb{F}$ are used to denote the truth values True and False, respectively. The syntax of $ACTLK_n$ is given by the following grammar [1] :

$$\gamma :== p \mid \neg p \mid \alpha \vee \beta \mid \alpha \wedge \beta \mid AX\alpha \mid AF\alpha \mid AG\alpha \mid A(\alpha U\beta) \mid K_i\alpha$$

where $p \in Prop$, and $i \in Ags$. Similarly, the syntax of $ECTLK_n$ is given by the grammar:

$$\gamma :== p \mid \neg p \mid \alpha \vee \beta \mid \alpha \wedge \beta \mid EX\alpha \mid EF\alpha \mid EG\alpha \mid E(\alpha U\beta) \mid \overline{K}_i\alpha$$

where $p \in Prop$, and $i \in Ags$. The connection between the two languages is given by the following equivalences: $\neg AX\alpha = EX\neg\alpha$, $\neg AF\alpha = EG\neg\alpha$, $\neg AG\alpha = EF\neg\alpha$, $\neg A(\alpha U\beta) = EG\neg\beta \vee E(\neg\beta U(\neg\alpha \wedge \neg\beta))$, $\neg K_i\alpha = \overline{K}_i\neg\alpha$. These equivalences may be used together with DeMorgans laws to transform $\neg\phi$, for any $ACTLK_n$ formula ϕ, into an equivalent $ECTLK_n$ formula.

We use a semantics for $ECTLK_n$ that is based on a variant of the *interpreted systems* model for the logic of knowledge [5]. Let W be a set, which we call the set of global states. A *run* over W is a function $r : \mathbf{N} \to W$. An *interpreted system* over W for n agents is a tuple $\mathcal{I} = (\mathcal{R}, \sim^1, \ldots, \sim^n, \pi)$, where $\mathcal{R}$ is a set of runs over W, each $\sim^i$ is an equivalence relation on W, and $\pi : W \to \mathcal{P}(Prop)$ is an interpretation function.

A *point* of $\mathcal{I}$ is a pair (r, m) where $r \in \mathcal{R}$ and $m \in \mathbf{N}$. We say that a run r' is *equivalent to a run r up to time* $m \in \mathbf{N}$ if $r'(k) = r(k)$ for $0 \leq k \leq m$. We define the semantics of $ECTLK_n$ by means of a relation $\mathcal{I}, (r, m) \models \phi$, where $\mathcal{I}$ is an intepreted system, (r, m) is a point of $\mathcal{I}$, and ϕ is a formula. This relation is defined inductively as follows:

- $\mathcal{I}, (r, m) \models p$ if $p \in \pi(r(m))$,
- $\mathcal{I}, (r, m) \models \neg p$ if not $\mathcal{I}, (r, m) \models p$
- $\mathcal{I}, (r, m) \models \alpha \vee \beta$ if $\mathcal{I}, (r, m) \models \alpha$ or $\mathcal{I}, (r, m) \models \beta$
- $\mathcal{I}, (r, m) \models \alpha \wedge \beta$ if $\mathcal{I}, (r, m) \models \alpha$ and $\mathcal{I}, (r, m) \models \beta$
- $\mathcal{I}, (r, m) \models EX\alpha$ if there exists a run $r' \in \mathcal{R}$ equivalent to r up to time m such that $\mathcal{I}, (r', m + 1) \models \alpha$
- $\mathcal{I}, (r, m) \models EF\alpha$ if there exists a run $r' \in \mathcal{R}$ equivalent to r up to time m and $m' \geq m$ such that $\mathcal{I}, (r', m') \models \alpha$.
- $\mathcal{I}, (r, m) \models EG\alpha$ if there exists a run $r' \in \mathcal{R}$ equivalent to r up to time m such that $\mathcal{I}, (r, m') \models \alpha$ for all $m' \geq m$
- $\mathcal{I}, (r, m) \models E(\alpha U\beta)$ if there exists a run $r' \in \mathcal{R}$ equivalent to r up to time m and a time m' such that $\mathcal{I}, (r, m') \models \beta$ and $\mathcal{I}, (r, m'') \models \alpha$ for all m'' with $m \leq m'' < m'$
- $\mathcal{I}, (r, m) \models \overline{K}_i\phi$ if for some point (r', m') of $\mathcal{I}$ such that $r(m) \sim_i r'(m')$ we have $\mathcal{I}, (r', m') \models \phi$

---

[1] In a longer version of the paper we include common knowledge operators, which we omit here for brevity.

For the knowledge operators, this semantics is essentially the same as the usual (observational) interpreted systems semantics. For the temporal operators, it corresponds to a semantics for branching time known as the *bundle semantics* [2,12].

While they give a clean and coherent semantics to the logic, interpreted systems are not suitable as inputs for a model checking program, since they are infinite structures. We therefore also work with an alternate semantic representation based on transition systems with epistemic indistinguishability relations and fairness condition. A (finite) *system* is a tuple $M = (W, I, \Rightarrow, \sim^1, \ldots, \sim^n, \pi, \chi)$ where W is a (finite) set of global states, $I \subseteq W$ is the set of initial states, $\Rightarrow \subseteq W \times W$ is a serial temporal transition relation, each $\sim_i \subseteq W \times W$ is an equivalence relation representing epistemic accessibility for agent $i \in Ags$, $\pi : W \to \mathcal{P}(Prop)$ is a propositional interpretation, and $\chi \subseteq \mathcal{P}(W) \setminus \emptyset$ is a *generalized Büchi fairness condition*. The system M can also be regarded as a generalized Büchi automaton with χ the set of acceptance sets.

Given a system M over global states W, we may construct an interpreted system $I(M) = (\mathcal{R}, \sim_1, \ldots, \sim_n, \pi)$ over global states W, as follows. The components $\sim^i$ and π are identical to those in M. The set of runs is defined as follows. We say that a *fullpath* from a state w is an infinite sequence of states $w_0 w_1 \ldots$ such that $w_0 = w$ and $w_i \Rightarrow w_{i+1}$ for all $i \geq 0$. We use $Path(w)$ to denote the set of all fullpaths from state w. The fairness condition is used to place an additional constraint on fullpaths. A fullpath $w_0 w_1 \ldots$ is said to be *fair* if for all $Q \in \chi$, there exists a state $w \in Q$ such that $w = w_i$ for infinitely many i. A *run* of the system is a fair fullpath $w_0 w_1 \ldots$ with $w_0 \in I$. We define $\mathcal{R}$ to be the set of runs of M. A formula ϕ of ACTLK$_n$ is said to hold in M, written $M \models_A \phi$, if $I(M), (r, 0) \models \phi$ for all $r \in \mathcal{R}$. Dually, a formula ϕ of ECTLK$_n$ is said to be satisfiable in M, written $M \models_E \phi$, if $I(M), (r, 0) \models \phi$ for some $r \in \mathcal{R}$.

We say that a state w is *fair* if it is the initial state of some fair fullpath, otherwise the state is *unfair*. A state w is *reachable* if there exists a sequence $w_0 \Rightarrow w_1 \Rightarrow \ldots w_k = w$ where $w_0 \in I$. (Some care with this is required because of the epistemic operators.) A state is fair and reachable iff it occurs in some run. Note that some reachable states may be unfair — we cannot always assume that a transition takes us to a fair state.

2.1 Model Checking Input Format

From now on, we fix a system M, a specification ψ in ACTLK$_n$. We are interested in determining whether $M \models_A \psi$, or equivalently, whether $M \models_E \phi$ for the ECTLK$_n$ formula ϕ corresponding to $\neg\psi$.

We will assume that the system M is presented in a particular format, in which the states of the system are viewed as assignments to a set of boolean variables, and the other components of M are represented by means of propositional logic formulas. In particular, we assume that there are N boolean variables making up a state. A state can therefore be represented as a boolean vector of length N. To refer to an arbitrary state, we may use a vector $s = (s_1, \ldots, s_N)$ of N boolean variables s_i. Given such a vector, let $s' = (s'_1, \ldots, s'_N)$ be the "primed" vector of symbols obtained by adding a prime symbol to each variable name to create N distinct variable names. We assume that the system M is presented as a tuple $\langle s, I(s), T(s, s'), H_1(s, s'), \ldots, H_n(s, s'), \chi \rangle$, where

- s identifies the variables that make up the state, or are used to compute state transitions,

- $I(s)$ is a propositional logic formula; a state is initial if it satisfies this formula,
- $T(s, s')$ is a propositional logic formula representing the transition relation $\Rightarrow$; there is a transition for a state represented by an assignment to s to the state represented by an assignment s' if this formula holds with respect to the union of these assignments.
- $H_i(s, s')$ is a propositional logic formula representing the indistinguishability relation $\sim_i$ for agent i,
- $\chi = \{F_1(s), \ldots, F_m(s)\}$ is a set (possibly empty) of propositional logic formulas $F_i(s)$, each representing one of the sets of states in a generalized Büchi fairness condition χ.

In addition to these formulas, we will make use of the formula $H(s, s') = \bigwedge_{i=1}^{N} s_i \Leftrightarrow s'_i$ which asserts the the states represented by s and s' are identical.

Given this representation of a system, we may represent length k fragments of runs of the system using a sequence $r = r(0), r(1), \ldots, r(k-1)$, where each $r(i) = (r(i)_1, \ldots, r(i)_N)$ is a vector of N variables. We use the following formulas to express properties of such sequences:

1. $\mathrm{Runf}_k(r) = \bigwedge_{i=0}^{k-2} T(r(i), r(i+1))$ expresses that r is a run fragment, in the sense that there is a transition from each state to the next,

2. $\mathrm{CRunf}_k(r, l) = \mathrm{Runf}_k(r) \wedge \bigvee_{h=0}^{k-1}(h = l \wedge T(r(k-1), r(h)))$ expresses that r is a cyclic run fragment. Here l is an additional variable of type $\{0 \ldots k-1\}$, representing the point at which the cycle starts.

3. $\mathrm{FCRunf}_k(r, l) = \mathrm{CRunf}_k(r, l) \wedge \bigwedge_{t=1}^{m} \bigvee_{h=0}^{k-1}(h \geq l \wedge F_t(r(h)))$ expresses that r is a *fair* cyclic run fragment. Fairness is obtained from the fact that each condition F_t in the generalized Büchi fairness condition holds at some point in the cycle. This implies that when we unfold the cyclic run to an infinite run, each condition F_i will be satisfied infinitely often, as required. (We remark that the use of the variable l helps to reduce the size of this formula by a factor of k.)

3 Previous Bounded Model Checking Algorithms for ACTLK$_n$

Bounded model checking approaches the problem of model checking a formula ψ in a system M via a search for counter-examples to the validity of the formula. These counter-examples are parameterized by their size k, and the existence of a counter-example of size k satisfying the formula $\phi = \neg\psi$ is encoded as a propositional logic formula $[M, \phi]_k$. Propositional logic SAT-solvers are then used to search for a satisfying assignment of this formula.

The details of the encoding depend upon the specification logic in question, and for a number of logics there have been several distinct proposals for encodings, with different complexity properties. In this section, we describe two encodings that have been proposed in the past for branching-time temporal and epistemic logics. This sets the context for our proposed optimizations.

3.1 Encoding of Penczeck et al

Penczeck et al [14] first proposed a BMC encoding for the logic ECTL, i.e., the logic $ECTLK_n$ described above, but without the knowledge operators. This encoding was later extended for $ECTLK_n$ [13]. In both cases, the encodings were for systems without fairness conditions, i.e., systems in which $\chi = \emptyset$ in the presentation above.

The basis for the encoding is a representation of forest-like counter-examples as set of run fragments. Intuitively, each time that the encoding needs to deal with an existential formula (such as $EF\alpha$, which requires the existence of a branch from the present point on which α is eventually satisfied), it uses a new run fragment (in the case of $EF\alpha$, this fragment is required to contain a point at which α holds). The BMC parameter k is taken to be the length of the run fragments. The total number of run fragments required to express the expected shape of the counter-example for a given value k for the formula is $1 + f_k(\phi)$, where the function f_k is defined recursively as follows: $f_k(p) = f_k(\neg p) = 0$ for $p \in Prop$, $f_k(\alpha \vee \beta) = max\{f_k(\alpha), f_k(\beta)\}$, $f_k(\alpha \wedge \beta) = f_k(\alpha) + f_k(\beta)$, $f_k(Y\alpha) = f_k(\alpha) + 1$ with $Y \in \{EX, EF, \overline{K_i}\}$, $f_k(EG\alpha) = k \cdot f_k(\alpha) + 1$, $f_k(E(\alpha U\beta)) = (k - 1) \cdot f_k(\alpha) + f_k(\beta) + 1$. A uniform notation is used for these run fragments. We write r_i for the ith run fragment. (For $i \neq j$, no variable is shared between the run fragments r_i and r_j.)

The whole encoding is made up of two parts as follows.

$$[M, \phi]_k \equiv I(r_0(0)) \wedge \bigwedge_{j=0}^{f_k(\phi)} \text{Runf}_k(r_j) \wedge [\phi]_k^{0,0} \tag{1}$$

The first part simply says that each r_j is a run fragment, and that the first state of r_0 is an initial state of the system. The second part states that this structure supports the formula ϕ. The notation $[\alpha]_k^{m,n}$ is defined in Table 1. Intuitively, this states that formula α holds at state m on run fragment r_n. We take p_i to be the i-th state variable, so that $(r_n(m))_i$ is the instance of this variable at the m-th state of the run fragment r_n.

Table 1. Encoding Function $[\gamma]_k^{m,n}$ for $ECTLK_n$ of Penczeck et al

$[p_i]_k^{m,n}$	$\equiv$	$(r_n(m))_i$
$[\neg p_i]_k^{m,n}$	$\equiv$	$\neg (r_n(m))_i$
$[\alpha \wedge \beta]_k^{m,n}$	$\equiv$	$[\alpha]_k^{m,n} \wedge [\beta]_k^{m,n}$
$[\alpha \vee \beta]_k^{m,n}$	$\equiv$	$[\alpha]_k^{m,n} \vee [\beta]_k^{m,n}$
$[EX\alpha]_k^{m,n}$	$\equiv$	$\bigvee_{j=1}^{f_k(\phi)} (H(r_n(m), r_j(0)) \wedge [\alpha]_k^{1,j})$
$[EG\alpha]_k^{m,n}$	$\equiv$	$\bigvee_{j=1}^{f_k(\phi)} (H(r_n(m), r_j(0)) \wedge \bigwedge_{l=0}^{k-1} [\alpha]_k^{l,j})$
$[EF\alpha]_k^{m,n}$	$\equiv$	$\bigvee_{j=1}^{f_k(\phi)} (H(r_n(m), r_j(0)) \wedge \bigvee_{l=0}^{k-1} [\alpha]_k^{l,j})$
$[E(\alpha U\beta)]_k^{m,n}$	$\equiv$	$\bigvee_{j=1}^{f_k(\phi)} (H(r_n(m), r_j(0)) \wedge \bigvee_{l=0}^{k-1} ([\beta]_k^{l,j} \wedge \bigwedge_{t=0}^{l-1} [\alpha]_k^{t,j}))$
$[\overline{K_i}\alpha]_k^{m,n}$	$\equiv$	$\bigvee_{j=1}^{f_k(\phi)} (I(r_j(0)) \wedge \bigvee_{l=0}^{k-1} ([\alpha]_k^{l,j} \wedge H(r_n(m), r_j(l))))$

For purposes of comparison with our encoding below, which takes fairness conditions into account, we note that fairness may be incorporated into this encoding by means of a simple change, using $\text{FCRunf}_k(r_j)$ where the encoding above uses $\text{Runf}_k(r_j)$.

We note that this use of cyclic runs is similar to their use in the BMC encodings for ACTL* [16] or ACTL*K_n [11].

3.2 Improved Encoding for ECTL by Zbrzezny

Zbrzezny [17] noted that the ECTL encoding of Penczeck et al [14] assumes that there exist sufficient run fragments in the counter-example to satisfy the existential subformulas encountered, but it needs to evaluate *all* of these fragments to check whether it provides the required witness. For example, in the clause for $EG\alpha$ in Table 1 the purpose of the top level disjunction over $j = 1 \ldots f_k(\phi)$ is to assert that one of the run fragments in the counter-example satisfies α at all points. This is inefficient: since the number $f_k(\phi)$ of run fragments is deliberately chosen to be large enough to supply all the witnesses required, we can allocate a *specific* run fragment to each witness ahead of time, and replace the check against all run fragments by a check against the specific run fragment that is supposed to provide the witness.

Zbrzezny gives a BMC encoding for ECTL that is based on this observation, and shows that his encoding leads to improved performance for model checking ECTL. We skip the full details of his encoding here: it requires some careful bookkeeping of run numbers during the encoding. Our own encoding below incorporates this idea with a slightly different formulation, but goes on to deal with the full logic ECTLK$_n$ in a way that incorporates further optimizations. For purposes of comparison we give just the clause for $EF\alpha$ (a simplication of the clause for $E(\alpha U\beta)$ actually presented), which defines the encoding $[EF\alpha]_k^{[m,n,A]}$ as

$$H(r_n(m), r_{min(A)}(0)) \wedge \bigvee_{j=0}^{k-1} [\alpha]_k^{[j,min(A),A\setminus\{min(A)\}]} .$$

Intuitively, A is a set of indices of free run fragments, $min(A)$ is index of the next available run fragment, and $A \setminus \{min(A)\}$ is the set of run fragments remaining for the encoding of witnesses required by α.

4   Improved encoding for ACTLK$_n$

In this section we define an encoding for ACTLK$_n$ that improves upon the encodings discussed in the previous section. We begin by noting some inefficiencies in these encodings, and noting some opportunities for optimization.

4.1   Motivation

Note that both the encodings of Penczeck et al and Zbrzezny construct the encoding $[\alpha]_k$ recursively, but in the process introduce some large disjunctions or conjunctions when dealing with modal operators. For example, for $[EF\alpha]_k$, both encodings use a subformula of the form $\bigvee_{j=0}^{k-1}[\alpha]_k^j$. In the case of formulas with deeply nested operators, this leads to an exponential blowup. For example for the formula ϕ_h defined by $\phi_0 = p_0$

and $\phi_{i+1} = p_{i+1} \wedge EF(\phi_i)$, even using the more efficient Zbrzezny approach we would obtain an encoding $[\phi_h]_k$ of the structure

$$\ldots \bigvee_{j_1=0}^{k-1} (\ldots \bigvee_{j_2=0}^{k-1} \ldots (\ldots \bigvee_{j_h=0}^{k-1} (\ldots)))))$$

which has size of the order k^h. On the other hand, the set of run fragments $\{r_0 \ldots r_h\}$ necessary for this encoding is of size merely $h + 1$, and each run fragment has k states. (Although Zbrzezny does not discuss knowledge, application of his ideas would involve dropping only the outer disjunction in the case for $\overline{K}_i$ in Table 1, so a similar blowup would be obtained for formulas such as $(K_a K_b)^h p$ that have been of interest when dealing with knowledge.)

We note that it is possible to encode this example more efficiently by introducing propositions $e_\phi^{r,n}$ representing that ϕ holds at the point (r, n). By Zbrzezny's ideas, we can witness each subformula ϕ_i by a particular run r_{h-i}, so we would like to have that

$$e_{\phi_h}^{r_0,0} \wedge \bigwedge_{j=1}^{h} \bigvee_{i=1}^{k} e_{\phi_{h-j}}^{r_j,i}$$

which states that ϕ_h holds at $(r_0, 0)$ and ϕ_{h-j} holds at some point i of r_j, plus

$$\bigwedge_{j=0}^{h-1} \bigwedge_{i=0}^{k-1} e_{\phi_{h-j}}^{r_j,i} \Rightarrow (r_j(i)_{h-j} \wedge H(r_j(i), r_{j+1}(0)))$$

i.e., p_{h-j} holds at (r_j, i) and r_{j+1} is a branch extending from (r_j, i). This gives an encoding that is of size $O(h \cdot k)$ rather than exponential. (We remark that since we only seek to *construct one* counter-example, rather than *detect all*, the converse implications are not needed.)

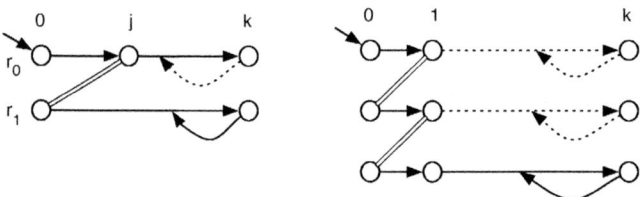

Fig. 1. Shapes of Counterexamples

We also note that a further optimization opportunity arises from considerations concerning loops and fairness conditions. Consider the specification $\psi_3 = AGAF \neg p$ in a system with fairness condition. Following the BMC approaches describe above, the expected shape of the counterexample is shown in the left graph of Figure 1. (Lines with arrows indicate transitions, double lines indicate identity of states.) However, we can in fact drop the cycle on the run fragment r_0, since we need it only to justify fairness of states up to the point j where we switch to the run fragment r_1, which contains a cycle that justifies fairness of all states that can reach this cycle. A similar consideration applies to the specification $AXAX\neg p$, whose counter-example form, consisting of 3 run fragments, is depicted on the right in Figure 1. However, not only can we drop loops here, we in fact need only the first step of the first two fragments.

4.2 Encoding

We now develop a new encoding for bounded model checking $ACTLK_n$. The encoding is based on the optimization ideas discussed above.

The encoding uses three types of resources: singleton run fragments, acyclic run fragments and cyclic run fragments, for which we use the symbols s, a, c respectively. We use the symbol r to represent an instance of any type of resource. Each resource r is associated with a length, denoted $|r|$, which depends on the BMC parameter. For BMC parameter k, singleton run fragment has length 1, and acyclic and cyclic run fragments have length k. We use the term *point* to represent a pair (r, n) where r is a resource and $n < |r|$ is an index, up to the length of that resource. Intuitively, these points will correspond to points of the system being model checked.

A *context* is a triple $R = (n_s, n_a, n_c)$ of numbers, representing the index number of the state, acyclic run fragment and cyclic run fragment that is the next free resource available for consumption by the encoding. For a resource type $T \in \{s, a, c\}$, we write $new_T(R)$ for the resource of type T with index n_T. We treat contexts as elements of the lattice $\mathbb{N}^3$, with basis $s = (1, 0, 0)$, $a = (0, 1, 0)$, $c = (0, 0, 1)$. Thus, we can represent a situation in which we consume one singleton run fragment in context R as consuming $new_s(R)$ and changing the context to $R + s$.

The encoding of each formula α consumes some number of each type of resource. We denote these numbers by $u_s^k(\alpha)$, $u_a^k(\alpha)$ and $u_c^k(\alpha)$, respectively. The definitions of these functions can be read from the encoding rules: we describe how this can be done after we have given these rules. Using the lattice representation, we also write $u^k(\alpha) = (u_s^k(\alpha), u_a^k(\alpha), u_c^k(\alpha))$.

We work with "obligations", which are tuples $\langle r, n, \psi, R \rangle$ representing that the encoding is required to contain components sufficient to express that formula ψ holds at the point (r, n) in the counter-example, with the encoding operating with respect to context R. The latter is used to determine precisely which resource instances will be used in the encoding.

Associated to these obligations are atomic propositions of the form $e_\psi^{r,n}$. We call these atomic propositions *skeleton variables*. (We note that because the encoding shares resources for disjunctive cases, a run fragment may be a potential witness for several different subformulas, so we do not take the extra step of indexing run fragments by subformulas.) In general, satisfying the obligation $\langle r, n, \psi, R \rangle$ recursively requires the introduction of new obligations, and a formula that relates the atomic proposition $e_\psi^{r,n}$ to other atomic propositions in the encoding. This formula uses several other atomic propositions as abbreviations of various formulas that need to be represented: $b_H^{r,n,r',n'}$ expresses $H(r(n), r'(n'))$, $b_{H_i}^{r,n,r',n'}$ expresses $H_i(r(n), r'(n'))$, $b_X^{r,n,r',n'}$ expresses $T(r(n), r'(n'))$, $b_I^{r,n}$ expresses $I(r(n))$.

We present a set of obligation rewrite rules, parameterized by the BMC parameter k, which represents the maximal run length in the counterexamples to be encoded. Each rule is of the form $o \rightarrow_k f, O$, where o is an obligation, f is a propositional logic formula, and O is a set of obligations. Intuitively, this rule means the obligation o can be satisfied by including in the encoding the formula f, but that the additional obligations in O need to be satisfied. The obligation rewrite rules are represented in Table 2. Some of the rules consume resources, at most one item in each case, the type T of which is given in the 3rd column. However, recursive satisfaction of the new obligations introduced by a rule leads to further resource consumption. The total resource consumption when rewriting each type of formula, including this recursive consumption, is given in the second column, which gives the recursive definition of the resource consumption function u^k with range $\mathbf{N}^3$.

The encoding uses several boolean functions of formulas to handle fairness issues. Define $tf(\gamma) = \mathbb{T}$ if γ is in the form $EY\alpha$ with $Y \in \{X, F, G\}$ or $E(\alpha U\beta)$. Then let $tpf(\gamma) = \mathbb{T}$ if $tf(\gamma)$, or $\gamma = \alpha \wedge \beta$ and either $tpf(\alpha)$ or $tpf(\beta)$, or $\gamma = \alpha \vee \beta$ and both $tpf(\alpha)$ and $tpf(\beta)$. Intuitively, this expresses that all ways of satisfying the formula involve satisfying a temporal formula at some point. We also use the boolean variable ϵ to represent that the fairness condition χ in the system is non-trivial, i.e., $\chi \neq \emptyset$. The condition $\epsilon \wedge \neg tpf(\alpha)$ is used to capture situations where fairness constraints need to be applied to states in the present run fragment, but we cannot rely upon the fact that some other run fragment will ensure that all relevant states on the present run are fair.

These rules, which operate on individual obligations, are lifted to *set* rewriting rules, that operate on pairs F, O consisting of a set of propositional formulas F and a set of obligations O, as follows: $F, O \rightarrow_k F', O'$ if there exists an obligation $o \in O$, a rule $o \rightarrow_k f, O''$ and $F' = F \cup \{f\}$ and $O' = (O \setminus \{o\}) \cup O''$.

For a formula ϕ, we start with an initial set of formulas F_0 and set of obligations O_0 that depend on the type of ϕ and the existence of fairness constraints. If $\epsilon \wedge \neg tpf(\alpha)$, then we take r_0 to be the individual state with index 0, and $O_0 = \langle r_0, 0, \phi, \mathsf{s} \rangle$. Otherwise we take r_0 to be the cyclic run fragment with index 0, and $O_0 = \langle r_0, 0, \phi, \mathsf{c} \rangle$. In either case, we take $F_0 = \{e_\phi^{r_0,0}\}$. If there is a sequence of set rewrites $F_0, O_0 \rightarrow_k^* F_k(\phi), \emptyset$ to a pair in which the set of obligations is empty, then we take $F_k(\phi)$ to be the set of propositional logic formulas that represents the semantics of ϕ on the counterexample. Let $\mathcal{B}_k(\phi)$ be the set of skeleton variables occurring in $F_k(\phi)$.

The complete encoding of the model checking problem is then

$$[M, \phi]_k = b_I^{r_0,0} \wedge \bigwedge_{f \in F_k(\phi)} f \wedge Resources_k(\phi) \wedge Encode(\mathcal{B}_k(\phi)).$$

Here $Resources_k(\phi)$ expresses that the resources used in the encoding of ϕ have the proper structure, and $Encode(\mathcal{B})$ expresses that the boolean variables in $\mathcal{B}$ have the intended meaning. More specifically, for each acyclic run fragment r with index $j \leq u_a^k(\phi)$ (cyclic run fragment r with index $j \leq u_c^k(\phi)$), $Resources(\phi)$ contains a conjunct $\mathsf{Runf}_k(r)$ (respectively, $\mathsf{FCRunf}_k(r)$). Similarly, for each $b \in \mathcal{B}_k(\phi)$, the formula $Encode(\mathcal{B}_k(\phi))$ contains a conjunct $b \Rightarrow f$, where f is its intended meaning. For example, for $b = b_H^{r,m,r',m'}$ we include the conjunct $b_H^{r,m,r',m'} \Rightarrow H(r(m), r'(m'))$. See above for the meanings of the remaining cases.

The correctness of the encoding is stated in the following theorem. Note that the bound on the parameter k also establishes termination (in principle) of BMC.

Table 2. Obligation rewriting rules $\langle r, n, \gamma, R\rangle \to_k f, O$, where $r' = new_T(R)$

γ	$u^k(\gamma)$	T	f	O	conditions
p_i	0		$e_\gamma^{r,n} \Rightarrow r(n)_i$		$p_i \in Prop$
$\neg p_i$	0		$e_\gamma^{r,n} \Rightarrow \neg r(n)_i$		$p_i \in Prop$
$\alpha \wedge \beta$	$u^k(\alpha) + u^k(\beta)$		$e_\gamma^{r,n} \Rightarrow e_\alpha^{r,n} \wedge e_\beta^{r,n}$		
$\alpha \vee \beta$	$max(u^k(\alpha), u^k(\beta))$		$e_\gamma^{r,n} \Rightarrow e_\alpha^{r,n} \vee e_\beta^{r,n}$		
$EX\alpha$	$c + u^k(\alpha)$	c	$e_\gamma^{r,n} \Rightarrow b_X^{r,n,r',0} \wedge e_\alpha^{r',0}$	$\langle r', 0, \alpha, R+c\rangle$	$\epsilon \wedge \neg tpf(\alpha)$
	$s + u^k(\alpha)$	s	$e_\gamma^{r,n} \Rightarrow b_X^{r,n,r',0} \wedge e_\alpha^{r',0}$	$\langle r', 0, \alpha, R+s\rangle$	otherwise
$EG\alpha$	$c + k \cdot u^k(\alpha)$	c	$e_\gamma^{r,n} \Rightarrow b_H^{r,n,r',0} \wedge \bigwedge_{i=0}^{k-1} e_\alpha^{r',i}$	$\langle r', i, \alpha, R+c+i\cdot u^k(\alpha)\rangle, i = 0\ldots k-1$	
$EF\alpha$	$c + u^k(\alpha)$	c	$e_\gamma^{r,n} \Rightarrow b_H^{r,n,r',0} \wedge \bigvee_{i=0}^{k-1} e_\alpha^{r',i}$	$\langle r', i, \alpha, R+c\rangle, i = 0\ldots k-1$	$\epsilon \wedge \neg tpf(\alpha)$
	$a + u^k(\alpha)$	a	$e_\gamma^{r,n} \Rightarrow b_H^{r,n,r',0} \wedge \bigvee_{i=0}^{k-1} e_\alpha^{r',i}$	$\langle r', i, \alpha, R+a\rangle, i = 0\ldots k-1$	otherwise
$\overline{K}_i\alpha$	$c + u^k(\alpha)$	c	$e_\gamma^{r,n} \Rightarrow b_I^{r,n,0} \wedge \bigvee_{j=0}^{k-1}(b_{H_i}^{r,n,r',j} \wedge e_\alpha^{r',j})$	$\langle r', i, \alpha, R+c\rangle, i = 0\ldots k-1$	$\epsilon \wedge \neg tpf(\alpha)$
	$a + u^k(\alpha)$	a	$e_\gamma^{r,n} \Rightarrow b_I^{r,n,0} \wedge \bigvee_{j=0}^{k-1}(b_{H_i}^{r,n,r',j} \wedge e_\alpha^{r',j})$	$\langle r', i, \alpha, R+a\rangle, i = 0\ldots k-1$	otherwise
$E[\alpha U\beta]$	$c + u^k(\beta) + (k-1)u^k(\alpha)$	c	$e_\gamma^{r,n} \Rightarrow b_H^{r,n,r',0} \wedge \bigwedge_{i=0}^{k-1} (\bigvee_{j=0}^{i-1} e_\alpha^{r',j} \wedge e_\beta^{r',i})$	$\langle r', j, \alpha, R+c+j\cdot u^k(\alpha)\rangle, \langle r', i, \beta, R+c+(k-1)\cdot u^k(\alpha)\rangle,$ $i = 0\ldots k-1, j = 0\ldots k-2$	$\epsilon \wedge \neg tpf(\beta)$
	$c + u^k(\beta) + ku^k(\alpha)$	a	$e_\gamma^{r,n} \Rightarrow b_H^{r,n,r',0} \wedge \bigwedge_{i=0}^{k-1} (\bigvee_{j=0}^{i-1} e_\alpha^{r',j} \wedge e_\beta^{r',i})$	$\langle r', j, \alpha, R+c+j\cdot u^k(\alpha)\rangle, \langle r', i, \beta, R+c+k\cdot u^k(\alpha)\rangle,$ $i = 0\ldots k-1, j = 0\ldots k-2$	otherwise

Theorem 1. *Let M be a (finite) system, ψ an $ACTLK_n$ formula. Then $M \not\models \psi$ iff $[M, \phi]_k$ is satisfiable for some $k \leq |M|$, where $\phi = \neg\psi$.*

We can also state a general result on the size of the encoding, compared with the complexity of the previous encodings.

Theorem 2. *For our new encoding, the size of $[M, \phi]_k$ is $O(lrk^2)$, where r is the number of consumed run fragments and l is the size of formula ϕ.*

This is to be compared with a size of $O(lr^{d+2}k^{d+2})$ for the encoding of Penczek and $O(lrk^{d+2})$ for the encoding of Zbrzezny, where d is the depth of nesting of modalities in ϕ.

5   Experimental Results

We argued above that it is possible to obtain an exponential improvement in the size of the encoding, so there are good theoretical grounds to believe that our approach will improve the performance of bounded model checking, particularly as the encoding is an input to a SAT-solver, which deals with an NP-complete problem. In this section we experimentally validate the expectation that our encoding yields a performance improvement over the earlier BMC encodings.

We conducted experiments using several classical multi-agent protocols, varying several aspects of the model checking problem. Each experiment measured runtime as a function of some parameter n of the problem: in some cases n was the number of agents, in others it concerned the depth of nesting, in others it was the size of the state space. Information about protocols, specifications and fairness conditions is listed in Table 3. Here n is the problem scale, NoS is the size of state space, and NoV is the number of state variables. For each of these protocols, we collect data on three specifications. The specifications all have the form $AG(\kappa)$ or $AF(\kappa)$ where κ is a formula that uses epistemic operators, but no temporal operators. For these specifications, we state the depth of modality nesting d. All the specifications are invalid, and we state the number of run fragments NoR in the BMC encoding as a function of the problem scale n and BMC parameter k. The minimal value of the BMC parameter yielding a counterexample is also stated (bound[k]).

Each specification is model checked using a BDD-based model checker (MCK based on CUDD [15] with sifting optimization), and three different BMC encodings: that of Penczek et al (BMC_P), Zbrzezny (BMC_Z), and our new BMC encoding (BMC_H), all implemented as extensions to MCK, so that the inputs to all four algorithms are the same. We included our fairness optimization in the BMC_Z implementation.

We report performance results on a 2× 3GHz Quad-core Intel Xeon MacPro with 16GB 667 MHz RAM. (Parallelism in the architecture is not used by the implementation.) BMC performance results are the cumulative timing for all values of the parameter k until a counter-example is found. Since the examples show exponential growth patterns as a function of the problem scale n, we plot results using a log-scale for run-times s. Thus, fitting a line $s = an + b$ to the data corresponds to a model of $O(e^{an})$, and an increase in the slope a corresponds to a polynomial order increase in running time.

Table 3. Parameter values in the experiments

Sys	scale[n]	NoS	NoV	fair.	spec.	depth[d]	valid	NoR[r]	bound[k]
DC	agents	$O(2^{2n})$	$O(n\log n)$		ψ_{dc1}	2		2	2
	≥ 3				ψ_{dc2}	2		n	2
					ψ_{dc3}	2		$k+1$	3
BG	msgs	$O(2n)$	$O(n\log n)$	χ_{bg1}	ψ_{bg1}	3		3	6
	≥ 2			χ_{bg2}	ψ_{bg2}	n		n	$n+3$
					ψ_{bg3}	2		$2k+1$	3
PE	length	$O(6n^2)$	$O(\log n)$		ψ_{pe1}	2		3	$\lfloor n/2 \rfloor + 2$
	≥ 3				ψ_{pe2}	2		$n+2$	$\lfloor n/2 \rfloor + 2$
					ψ_{pe3}	2		$k+1$	$2n+1$

The first protocol (DC) is Chaum's Dining Cryptographers [3], a protocol for anonymous broadcast. In this protocol, n agents first share the outcomes of coins they flip in a pairwise fashion around a ring, and then each agent i makes a public announcement determined from the two coinflips for which they know the outcome and a proposition $paid_i$ (representing whether or not they paid for the meal – at most one is assumed to have paid.) The proposition $stop$ is used to indicate completion of the protocol. This protocol is scaled according to the number of agents, i.e., the problem parameter n is the number of agents. The characteristics of this protocol are that the size of its state space is $O(2^{2n})$ and the number of state variables is $O(n\log n)$. The formulas we consider are given in Table 4.

Table 4. Specifications for Dinning Cryptographers

ψ_{dc1}	$AG((stop \wedge \neg paid_0) \Rightarrow K_0(\bigvee_{i=1}^{n-1} paid_i))$
ψ_{dc2}	$AG((stop \wedge \neg paid_0 \wedge odd) \Rightarrow \bigvee_{i=1}^{n-1} K_0 paid_i)$
ψ_{dc3}	$AF(\neg paid_0 \Rightarrow K_0(\bigvee_{i=1}^{n-1} paid_i)))$

Performance results for these formulas are given in Figure 2. (In all these figures, f, g and g_i are propositional logic formulas used as abbreviations.) Counterexamples for these formulas require only small bounds of k but may need a large number of runs.

The second protocol (BG) is the two agent Byzantine Generals Problem, first proposed in [9], in which two agents repeatedly send each other acknowledgements through a lossy channel to increase their mutual knowledge of receipt of a message. This protocol is scaled according to the total number of messages sent by the agents. The characteristics of this protocol are that the size of its state space is $O(2n)$ and the number of state variables is $O(n\log n)$. The formulas for this protocol are given in Table 5, and performance results for these formulas are given in Figure 3.

Table 5. Specifications for Byzantine Generals

ψ_{bg1}	$AG(sndmsg_0 \Rightarrow K_{Alice}K_{Bob}sndmsg_0)$
χ_{bg1}	$\{\neg sndmsg_0 \vee rcvmsg_0, \neg sndack_0 \vee rcvack_0\}$
ψ_{bg2}	$\begin{cases} AG(rcvmsg_{\frac{n}{2}-1} \wedge \neg rcvack_{\frac{n}{2}-1} \Rightarrow (K_{Alice}K_{Bob})^{\frac{n-2}{2}}K_{Alice}rcvmsg_0) & \text{if } n \text{ is even} \\ AG(rcvack_{\frac{n-3}{2}} \wedge \neg rcvmsg_{\frac{n-1}{2}} \Rightarrow (K_{Bob}K_{Alice})^{\frac{n-1}{2}}rcvmsg_0) & \text{if } n \text{ is odd} \end{cases}$
χ_{bg2}	$\begin{cases} \displaystyle\bigcup_{i=0}^{\frac{n}{2}-1}\{\neg sndmsg_i \vee rcvmsg_i, \neg sndack_i \vee rcvack_i\} & \text{if } n \text{ is even} \\[6pt] \{\neg sndmsg_{\lfloor\frac{n}{2}\rfloor} \vee rcvmsg_{\lfloor\frac{n}{2}\rfloor}\} \cup \displaystyle\bigcup_{i=0}^{\lfloor\frac{n}{2}\rfloor-1}\{\neg sndmsg_i \vee rcvmsg_i, \neg sndack_i \vee rcvack_i\} & \text{if } n \text{ is odd} \end{cases}$
ψ_{bg3}	$AF(K_{Bob}sndmsg_0 \vee K_{Alice}rcvmsg_0)$

The third protocol (PE) is a two agent Pursuit-Evasion Game on a very simple discrete linear terrain consisting of positions 0 to n — the pursuer needs to determine if the evader is in the terrain or not, and has perfect visibility on its present location. The game starts with the evader at the rightmost position n and the pursuer at leftmost position 0. The evader moves randomly between position 0 and n, while the pursuer patrols between position 0 and $n-1$. The game ends with a successful capture when they are either at the same position or cross over, exchanging their positions in two successive rounds. This example is scaled according to the length of terrain. The characteristics of this protocol are that the size of its state space is $O(6n^2)$ and the number of state variables is only $O(\log n)$. Formulas for this protocol are given in Table 6. Here ep is the Evader's position, pp is the Pursuer's position and n is the length of terrain. Performance results for these formulas are given in Figure 4. The specifications need large but linear bounds to find their counterexamples.

Table 6. Specifications for Pursuit Evation Game

ψ_{pe1}	$AG(found \wedge direction = 0 \Rightarrow (K_{pursuer}ep = pp) \vee (K_{pursuer}ep = pp - 1))$
ψ_{pe2}	$AG(found \Rightarrow \displaystyle\bigvee_{i=0}^{n} K_{pursuer}ep = i)$
ψ_{pe3}	$AF(K_{pursuer}ep = pp)$

In all cases, our new BMC encoding (BMC_H) gives a significant improvement in running time over the Penczek et al encoding (BMC_P). In some cases, we find a constant factor improvement, indicated by parallel curves in the logscale plot with differing initial points. E.g., for ψ_{bg1} and ψ_{bg3} we have roughly a 100-fold speedup, and for ψ_{dc1} and ψ_{dc3} we have roughly a 10-fold speedup. In other cases, we see in the logscale plot roughly linear curves in both cases but with a lower slope for our encoding, implying that for some $c > 1$, the new encoding performs as $f(n)^{1/c}$ where the Penczek et al encoding performs as $f(n)$, e.g., for ψ_{dc2}, ψ_{bg2} and ψ_{pe1}- ψ_{pe3}. In the latter cases, we

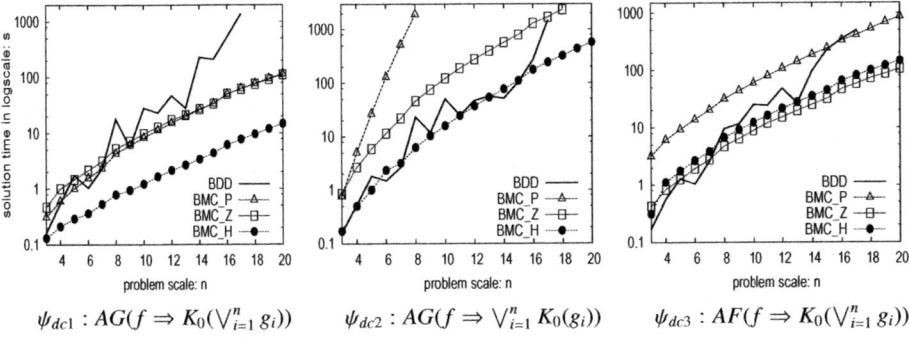

$\psi_{dc1} : AG(f \Rightarrow K_0(\bigvee_{i=1}^{n} g_i))$ $\psi_{dc2} : AG(f \Rightarrow \bigvee_{i=1}^{n} K_0(g_i))$ $\psi_{dc3} : AF(f \Rightarrow K_0(\bigvee_{i=1}^{n} g_i))$

Fig. 2. Dining Cryptographers

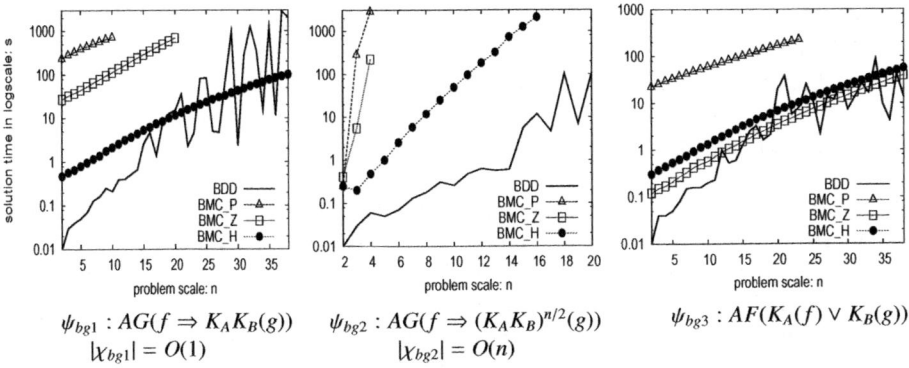

$\psi_{bg1} : AG(f \Rightarrow K_A K_B(g))$ $\psi_{bg2} : AG(f \Rightarrow (K_A K_B)^{n/2}(g))$ $\psi_{bg3} : AF(K_A(f) \vee K_B(g))$
$|\chi_{bg1}| = O(1)$ $|\chi_{bg2}| = O(n)$

Fig. 3. Byzantine Generals

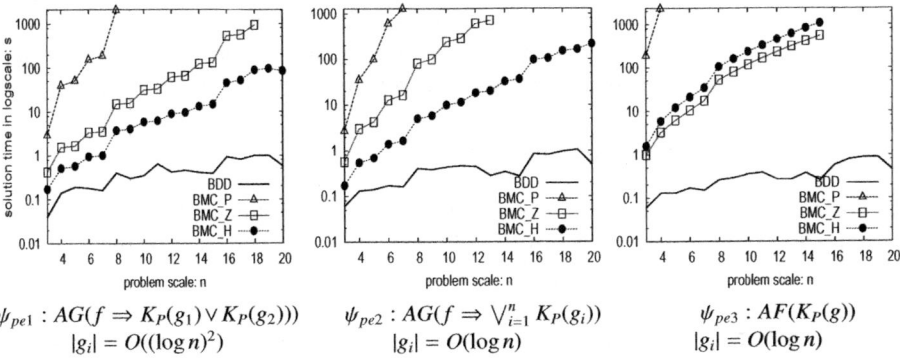

$\psi_{pe1} : AG(f \Rightarrow K_P(g_1) \vee K_P(g_2)))$ $\psi_{pe2} : AG(f \Rightarrow \bigvee_{i=1}^{n} K_P(g_i))$ $\psi_{pe3} : AF(K_P(g))$
$|g_i| = O((\log n)^2)$ $|g_i| = O(\log n)$ $|g_i| = O(\log n)$

Fig. 4. Pursuit-Evasion Games

obtain a very substantial improvement in the scale of example that the method is able to handle in reasonable running times.

Performance of the Zbrzezny BMC encoding (BMC_Z) is generally intermediate between the Penczek et al BMC encoding and ours. On deeply nested examples (e.g., ψ_{bg2}) our encoding performs significantly better, as expected. However, the depth of nesting does not need to be deep for an order of magnitude improvement to be visible (e.g., ψ_{dc1}, ψ_{dc2}, ψ_{pe1} and ψ_{pe2}). Finally, in some shallowly nested cases (ψ_{dc3}, ψ_{bg3} and ψ_{pe3}) the performance is very similar to ours, and slightly faster by a small factor. (This may be due to the overhead of constructing our slightly more intricate encoding.)

The performance comparison between the bounded model checking approaches and the BDD approach depends on the example. BDD model checking outperforms all the BMC approaches in all the pursuit-evasion game examples. On the Dining Cryptographers example, the BDD model checker initially has comparable performance to BMC_H, but eventually BMC_H wins out, and by more than a constant factor: we did not get termination for the BDD on problems of scale >18, whereas BMC continued to perform steadily in logscale. For the Byzantine Generals, the BDD approach sometimes (the deeply nested example ψ_{bg2}) performs significantly better, or (ψ_{bg1} and ψ_{bg3}) performs better on small examples but eventually performs chaotically around our BMC approach, but still better than the older BMC encodings.

6   Related Work

Kacprzak et al [7] have previously compared performance of the Penczek et al BMC encoding, as implemented in the model checker Verics [8], with BDD based model checking, implemented in MCMAS [10]. They study the Dining cryptographers protocol. We note that whereas we work from a single common model representation, they need to work with different input representations. For BMC they report only 5 data points, for BDD, up to 11. They conclude that the BDD approach is generally faster, but that BMC may handle larger models. By contrast, we find that with our new encoding, BMC eventually has better performance. (This also seems to hold for BMC_Z, though for ψ_{dc2} this is not clear.)

Another comparison of epistemic model checkers is by van Ditmarsch et al [4], who compare MCK, MCMAS and DEMO, principally from the point of view of ease of encoding of specifications of the Russian cards problem. In fact, the encodings developed are somewhat different and are not directly comparable for performance purposes.

7   Conclusion and Future Work

In this paper, we have proposed a new BMC encoding function for fair $ACTLK_n$. Compared with previous encodings [14,13] whose complexity increases exponentially with respect to the bound k and the number r of runs, the complexity of our encoding is only quadratic on k and linear on r. We conduct experiments on it for several protocols, including Dining Cryptographer, Byzantine Generals, and a Pursuit-Evasion Game. These experiments show that the new encoding often performs much better than the old encodings. The performance comparison with BDD model checking gives mixed results, but we note that unlike BDD model checking, BMC is able to return a counterexample.

For future work, we are investigating generalizing this counterexample-based encoding to some more expressive logics, e.g., an universal fragment of modal μ-calculus with epistemic operators. We have already developed an encoding function for synchronous systems with perfect recall semantics, and will report on its performance elsewhere.

References

1. Biere, A., Cimatti, A., Clarke, E.M., Strichman, O., Zhu, Y.: Bounded model checking. Advances in Computers 58, 118–149 (2003)
2. Burgess, J.P.: Logic and time. J. Symb. Log. 44(4), 566–582 (1979)
3. Chaum, D.: The dining cryptographers problem: Unconditional sender and recipient untraceability. J. Cryptology 1(1), 65–75 (1988)
4. van Ditmarsch, H.P., van der Hoek, W., van der Meyden, R., Ruan, J.: Model checking russian cards. Electronic Notes in Theoretical Computer Science 149(2), 105–123 (2005); Proc. of MoChart 2005
5. Fagin, R., Halpern, J.Y., Moses, Y., Vardi, M.Y.: Reasoning about Knowledge. MIT Press, Cambridge (1995)
6. Gammie, P., van der Meyden, R.: MCK: Model checking the logic of knowledge. In: Alur, R., Peled, D.A. (eds.) CAV 2004. LNCS, vol. 3114, pp. 479–483. Springer, Heidelberg (2004)
7. Kacprzak, M., Lomuscio, A., Niewiadomski, A., Penczek, W., Raimondi, F., Szreter, M.: Comparing BDD and SAT based techniques for model checking Chaum's dining cryptographers protocol. Fundam. Inform. 72(1-3), 215–234 (2006)
8. Kacprzak, M., Nabialek, W., Niewiadomski, A., Penczek, W., Pólrola, A., Szreter, M., Wozna, B., Zbrzezny, A.: Verics 2007 - a model checker for knowledge and real-time. Fundam. Inform. 85(1-4), 313–328 (2008)
9. Lamport, L., Shostak, R.E., Pease, M.C.: The byzantine generals problem. ACM Trans. Program. Lang. Syst. 4(3), 382–401 (1982)
10. Lomuscio, A., Qu, H., Raimondi, F.: MCMAS: A model checker for the verification of multi-agent systems. In: Bouajjani, A., Maler, O. (eds.) CAV 2009. LNCS, vol. 5643, pp. 682–688. Springer, Heidelberg (2009)
11. Luo, X., Su, K., Sattar, A., Reynolds, M.: Verification of multi-agent systems via bounded model checking. In: Sattar, A., Kang, B.-h. (eds.) AI 2006. LNCS (LNAI), vol. 4304, pp. 69–78. Springer, Heidelberg (2006)
12. van der Meyden, R., Wong, K.: Complete axiomatizations for reasoning about knowledge and branching time. Studia Logica 75(1), 93–123 (2003)
13. Penczek, W., Lomuscio, A.: Verifying epistemic properties of multi-agent systems via bounded model checking. In: AAMAS, pp. 209–216. ACM, New York (2003)
14. Penczek, W., Wozna, B., Zbrzezny, A.: Bounded model checking for the universal fragment of CTL. Fundam. Inform. 51(1-2), 135–156 (2002)
15. Fabio Somenzi. CUDD: CU Decision Diagram Package, http://vlsi.colorado.edu/~fabio/CUDD
16. Wozna, B.: ACTLS properties and bounded model checking. Fundam. Inform. 63(1), 65–87 (2004)
17. Zbrzezny, A.: Improving the translation from ECTL to SAT. Fundam. Inform. 85(1-4), 513–531 (2008)

Symbolic Model Checking the Knowledge in Herbivore Protocol

Xiangyu Luo[1,2], Kaile Su[3,4,*], Ming Gu[2], Lijun Wu[5], and Jinji Yang[6]

[1] College of Computer Science & Technology, Huaqiao University, Xiamen, China
shiangyuluo@gmail.com
[2] School of Software, Tsinghua University, Beijing, China
[3] College of Mathmatics Physics and Information Engineering, Zhejiang Normal University, Jinhua, China
[4] Institute for Integrated and Intelligent Systems, Griffith University, Brisbane, Australia
[5] School of Computer Science and Engineering, University of Electronic Science and Technology of China, Chengdu, China
[6] School of Computer, South China Normal University, Guangzhou, China

Abstract. The importance of anonymity has increased over the past few years in many applications. Herbivore is a distributed anonymous communication system, providing private file sharing and messaging over the Internet. In this paper, we utilize MCTK to model the round protocol of the Herbivore system and verify the anonymity and other knowledge properties that the protocol should provide, where MCTK is an OBDD-based symbolic model checker for temporal logic of knowledge developed by us, under the semantics of interpreted systems with local propositions. We model the round protocol of the Herbivore system in MCTK under the assumption that all agents have perfect recall of all observations. We implement the round protocol of the Herbivore system in MCTK and another epistemic model checker MCK. The encouraging experimental results show the validity of our MCTK.

Keywords: symbolic model checking, temporal logic of knowledge, multi-agent systems, the Herbivore system, anonymity.

1 Introduction

The security of cryptographic protocols, such as SSL, mainly depends on the assumption that all agents are computationally limited and that certain computational problems are intractable under these computational limits. So it is computationally difficult for attackers to decipher what was sent. However, these cryptographic protocols cannot provide anonymity, that is to say, they cannot mask the identity of communication agents. In recent years, the importance of anonymity has increased in many applications, such as Web-browsing, message-sending and file-sharing. A typical system of such applications is Herbivore [1], which is a distributed anonymous communication system that provides private file sharing and messaging over the Internet. It simultaneously provides scalability, efficiency and strong anonymity. In this paper, we focus on constructing a

---

* Corresponding author.

R. van der Meyden and J.-G. Smaus (Eds.): MoChArt 2010, LNAI 6572, pp. 112–129, 2011.

formal framework in which to reason about the anonymity and other properties that the Herbivore system provides.

Knowledge provides a natural way to express information-hiding properties, that is to say, a message is hidden from a if a does not know about it. As for anonymity, it says that an agent performing an action maintains anonymity with respect to an observer if the observer never learns certain facts having to do with whether or not the agent performed the action. The logic of knowledge is a type of modal logic, which can express information flow among agents. This logic contains, for each agent i in a system, a modal operator K_i, with the intuitive meaning of formula $K_i\varphi$ that agent i knows that φ is true. In this paper, we will apply MCTK, a symbolic model checker for the temporal logic of knowledge developed by us, to reasoning about agents' knowledge in the Herbivore system.

Model checking is most widely understood as a technique for automatically verifying that finite state systems satisfy formal specifications. The formal specifications for finite state systems are most commonly expressed as formulas of temporal logics such as LTL (Linear Temporal Logic) in the case of SPIN and CTL (Computation Tree Logic) in the case of SMV. The application of model checking within the context of the logic of knowledge was first mooted by Halpern and Vardi [2]. A number of algorithms for model checking epistemic specifications and the computational complexity of the related problems were studied in [3]. To represent the evolution of knowledge, some state-of-the-art model checkers combine the logic of knowledge with LTL and/or CTL temporal logics. For example, the model checker MCK [4] deals with the logic of knowledge and both linear and branching time. The model checker MCMAS [5] handles the logic of knowledge and branching time. Both MCK and MCMAS are implemented by using OBDD-based symbolic algorithms.

In [6,7], based on the semantics of *interpreted systems* with *local propositions* [8], we proposed a methodology of symbolic model checking for Halpern and Vardi's logic of CKL_n with path quantifiers, which leads to a "direct" implementation of model checking for the CTL^*-based temporal logic of knowledge, where CTL^* is the combination of LTL and CTL. Moreover, the corresponding symbolic model checker MCTK [7,9] was implemented by Xiangyu Luo by using OBDD (Ordered Binary Decision Diagram [10]). This paper attempts to apply our model checker MCTK to modeling and verification of the Herbivore system.

The structure of this paper is as follows. Section 2 introduces the framework of interpreted system with local variables in our model checker MCTK. Section 3 briefly introduces the implementation of MCTK. Section 4 introduces the round protocol of the Herbivore system and then models this protocol in MCTK and MCK. The experimental results from MCTK and MCK will be presented in Section 5. Finally we conclude this paper in Section 6.

2   A Brief Review of Knowledge and Time in Multi-agent Systems

In this section, we briefly summarize the framework of the interpreted systems with local variables as implemented in MCTK. We first introduce the interpreted systems, and then give the syntax and semantics of the temporal logic of knowledge $ECKL_n$ in terms of the interpreted systems with local variables.

The systems we are modeling are composed of multiple agents, each of which is in some state at any point of time. We refer to this as the agent's *local* state, in order to distinguish it from the system's state, the *global* state. Without loss of too much generality, we make the system's state a tuple $(s_1, \cdots, s_n)$, where s_i is agent i's state.

Let L_i be a set of possible local states for agent i, for $i = 1, \cdots, n$. We take $G \subseteq L_1 \times \cdots \times L_n$ to be the set of *reachable global* states of the system. A *run* over G is a function from the time domain–the natural numbers in our case–to G. Thus, a run over G can be identified with a sequence of global states in G. We refer to a pair (r, m) consisting of a run r and time m as a *point*. We denote the i'th component of the tuple $r(m)$ by $r_i(m)$. Thus, $r_i(m)$ is the local state of agent i in run r at "time" m.

The idea of the interpreted system semantics is that a run represents one possible computation of a system and a system may have a number of possible runs, so we say a *system* is a set of runs. Assume that we have a set Φ of primitive propositions, which we can think of as describing basic facts about the system. An *interpreted system* $\mathcal{I}$ consists of a pair $(\mathcal{R}, \pi)$, where $\mathcal{R}$ is a set of runs over a set of global states and π is a valuation function, which gives the set of primitive propositions true at each point in $\mathcal{R}$ [11].

To define knowledge in interpreted systems, we associate every agent i with an equivalence relation $\sim_i$ over the set of points [11]:

$$(r, u) \sim_i (r', v) \quad \text{iff} \quad r_i(u) = r'_i(v).$$

If $(r, u) \sim_i (r', v)$, then we say that (r, u) and (r', v) are indistinguishable to agent i, or, alternatively, that agent i carries exactly the same information in (r, u) and (r', v). Further, we associate the "distributed knowledge" and "common knowledge" among a group Γ of agents respectively with two relations $\sim_\Gamma^D$ and $\sim_\Gamma^C$ [11], where $\sim_\Gamma^D = \bigcap_{i \in \Gamma} \sim_i$ and $\sim_\Gamma^C$ is the transitive closure of $\bigcup_{i \in \Gamma} \sim_i$.

We can now define what it means for a formula φ to be true at a point (r, m) in an interpreted system $\mathcal{I}$. The logic language adopted in the model checker MCTK is an extension of *temporal logic of knowledge* CKL_n by incorporating two path quantifiers A (for all paths) and E (for some path). We call the resulting logic $ECKL_n$. The syntax of $ECKL_n$ involves two classes of formulae:

- *state formulas*, which are evaluated in states:

$$\phi ::= p \mid \neg\phi \mid \phi \wedge \phi \mid A\alpha \mid E\alpha \mid K_i\phi \mid D_\Gamma\phi \mid C_\Gamma\phi$$

  where p is any primitive proposition in Φ and α any path formula; and
- *path formulas*, which are evaluated along paths:

$$\alpha ::= \phi \mid \neg\alpha \mid \alpha \wedge \alpha \mid \bigcirc\alpha \mid \alpha U\alpha$$

  where ϕ is any state formula.

Intuitively, $E\alpha$ is true if there exists a path fulfilling α; and $A\alpha$ is true if all paths fulfill α. Thus $A\alpha$ can be defined by $\neg E\neg\alpha$. $\bigcirc\varphi$ is true if φ is true at the next step; and $\varphi U\psi$ is true if φ is true until ψ is true. The other future-time connectives $\Diamond$ (sometime or eventually) and $\square$ (always) can be derived from the basic temporal connective U by the following equivalences: $\Diamond\varphi \equiv trueU\varphi$ and $\square\varphi \equiv \neg\Diamond\neg\varphi$.

The state formulas of $ECKL_n$ involve three epistemic modal operators: K_i for each agent i's knowledge, D_Γ for distributed knowledge and C_Γ for common knowledge, where Γ is a group of agents.

The semantics of $ECKL_n$ is given via the satisfaction relation "$\models$". Given an interpreted system $\mathcal{I} = (\mathcal{R}, \pi)$ and a point (r, u) in $\mathcal{I}$, we define $(\mathcal{I}, r, u) \models \psi$ by induction on the structure of ψ.

$$(\mathcal{I}, r, u) \models p\ ` \quad \text{iff}\ \ p \in \pi(r(u)), \text{where } p \in \Phi.$$
$$(\mathcal{I}, r, u) \models \neg\varphi \quad \text{iff}\ \ \text{it is not } (\mathcal{I}, r, u) \models \varphi.$$
$$(\mathcal{I}, r, u) \models \varphi_1 \wedge \varphi_2 \quad \text{iff}\ \ (\mathcal{I}, r, u) \models \varphi_1 \text{ and } (\mathcal{I}, r, u) \models \varphi_2.$$
$$(\mathcal{I}, r, u) \models \bigcirc\varphi \quad \text{iff}\ \ (\mathcal{I}, r, u+1) \models \varphi$$
$$(\mathcal{I}, r, u) \models \varphi U \varphi' \quad \text{iff}\ \ (\mathcal{I}, r, u') \models \varphi' \text{ for some } u' \geq u \text{ and } (\mathcal{I}, r, u'') \models \varphi \text{ for}$$
$$\text{all } u'' \text{ with } u \leq u'' < u'.$$
$$(\mathcal{I}, r, u) \models E\varphi \quad \text{iff}\ \ \text{there exists a run } r' \text{ such that } r'(u') = r(u) \text{ for some } u',$$
$$\text{and } (\mathcal{I}, r', u') \models \varphi.$$
$$(\mathcal{I}, r, u) \models A\varphi \quad \text{iff}\ \ \text{for all runs } r' \text{ such that } r'(u') = r(u) \text{ for some } u', \text{ we}$$
$$\text{have } (\mathcal{I}, r', u') \models \varphi.$$
$$(\mathcal{I}, r, u) \models K_i\varphi \quad \text{iff}\ \ (\mathcal{I}, r', u') \models \varphi \text{ for all } (r', u') \text{ such that } (r, u) \sim_i (r', u').$$
$$(\mathcal{I}, r, u) \models D_\Gamma\varphi \quad \text{iff}\ \ (\mathcal{I}, r', u') \models \varphi \text{ for all } (r', u') \text{ such that } (r, u) \sim_\Gamma^D (r', u').$$
$$(\mathcal{I}, r, u) \models C_\Gamma\varphi \quad \text{iff}\ \ (\mathcal{I}, r', u') \models \varphi \text{ for all } (r', u') \text{ such that } (r, u) \sim_\Gamma^C (r', u').$$

Intuitively, from the semantics above, agent i knows φ ($K_i\varphi$) in state $r(u)$ exactly if φ is true at all states that i considers possible in s; A group Γ of agents has distributed knowledge of φ ($D_\Gamma\varphi$) exactly if the "combined" knowledge of the members of Γ implies φ; and a group Γ of agents has common knowledge of φ ($C_\Gamma\varphi$) exactly if everyone in Γ knows φ, everyone in Γ knows that everyone in Γ knows φ, etc.

We say that φ is valid in $\mathcal{I}$, denoted by $\mathcal{I} \models \varphi$, if $(\mathcal{I}, r, u) \models \varphi$ for every point (r, u) in $\mathcal{I}$. For a propositional formula φ, we use $\models \varphi$ to express that φ is a valid formula or tautology.

3   MCTK: A Symbolic Model Checker for Temporal Logic of Knowledge $ECKL_n$

In this section we briefly introduce the implementation of our symbolic model checker MCTK for $ECKL_n$. We will introduce the finite-state program with n agents as the modelling language of MCTK. It is a symbolized and finite-state transition representation for the interpreted systems with local variables.

The problem of model checking can be defined as establishing whether or not a model M satisfies a formula φ ($M \models \varphi$). OBDDs are an efficient representation for the manipulation of boolean functions. OBDDs of different functions can be composed efficiently: in [12] algorithms are provided for the manipulation and the composition of OBDDs. Model checking techniques using OBDDs are called *symbolic model checking*. The use of OBDDs in model checking resulted in a significant breakthrough in verification in the early 1990s, because they have allowed systems with much larger state spaces to be verified.

To be convenient for representing an interpreted system as an input language of MCTK, we first formally define a *(symbolic) finite-state program with n agents*, a tuple

$$\mathcal{P} = (\mathbf{x}, \theta(\mathbf{x}), \tau(\mathbf{x}, \mathbf{x}'), O_1, \cdots, O_n)$$

where

- $\mathbf{x} = \{x_1, \ldots, x_k\}$ is a set of boolean variables. A state can be encoded as an assignment for $\mathbf{x}$, thus a set of states can be represented as a boolean formula over $\mathbf{x}$ or a subset of $\mathbf{x}$;
- θ is a boolean formula over $\mathbf{x}$ representing the set of initial states, called the *initial condition*;
- τ is a boolean formula over $\mathbf{x} \cup \mathbf{x}'$, called the *transition relation*, where $\mathbf{x}' = \{x_1', \ldots, x_k'\}$ is a copy of $\mathbf{x}$, encoding the next state in a transition relation; and
- for each i, $O_i \subseteq \mathbf{x}$ is the set of agent i's *local variables*, or *observable variables*.

Given a state s, we define agent i's local state at state s to be $s \cap O_i$. For convenience, we denote $(s \cap O_1, \cdots, s \cap O_n)$ by $g(s)$. We associate with $\mathcal{P}$ the interpreted system $\mathcal{I}_\mathcal{P} = (\mathcal{R}, \pi)$, where $\mathcal{R}$ is a set of those runs r satisfying that

1. for each m, $r(m)$ is of the form $g(s) = (s \cap O_1, \cdots, s \cap O_n)$ where s is a state in $\mathcal{P}$ and the assignment $\pi(s)$ is the same as s;
2. $r(0)$ is $g(s)$ for some assignment s that satisfies θ; and
3. for each natural number m, if $r(m) = g(s)$ and $r(m + 1) = g(s')$ for some assignments s and s' for $\mathbf{x}$, then $s \cup N(s')$ is an assignment satisfying $\tau(\mathbf{x}, \mathbf{x}')$, where $N(s')$ denotes $\{x_j' \mid x_j \in s' \text{ and } 0 < j \leq k\}$.

The interpreted system $\mathcal{I}_\mathcal{P}$ is called *the generated interpreted system of $\mathcal{P}$*. The model checking problem for $ECKL_n$ we are concerned with is to determine whether, given a finite-state program with n agents $\mathcal{P}$ and a formula φ, the formula φ is true in the initial state of every run in the $\mathcal{R}$ of the generated interpreted system $\mathcal{I}_\mathcal{P} = (\mathcal{R}, \pi)$. More concisely, we say that $\mathcal{I}_\mathcal{P}$ realizes φ if $(\mathcal{I}_\mathcal{P}, r, 0) \models \varphi$ for every run r in $\mathcal{I}_\mathcal{P}$.

A key idea of symbolic model checking a logic by using OBDDs is to represent the sets of states and the transition relations in a model by means of boolean formulae. The first problem of our model checking approach is to represent a finite-state program with n agents as a dedicated programming language, such as PROMELA [13] and NuSMV [14]. Because the NuSMV input language is a natural representation of finite-state transition system, we adopt the NuSMV input language and extend the NuSMV syntax descriptions for defining each agent's observable variables and the $ECKL_n$ logic language to the input language. Therefore, by making use of and fixing the compilation unit in the open source of NuSMV, we can get an OBDD-based representation of a finite-state program with n agents.

We do not introduce the entire symbolic model checking algorithm for $ECKL_n$ here and refer to [6,7] for more details. Roughly speaking, the symbolic model checking algorithm for $ECKL_n$ is based on the idea of *local proposition* [8] and the tableau construction described in [15] and [16], and implemented by using OBDDs. An i-local proposition is one whose interpretation is the same in each of the points in each equivalence class induced by the $\sim_i$ relation. The intuition of our model checking approach to a formula of the form $K_i\varphi$ is to automatically replace the formula by some i-local formula ψ over the variables in O_i, even in the case that the formula φ contains temporal operators. the formula ψ is achieved by composing OBDDs, quantifying over OBDDs variables, and computing fix-points of operators on OBDDs.

The MCTK model checker is an extension of NuSMV 2.1.2, so it supports all functions of NuSMV. The OBDD package exploited in MCTK is the CUDD library developed by Fabio Somenzi at Colorado University. MCTK can be run from the command line and accepts various options to modify verbosity, to inspect OBDDs statistics and memory usage, and to enable variable reordering in CUDD. MCTK is written in the C programming language and has been compiled with gcc/g++ on x86 platform under Linux. In the next section we will show how the MCTK model checker can be applied to the verification of the Herbivore protocol.

4   The Herbivore Protocol

There are two components in the Herbivore system. At the lowest level, a *round protocol* governs how bits are sent among the participating nodes. This protocol achieves strong anonymity by building on DC-nets at the wire level. DC-nets were introduced in 1988 [17], which use unconditional secrecy channels to provide an unconditionally secure untraceable-sender system. To scale well in the face of planetary scale networks and malicious participants, Herbivore employs a *global topology control algorithm* to divide the network into smaller anonymizing cliques. Herbivore guarantees that each clique will have at least k nodes, where k is a predetermined constant that describes the degree of anonymity offered by the system.

In this paper, we are mainly concerned about honest agents' knowledge during the execution of the round protocol. As Sharad Goal *et al.* described in [1], the round protocol governs the behavior of nodes within a given clique. It ensures that nodes can transmit data anonymously, reserve bandwidth and detect tampering. In each round, fixed amounts of data, corresponding to packets, are anonymously transferred in consecutively numbered slots. A round then proceeds in the following three phases.

Reservation Phase. This phase assigns transmission slots to nodes in order to reduce collisions and improve bandwidth utilization. Let m_r be the number of bits used in the reservation phase, each node that would like to transmit during this round uniformly at random picks a number i from $\{1, \ldots, m_r\}$, and then anonymously transmits the m_r-bit vector with a 1 in the ith bit and zeros everywhere else. All others anonymously transmit the 0 vector. The vector broadcast (transmitted to all participants) by the clique indicates the order of sending in the next phase. Since multiple nodes broadcast the reservation block simultaneously, it is possible for their transmissions to collide. If an even number of nodes attempt to reserve a given slot, the collision will be evident in the reservation phase, and they will simply wait until the next round to transmit. If an odd number of nodes collide, the collision will occur during the transmission phase.

Transmission Phase. This is the phase in which data transmission occurs. Each node that has reserved a slot anonymously transmits its packet in the appropriate slot;

all other nodes anonymously transmit 0. Each node is both transmitting and receiving in this phase. Specifically, the nodes who have reserved a slot monitor the anonymous channel and monitor the packet sent anonymously. They can thus detect bona-fide collisions and tampering by malicious nodes: The packet received over the anonymous channel will simply not match the data they intended to send in that slot. This is akin to collisions in an Ethernet. A node that detects a collision waits until the next round to try to retransmit. After a fixed number of unsuccessful retries, it joins the network in a different location. The integrity of the transmitted data is protected by an MD5 checksum attached to each packet.

Exit Phase. The purpose of the exit phase is to ensure that long-running network transactions are protected from traffic analysis. This phase consists of a vote to check if the current round is a suitable time for changes in clique membership. A node may use this phase to anonymously signal to other nodes that it is in the midst of a long-running transaction, and that they should delay their departure from the clique if possible. This process is quite efficient, requiring a constant number (m_v) of bits independent of clique size, but it is not binding, as nodes may leave or crash at any time.

We now show how the round protocol can be modeled and verified by using MCTK. To abstract the practical round protocol to a model that can be checked by MCTK, we make the following simplifications:

- We don't formalize the exit phase here because it is only used to protect long-running transactions from *intersection attack*, which is not considered in this paper.
- We adopt key ring, instead of the fully-connected key graph used in the practical protocol. Logically, all agents form a ring, and each agent only has two shared keys with his left and right neighbor, respectively. This simplification also preserves anonymity of one agent's message because coordinated attacks made by all other agents in the same clique aren't considered here. Figure 1 is the key and network topology of a five node clique in our framework.
- We use one bit, instead of a m_r-bit vector, to describe the transmission slot(s). That is, there is only one slot in our model. This simplification can greatly reduce the size of the model.

4.1   The Environment in MCTK

Figure 2 is the MCTK environment description of the round protocol with N agents and N shared keys (N $\geq$ 3). Logically, these N agents A_1, ... , A_N are arranged in turn and widdershins to form a clique. Each agent shares two different keys with his left and right neighbors, respectively. In addition, each key shared among two agents may be different in the reservation and transmission phases. To model these keys, we can define 2N boolean variables as Line 3-6 of Figure 2. For example, the keys shared between agent i and his neighbor j are key_i_j[1] and key_i_j[2], the former is for the reservation phase and the latter for the transmission phase. In Line 25 init(phase) denotes that the initial value of variable phase is equal to the right hand side of symbol ':=', that is reservation. In the input language, the sentences in the form of "next(var):=exp" mean that the value of variable var in the next state is equal

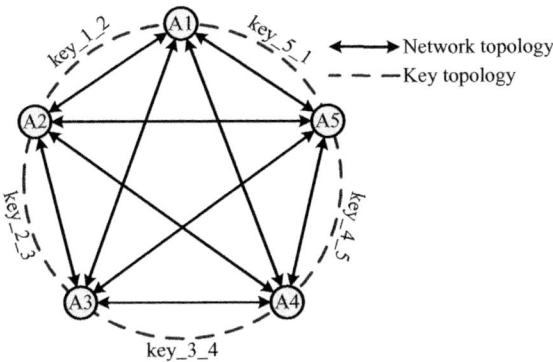

Fig. 1. A five node clique

to the current value of the expression exp. The "case" expression in Line 26-30 returns the value of the first expression on the right hand side of the symbol ":", such that the corresponding condition on the left hand side evaluates to be true. So, the assignments for variable phase in Line 25-30 represent that the protocol starts from the reservation phase, then arrives at the transmission phase after taking the first step, and will finish after the transmission phase.

In the environment, we don't assign any initial value to these keys used in the reservation phase and in Line 31-32 we specify the next value of them to be their current value, which means that these keys used in the reservation phase are nondeterministically chosen in the initial state and will keep invariant in the future. While in Line 33-37, these keys used in the transmission phase are nondeterministically chosen in the transmission phase and will keep invariant henceforth.

For each $i \in \{1, \ldots, N\}$, A_i is an agent that uses the protocol Agent, which will be shown in Figure 3. For the declaration of agent A_i, all of the actual parameters are observable for A_i itself. The parameter phase indicates whether the current phase is reservation, transmission or end, where end denotes that the execution of the round protocol finish. The two parameters key_{i-1}_i[1], key_i_{i+1}[1] and the other two parameters key_{i-1}_i[2], key_i_{i+1}[2] are the agent's left and right shared keys respectively used in the reservation and transmission phases. Note that in the actual input program, {i-1}, i or {i+1} is replaced by its value when its value is between 1 and N. But if its value is larger than N, it is replaced by 1; if its value is less than 1, it is replaced by N. The rest parameters are all other agent's local variables said[1] and said[2], which are used to record what an agent say in the reservation and transmission phases respectively. In other words, agent A_i can observe the messages that all other agents send in the two phases.

4.2 The Agent's Module in MCTK

We now present the MCTK module declaration for N agents in Figure 3. The name of agents' module is Agent, which is followed by its formal parameters that are listed

```
1   MODULE main()
2   VAR
3     key_1_2: array 1..2 of boolean;
4     key_2_3: array 1..2 of boolean;
5     ...
6     key_N_1: array 1..2 of boolean;
7     phase: {reservation, transmission, end};
8     A_1: Agent(phase, key_N_1[1], key_N_1[2],
9                       key_1_2[1], key_1_2[2],
10                      A_2.said[1], A_2.said[2],...,
11                      A_N.said[1], A_N.said[2]);
12    ...
13    A_i: Agent(phase, key_{i-1}_i[1], key_{i-1}_i[2],
14                      key_i_{i+1}[1], key_i_{i+1}[2],
15                      A_1.said[1], A_1.said[2],...,
16                      A_{i-1}.said[1], A_{i-1}.said[2],
17                      A_{i+1}.said[1], A_{i+1}.said[2],...,
18                      A_N.said[1], A_N.said[2]);
19    ...
20    A_N: Agent(phase, key_{N-1}_N[1], key_{N-1}_N[2],
21                      key_N_1[1], key_N_1[2],
22                      A_1.said[1], A_1.said[2],...,
23                      A_{N-1}.said[1], A_{N-1}.said[2]);
24  ASSIGN
25    init(phase) := reservation;
26    next(phase) := case
27      phase=reservation:      transmission;
28      phase=transmission:     end;
29      phase=end:              end;
30    esac;
31    next(key_1_2[1]) := key_1_2[1]; ...
32    next(key_N_1[1]) := key_N_1[1];
33    next(key_1_2[2]) :=
34      case phase=reservation: {1,0}; 1: key_1_2[2]; esac;
35    ...
36    next(key_N_1[2]) :=
37      case phase=reservation: {1,0}; 1: key_N_1[2]; esac;
```

Fig. 2. The MCTK environment of the round protocol

in parentheses. All of the formal parameters are observable for the agents using this module.

There are four local boolean variables defined in the module. Variable msg is the message that the agent wants to send in current round; Variable slot indicates whether or not this agent wants to send message msg. If slot = 1 then the agent wants to send it, otherwise the agent does not; Variables said[1] and said[2], the two elements of array said, records what the agent said in the reservation and transmission phases respectively.

```
1   MODULE Agent(observable phase,
2                    observable lkey1, observable lkey2,
3                    observable rkey1, observable rkey2,
4                    observable said_1_1, observable said_1_2,
5                    ...
6                    observable said_{N-1}_1, observable said_{N-1}_2)
7   VAR
8     msg: boolean;
9     slot: boolean;
10    said: array 1..2 of boolean;
11  ASSIGN
12    next(msg) := msg;
13    next(slot) := slot;
14    next(said[1]) := case
15      phase=reservation: lkey1 xor rkey1 xor slot;
16                      1: said[1];
17    esac;
18    next(said[2]) := case
19      phase=transmission: lkey2 xor rkey2 xor (slot & msg);
20             phase=end: said[2];
21    esac;
```

Fig. 3. The Agent protocol in MCTK

From the MCTK agent declaration language in [7], we know that the set O_i of agent i's observable variables is the set of agent i's local variables and his observable actual parameters. Therefore, we can present the set of observable variables of each agent of the round protocol as the set of boolean encoding variables of the corresponding actual parameters of phase, lkey1, lkey2, rkey1, rkey2, said_1_1, said_1_2, ... , said_{N-1}_1, said_{N-1}_2, as well as the local variables msg, slot, said[1] and said[2]. For agent A_1 for example, his observable variables are the boolean encoding variables of phase, key_N_1[1], key_N_1[2], key_1_2[1], key_1_2[2], A_2.said[1], A_2.said[2], ... , A_N.said[1], A_N.said[2], A_1.msg, A_1.slot, A_1.said[1] and A_1.said[2].

The assignment part of an agent's module specifies what happens in the two different phases of the execution of the round protocol. Line 12-13 keeps the values of variables msg and slot invariant in the execution of the protocol since their initial values are chosen nondeterministically.

Line 14-17 specifies that said[1], the message the agent wants to send in the reservation phase, is the XOR of slot, his left key lkey1 and his right key rkey1 for the reservation phase. The message will be sent in the second round of the protocol (because the initial value of phase is equal to reservation) and will keep invariant henceforth. Line 18-21 specifies that said[2], the message the agent wants to send in the transmission phase, is the XOR of his left key lkey2 and his right key rkey2 for the transmission phase, and the conjunction of his slot and msg. It means that if the agent does not want to send a message, then he simply sends (broadcasts) a "0" anonymously. The message will be sent in the next round of the transmission phase and will keep invariant henceforth.

4.3 The Specifications in MCTK

So far we finished the description of the round protocol in MCTK. We now list some specifications that are checked to be true in our model checker MCTK, and will explain how the agents' knowledge evolves in each phase via the agents' limited observation on the environment and other agents. Notice that in an $ECKL_n$ specification, a formula in the form of "X f" denotes that f will hold in the next state. Formula "ag K f" indicates that agent ag knows f. Formula "ags C f" denotes that f is the common knowledge of the agents in ags.

We introduce some expressions that will be used in the specifications at first. Expression `conflict` is defined as the expression that the sum of variable `slot` in each agent's module is lager than 1, i.e. `(A_1.slot+...+A_N.slot)>1`, so there is a collision if and only if `conflict` is true. Expression `xor_said1` is defined as the XOR of what all agents send in the reservation phase, i.e. `(A_1.said[1] xor ... xor A_N.said[1])`. Similarly, expression `xor_said2` is the XOR of what all agents send in the transmission phase and equal to `(A_1.said[2] xor ... xor A_N.said[2])`.

The first specification we check is that in the reservation phase, the sender's (for example A_1's) anonymity is a common knowledge among all agents in a clique:

```
(1)  X(A_1.slot -> ((A_1,...,A_N) C
                    (!(A_2 K A_1.slot) &...& !(A_N K A_1.slot))))).
```

We now check whether the reservation phase can reduce collisions or not. As Sharad Goal *et al.* [1] claimed for this phase, it is possible for agents' transmissions to collide since multiple agents broadcast the reservation message simultaneously. If there is an even number of agents who attempt to reserve the slot to send a message, the collision will be evident in the reservation phase; if there is an odd number of agents who attempt to reserve the slot, the collision will occur during the transmission phase. This claim can be checked by the following specification:

```
(2)  X(((A_1.slot & !xor_said1 ) -> (A_1 K conflict)) &
       ((A_1.slot & xor_said1 ) -> !(A_1 K conflict))).
```

Note that `xor_said1`, the broadcast by agent A_1 in the reservation phase, is equal to the XOR of all agents' `slot`, so `xor_said1 = 0` means that there is an even number of agents who want to send their messages. Therefore, the first line of spec. (2) says that if agent A_1 wants to send a message and he observes that there is an even number of agents who want to send their messages, he then knows that there exists a collision in the reservation phase. It is easy to prove that because in this precondition, agent A_1 knows that the XOR of all other agents' `slot` must be 1, which means that at least one of the other agents' `slot` is equal to 1, so agent A_1 is able to deduce the collision. The second line of spec. (2) says that in the reservation phase, if agent A_1 observes that there is an odd number of agents who want to send their messages, he can not know whether there exists a collision or not, which means that the collision will occur during the transmission phase.

When a sender observes there is an even number of the senders, or an agent that does not send a message observes there is an odd number of the senders, then he will know at least one of the other agents is the sender, but will not know who is the sender. This anonymity can be checked by the following spec. (3):

```
(3) X(((A_1.slot & !xor_said1) | (!A_1.slot & xor_said1)) ->
       ((A_1 K (A_2.slot | ... | A_N.slot)) &
       !(A_1 K A_2.slot) & ... & !(A_1 K A_N.slot)))).
```

Sharad Goal *et al.* [1] claimed that in the transmission phase, agents can detect bonafide collisions and tampering by malicious nodes when they observe the packet received over the anonymous channel does not match the data they intended to send. The claim can be checked by the following temporal epistemic spec. (4):

```
(4) X X((A_1.slot & (xor_said2!=A_1.msg)) -> (A_1 K conflict))
```

Spec. (4) says that if agent A_1 intends to send a message and observes that the broadcast he get in the transmission phase is not equal to his own message, then in the transmission phase, he will know there is a collision.

We are interested in an agent's knowledge about collision in the case that the broadcast he get in the transmission phase is equal to the conjunction of his slot and message, in this case agents should keep in ignorance of the collision in the transmission phase, no matter whether he is a sender or not:

```
(5) X X((xor_said1 & (xor_said2 <-> (A_1.slot & A_1.msg))) ->
       !(A_1 K conflict)).
```

Spec. (5) says that if there is an odd number of agents who want to send message and the broadcast in the transmission phase is equivalent to the conjunction of agent A_1's slot and message, then in the transmission phase he will not know there is a collision.

Now let's consider these specifications with two tiers of knowledge, by these specifications we can examine one agent's knowledge about other agents' knowledge. We first check that if agent A_1 knows there is a collision in the reservation phase, then he knows that all of the senders (such as agent A_2) also know the collision, but the other agents do not know the collision:

```
(6) X((A_1 K conflict) -> (A_1 K ((A_2.slot->(A_2 K conflict)) &
                                  (!A_2.slot->!(A_2 K conflict))))).
```

If agent A_1 doesn't know there is a collision in the reservation phase but will know the collision in the transmission phase, then he will know in the transmission phase that any agent having the same slot and message will know the collision in the transmission phase too:

```
(7) X((!(A_1 K conflict) & X(A_1 K conflict)) ->
      X(A_1 K ((A_2.slot=A1.slot & A_2.msg=A_1.msg) ->
               (A_2 K conflict)))).
```

If agent A_1, who intends to send message '1', doesn't know there is a collision in the reservation phase, but he will know the collision in the transmission phase, then he will know in the transmission phase that if agent A_2's message is '0', then agent A_2 will not know the collision in the transmission phase:

```
(8) X((!(A_1 K conflict) & X(A_1 K conflict) & A_1.slot &
      A_1.msg) -> X(A_1 K (!A_2.msg -> !(A_2 K conflict)))).
```

4.4   The Round Protocol in MCK

As mentioned in Section 1, besides MCTK, there are two state-of-the-art model checkers MCK and MCMAS for temporal logics of knowledge. Because we know that the knowledge modality in MCMAS and MCTK is evaluated only under the current observation of agents, we consider that the modelling and verifying method for the round protocol in MCMAS is similar to that in MCTK and not novel. We prefer to model and verify the round protocol in MCK and compare the running efficiency between MCK and MCTK.

MCK [4], for "Model Checking Knowledge", is a model checker for the logic of knowledge, developed at the School of Computer Science and Engineering at the University of New South Wales. Currently, the MCK system is primarily on OBDD-based model checking algorithms and supports both linear and branching time temporal operators. The novelty of this model checker is that it supports several different ways of defining knowledge given a description of a multi-agent system and the observations made by the agents: observation alone, observation and clock, and perfect recall of all observations. The first way of observation alone is to evaluate an agent's knowledge based just on its current observation, which is the same as the knowledge evaluating method in MCMAS and MCTK; the second way of observation and clock is to compute an agent's knowledge based both on its current observation and the current clock value; and the final way of perfect recall of all observations is to compute an agent's knowledge based on the complete record of all its observations. So, an agent can extract more information if it computes its knowledge in the last two ways. To the best of our knowledge, currently the last two ways are supported only in MCK. Because in the last two ways it is not necessary to model the clock explicitly, we consider the MCK model described in the last two ways is more succinct than that in the way of observation alone. Therefore, in this paper we are also interested in modelling the round protocol in MCK and verifying some MCK specifications that are formally similar to the MCTK specifications listed above in the way of observation and clock.

The MCK input program for the environment of the round protocol just includes some variables and agent declarations. We also define 2N boolean variables for representing keys:

```
key_1_2:Bool[2] key_2_3:Bool[2] ... key_N_1:Bool[2],
```

where the array elements with index 0 are the keys used in reservation phase, and the array elements with index 1 are the keys used in transmission phase. Two arrays said1:Bool[N] and said2:Bool[N] are defined for the messages sent by N agents respectively in the reservation phase and the transmission phase. For example, said1:Bool[i] is the message sent by agent i in the reservation phase. N agents are declared by

```
agent A_1 "prot" (key_N_1, key_1_2, said1, said2)
...
agent A_i "prot" (key_{i-1}_i, key_i_{i+1}, said1, said2)
...
agent A_N "prot" (key_{N-1}_N, key_N_1, said1, said2)
```

The name of the agent i is A_i. It uses the protocol "prot". Agent A_i can interact with, and potentially observe the variables between parentheses. The first two parameters are keys shared with its left and right neighbors, while said1 and said2 appear in all agent definitions, as they are publicly observable.

```
1   protocol "prot"(
2     keyl: observable Bool[2], --the agent's left key
3     keyr: observable Bool[2], --the agent's right key
4     said1: observable Bool[3],
5     said2: observable Bool[3])
6
7   msg: observable Bool  --the message the agent sends
8   slot: observable Bool --the slot the agent tries to use
9
10  begin
11    <<said1[self].write(keyl[0] xor keyr[0] xor slot)>>;
12    <<said2[self].write(keyl[1] xor keyr[1] xor (slot/\msg))>>
13  end
```

Fig. 4. The agent protocol in MCK

The agent protocol in MCK is shown in Fig. 4. The body of this protocol specifies, for the reservation and transmission phase, what happens in the two phases. In MCK, keyword self is the index of an agent using the agent protocol "prot", and any action between << and >> will be executed. Therefore, Line 11 means that the agent will send the XOR of his left key, right key and the slot he tries to send it in. Line 12 says that the agent will send the XOR of his left key, right key and the conjunction of his slot and message. It means that if the agent does not want to send a message, then he simply sends an "0" anonymously.

Now, we can list various temporal epistemic specifications syntactically similar to the above specifications in MCTK. We do not list all these specifications here. To make the execution efficiency of these specifications checked by MCTK and MCK more comparable, we check spec. (1)-(6) in MCK as the spec_clk_xn specifications, which indicates that the formula uses linear time temporal logic operators. First, we take the MCTK spec. (1) with 3 agents as an example, the corresponding MCK specification is

```
spec_clk_xn =
X(C1.slot =>
    (CK(neg (Knows C2 C1.slot) /\ neg (Knows C3 C1.slot))))).
```

Note that in MCK, the knowledge formula $K_{Agent}\varphi$ is written as "Knows $Agent\ \varphi$". The common knowledge formula $C_{all\_agents}\varphi$ is written as "CK φ", it means that φ is common knowledge to all agents. The temporal formula in the form of "X $n\ \varphi$" is evaluated under the semantics of taking n steps before evaluating φ, while φ must not contain temporal operators.

Below we take the MCTK spec. (4) with 3 agents as one more example, the corresponding MCK specification can be described as

```
spec_clk_xn =
X 2 ((A_1.slot /\
      ((said2[0] xor said2[1] xor said2[2]) xor A_1.msg))
      => (Knows A_1 ((A_1.slot /\ A_2.slot) \/
                     (A_1.slot /\ A_3.slot) \/
                     (A_2.slot /\ A_3.slot))))).
```

Besides, in MCK we check spec. (7) and (8) as the spec_clk_ctl_nested specifications, which indicates that the formula uses branching time temporal logic operators. For example, the MCK specification corresponding to the MCTK spec. (8) can be described as

```
spec_clk_ctl_nested =
( AX(neg (Knows C1 ((C1.slot /\ C2.slot) \/
                    (C1.slot /\ C3.slot) \/
                    (C2.slot /\ C3.slot)))) /\
  (AX AX (Knows C1 ((C1.slot /\ C2.slot) \/
                    (C1.slot /\ C3.slot) \/
                    (C2.slot /\ C3.slot)))) /\
  C1.slot /\ C1.msg
) => AX AX ( Knows C1 ((neg C2.msg) =>
             neg (Knows C2 ((C1.slot /\ C2.slot) \/
                            (C1.slot /\ C3.slot) \/
                            (C2.slot /\ C3.slot)))))).
```

The knowledge modality in the spec_clk_xn and spec_clk_ctl_nested specifications is evaluated under the *clock* semantics, that is agents compute knowledge using both of their current observation and the current global clock value.

5   Experimental Results

To show the effectiveness and the running efficiency of MCTK and MCK, it is interesting to model the round protocol in MCK and verify some of MCK's specifications equivalent to the specifications listed above.

Let's review the MCTK model of the round protocol, in which we explicitly simulate clock tick by a variable phase, which is observable for all agents. It means that all agents are sharing a global clock. In the MCTK model checker, we compute agents' knowledge in terms of their observable variables. Therefore, we can say that the knowledge in the above MCTK specifications is interpreted in *clock* semantics for knowledge, that is to say, agents compute knowledge using both their current observation and the current value of the global clock. Furthermore, for each agent in MCTK, he can get all information (including his left key, right key and what the other agents said in *both* of the reservation and transmission phases) via his observable formal parameters, so we can say these agents have "perfect recall" of all observations. Therefore, we can say that the knowledge evaluated under the MCTK model of the round protocol simulates the knowledge under the clock and perfect recall semantics in MCK. From the above analysis of knowledge evaluation in MCTK and MCK, we can say the following experimental comparison between them is reasonable.

Based on a laptop configuration Ubuntu 5.04 Pentium M 1.6GHz and 512M RAM, we verify that all of the specifications above are true in MCTK and MCK, both using OBDD dynamic ordering (add parameter '-dynamic' for MCTK and '-rs' for MCK). We directly use the binary file of MCK of version 0.1.0 that is available at the MCK website[1]. Table 1 shows the experimental results. Each specification is checked individually. Table 1 demonstrates that MCTK performs better than MCK, in particular for larger systems.

However, just based on the total time and space consumption for modeling and verification for a given specification, we can not conclude that the verification algorithm in MCTK must be more efficient than that in MCK. As far as we are concerned, there are at least four reasons. Firstly, we believe the high performance of MCTK is mainly due to the running efficiency of CUDD BDD package used in MCTK is much better than that of David Long's BDD package, which is used in MCK. Secondly, MCTK is an extension of NuSMV, in which some optimization modeling and verifying techniques, such as partitioned transition relations, can provide a much more concise OBDD-based representation of the formal model. We guess MCK seldom adopts these similar optimization techniques. Thirdly, the input language of MCK is customized for describing multi-agent systems, while the input language of MCTK is a minor extension of the input language of NuSMV 2.1.2, so we guess the OBDD-based formal model in MCK is more complicated than that in MCTK, which requires MCK create more BDD variables and larger OBDDs than MCTK. The second and third reasons can be demonstrated by Table 1, from it we can see that each MCK model needs more than two times the number of BDD variables for the corresponding MCTK model. It causes the state space of a MCK model is much larger than that of the corresponding MCTK model. Fourthly, we believe that different MCK specification forms such as spec_obs_ltl, spec_clk_xn and spec_clk_ctl_nested, execute quite different algorithms. So it is not fair, from this point of view, to evaluate agents' knowledge based just on the current observation in MCTK while based both on the current observation and the current clock value in MCK. In spite of this, the experimental results in this paper still convince us that evaluating knowledge based on the observational semantics usually gives better performance results than that based on the observational and clock semantics.

Therefore, it is hard to fairly compare the running efficiency of the verification algorithms within MCK and MCTK just based on the total time and space consumption for modeling and verification for a given specification. We may model some examples, including the Herbivore protocol, and verify some related temporal epistemic specifications only under the observational semantics in MCTK, MCK and MCMAS, to compare the running efficiency of the evaluating algorithms under the observational semantics in these three model checkers. Furthermore, to compare these model checkers completely, it is necessary to analyze their source codes. We leave these as our future works.

---

[1] http://www.cse.unsw.edu.au/~mck/Sources/mck

Table 1. Experimental results

20 agents					30 agents				
spec	tool	time	memory	BDD vars	spec	tool	time	memory	BDD vars
(1)	MCTK	0m26.352s	10.5MB	287	(1)	MCTK	1m0.717s	13.3MB	427
	MCK	15m36.113s	8.9MB	760		MCK	52m3.411s	7.1MB	1140
(2)	MCTK	0m16.773s	12.8MB	287	(2)	MCTK	0m57.961s	14.5MB	427
	MCK	7m51.958s	7.3MB	580		MCK	26m18.280s	15.2MB	870
(3)	MCTK	0m30.316s	9.3MB	287	(3)	MCTK	0m57.701s	14.4MB	427
	MCK	6m32.665s	3MB	580		MCK	34m12.154s	12.7MB	870
(4)	MCTK	0m12.191s	10.5MB	289	(4)	MCTK	0m31.327s	11.7MB	429
	MCK	8m14.593s	7.4MB	580		MCK	42m46.440s	29.2MB	870
(5)	MCTK	0m12.384s	11.2MB	289	(5)	MCTK	0m18.410s	11.6MB	429
	MCK	6m14.748s	3.2MB	580		MCK	42m54.903s	19.5MB	870
(6)	MCTK	1m14.791s	16.2MB	287	(6)	MCTK	2m46.860s	22.2MB	427
	MCK	6m19.799s	7.8MB	580		MCK	27m10.214s	28.1MB	870
(7)	MCTK	1m10.927s	16.2MB	291	(7)	MCTK	0m53.868s	13.1MB	431
	MCK	23m0.896s	25.2MB	580		MCK	94m25.166s	38.3MB	870
(8)	MCTK	1m20.062s	18.6MB	291	(8)	MCTK	1m9.040s	11.1MB	431
	MCK	20m45.827s	27MB	580		MCK	82m58.828s	46MB	870

6   Conclusions

In this paper, we have implemented and verified the round protocol of the Herbivore system in our model checker MCTK and MCK. The experimental results show that our MCTK is an efficient model checker for temporal logic of knowledge. As for future work for the Herbivore protocol, we will consider the formalization of the exit phase in MCTK to verify whether or not the phase is able to protect long-running network transactions from traffic analysis. We also intend to implement more complex protocols in MCTK and verify more complex properties, such as these for the analysis of coordinator attack, topology attacks, collusion and occupancy attacks, and so on. For these works, MCTK will be further extended and optimized.

Acknowledgments. We would like to thank the anonymous referees for their valuable comments. This work is supported by the National Natural Science Foundation of China (Nos.90718039, 60725207, 60763004 and 61073033), the Chinese National 973 Plan (No.2010CB328103), the Scientific Research Foundation of Huaqiao University (No.11BS108), and the ARC Future Fellowship FT0991785.

References

1. Goel, S., Robson, M., Polte, M., Sirer, E.G.: Herbivore: A Scalable and Efficient Protocol for Anonymous Communication. Technical Report TR2003-1890, Cornell Univeristy Computing and Information Science (2003)
2. Halpern, J., Vardi, M.Y.: Model Checking vs. Theorem Proving: A Manifesto. Technical Report, IBM Almaden Research Center(1991); An extended version of a paper in Proc. 2nd Int. Conf. on Principles of Knowledge Representation and Reasoning (1991)

3. van der Meyden, R.: Common Knowledge and Update in Finite Environments. Information and Computation 140(2), 115–157 (1998)
4. Gammie, P., van der Meyden, R.: MCK: Model Checking the Logic of Knowledge. In: Alur, R., Peled, D.A. (eds.) CAV 2004. LNCS, vol. 3114, pp. 479–483. Springer, Heidelberg (2004)
5. Lomuscio, A., Raimondi, F.: MCMAS: a Model Checker for Multi-Agent Systems. In: Hermanns, H. (ed.) TACAS 2006. LNCS, vol. 3920, pp. 450–454. Springer, Heidelberg (2006)
6. Su, K.: Model Checking Temporal Logics of Knowledge in Distributed Systems. In: Proceedings of the Nineteenth National Conference on Artificial Intelligence, Sixteenth Conference on Innovative Applications of Artificial Intelligence, pp. 98–103. AAAI Press / The MIT Press (2004)
7. Su, K., Sattar, A., Luo, X.: Model Checking Temporal Logics of Knowledge Via OBDDs. The Computer Journal 50(4), 403–420 (2007)
8. Engelhardt, K., van der Meyden, R., Moses, Y.: Knowledge and the Logic of Local Propositions. In: TARK 1998: Proceedings of the 7th Conference on Theoretical Aspects of Rationality and Knowledge, pp. 29–41. Morgan Kaufmann Publishers Inc., San Francisco (1998)
9. Luo, X.: Symbolic Model Checking Multi-Agent Systems. Phd Thesis, School of Information Science and Technology, Sun Yat-sen University (2006) (in Chinese)
10. Bryant, R.E.: Graph-Based Algorithms for Boolean Function Manipulation. IEEE Transactions on Computers 35(8), 677–691 (1986)
11. Fagin, R., Halpern, J., Moses, Y., Vardi, M.: Reasoning about Knowledge. MIT Press, Cambridge (1995)
12. Bryant, R.E.: Symbolic Boolean Manipulation with Ordered Binary-Decision Diagrams. ACM Computing Surveys 24(3), 293–318 (1992)
13. Holzmann, G.: The Model Checker SPIN. IEEE Transactions on Software Engineering 23(5), 279–295 (1997)
14. Cimatti, A., Clarke, E.M., Giunchiglia, E., Giunchiglia, F., Pistore, M., Roveri, M., Sebastiani, R., Tacchella, A.: NuSMV 2: An OpenSource Tool for Symbolic Model Checking. In: Brinksma, E., Larsen, K.G. (eds.) CAV 2002. LNCS, vol. 2404, pp. 359–364. Springer, Heidelberg (2002)
15. Lichtenstein, O., Pnueli, A.: Checking That Finite State Concurrent Programs Satisfy Their Linear Specification. In: POPL 1985: Proceedings of the 12th ACM SIGACT-SIGPLAN Symposium on Principles of Programming Languages, pp. 97–107. ACM Press, New York (1985)
16. Clarke, E.M., Grumberg, O., Hamaguchi, K.: Another Look at LTL Model Checking. In: Dill, D.L. (ed.) CAV 1994. LNCS, vol. 818, pp. 415–427. Springer, Heidelberg (1994)
17. Chaum, D.: The Dining Cryptographers Problem: Unconditional Sender and Recipient Untraceability. Journal of Cryptology 1, 65–75 (1988)

Author Index

GPSR Compliance

*The European Union's (EU) General Product Safety Regulation (GPSR)
is a set of rules that requires consumer products to be safe and our
obligations to ensure this.*

*If you have any concerns about our products, you can contact us on
ProductSafety@springernature.com*

In case Publisher is established outside the EU, the EU authorized
representative is:

Springer Nature Customer Service Center GmbH
Europaplatz 3
69115 Heidelberg, Germany

Batch number: 09478804

Printed by Printforce, the Netherlands